PUBLIC
VALUES
AND
PUBLIC
INTEREST

Public Management and Change Series

Beryl A. Radin, Series Editor

EDITORIAL BOARD

TITLES IN THE SERIES

Georgetown University Press, Washington, D.C. www.press.georgetown.edu
© 2007 by Georgetown University Press. All rights reserved. No part of this book may be repro-
duced or utilized in any form or by any means, electronic or mechanical, including photocopy-
ing and recording, or by any information storage and retrieval system, without permission in
writing from the publisher.

Library of Congress Cataloging-in-Publication Data

Bozeman, Barry.
   Public values and public interest : counterbalancing economic individualism / Barry Bozeman.
      p. cm. — (Public management and change series)
   Includes bibliographical references and index.
   ISBN 978-1-58901-177-9 (alk. paper)
   1. Public interest—Economic aspects.   2. Common good—Economic aspects.   3. Public
administration.   I. Title.
   JC330.15.B68 2007
   351.01—dc22

                                                                              2007007015

14 13 12 11 10 09 08 07   9 8 7 6 5 4 3 2
First printing

Printed in the United States of America

PUBLIC VALUES AND PUBLIC INTEREST

COUNTERBALANCING
ECONOMIC INDIVIDUALISM

BARRY BOZEMAN

Georgetown University Press
Washington, D.C.

I dedicate this book to the public administration and public policy students and practitioners who I have been privileged to teach and from whom I have been privileged to learn.

CONTENTS

ILLUSTRATIONS

ACKNOWLEDGMENTS

My thanks begin with Monica Gaughan. As faculty colleague, spouse, and critic, Monica contributed with heart and mind, inspiring me with her ideas, courage, integrity, and, most of all, her unique brand of outrageousness.

Two individuals who contributed a great deal to the book are designated as chapter coauthors. Mary Feeney (University of Georgia) has been working with me for several years on various aspects of the public values agenda and wrote much of chapter 2. In addition, she read the entire manuscript and offered valuable criticism, and she provided research assistance for the book. Ben Minteer (Arizona State University) is perhaps the world's premier scholar of John Dewey's philosophy as it pertains to public interest theory and environmental ethics. He helped shape the book and is a coauthor of chapter 4.

Torben Beck Jorgensen (University of Copenhagen) has served as an informal consultant, confidante, and critic. He read a complete first draft of the manuscript and provided excellent advice that led to many improvements.

Researchers at the Consortium for Science, Policy and Outcomes (CSPO), now centered at Arizona State University, have been instrumental in many ways, providing support, encouragement, and collaboration. I am particularly grateful to CSPO stalwarts Michael Crow, Daniel Sarewitz, and David Guston.

Three of my colleagues at Georgia Institute of Technology, my faculty home during most of the time I was writing this book, have been extremely helpful. Thanks to Bryan Norton, Gordon Kingsley, and Juan Rogers. They listened patiently as I struggled to develop rough ideas and provided many useful suggestions.

At my current academic home, University of Georgia, my colleague Hal Rainey provided his usual excellent advice and criticism. He read the entire first draft of the manuscript and provided excellent ideas for revision. Our decades-long dialogue about "publicness" has greatly influenced my thinking and, just as important, encouraged me to keep working on this endlessly fascinating topic. George Frederickson read and commented on the draft manuscript, and his efforts have helped me produce a book that is much better than it would have been without his advice. I have also been greatly influenced by reading the excellent body of theory and research he has produced on topics pertaining to citizenship, community, and public interest. Finally, I am grateful to the highly competent, professional, and congenial staff at Georgetown University Press, especially Gail Grella.

CHAPTER ONE
THE PRIVATIZATION
OF PUBLIC VALUE

It is in vain to say that enlightened statesmen will be able to adjust these clashing interests, and render them all subservient to the public good.

—JAMES MADISON, *The Federalist No. 10*

No deliberation of politics and political theory claims a more venerable heritage than the dialogues on the existence, nature, and requirements of the "public interest" or the "common good." In Aristotle's *Politics*, the "common interest" (*to koinei sympheron*) is the rationale for proper constitutions; St. Thomas Aquinas in *Summa Theologiae* identifies the common good (*bonum commune*) as the worthy goal of government; Locke's *Second Treatise of Government* declares that "the peace, safety, and public good of the people" are the transcendent political purposes.

We need not go back hundreds of years to find interest in public interest theory. In the early years of the twentieth century, many prominent political scientists paid homage to the idea of the public interest. Pendleton Herring's (1936) reconciliation theory was premised on public managers' ability to divine the common good; Emmette Redford (1954) viewed the public interest as the key to effective regulatory administration; Phillip Monypenny (1953) anchored his public administration ethical code in a concept of the public interest. Even the foundation stone of American public administration, Woodrow Wilson's (1955) *Study of Administration*, originally published in 1887, set its famous politics/administration dichotomy in a concept of the collective good (Rutgers 1997).

Nowadays, many sophisticates' reaction to public interest appeals is much the same as nonbelievers' responses to discussions of God and the afterlife: nervous embarrassment tempered by a faint hope for some alternative to the void. How did this happen? The reasons for a decline in public interest argument and theorizing are many and varied. Social and academic fashion seems to have played a role. The development of quantitative social sciences and its inexhaustible demand for empirical evidence lessened our patience for topics

1

that seem to hold little possibility of precise answers. The harshest critics of public interest theory rail loudest about its ambiguities and a seeming inability to determine when and if public interest theory has progressed.

Today, concern with the public interest has not disappeared, but public interest *theory* strikes many as an anachronism, a relic from another day's Zeitgeist when the public interest was a preoccupation of celebrity intellectuals such as Walter Lippman (e.g., 1955). Public interest theory seems at odds with the pace, demands, and give-and-take of today's public policy and management. Public interest theory seems out of place in polities dominated by fractious, interest group–based politics. What could public interest theory possibly say about policy domains rife with technical complexity and requiring teams of highly educated experts just to describe problems? And who could even think about *solving* a policy problem or "administering in the public interest" now that we know almost all problems have multiple, competing stakeholders seeking to maximize conflicting values?

The unpopularity of public interest theory is not entirely a product of contemporary cynicism. Scholars began to beat a hasty retreat in the 1950s. In the political science of the mid-twentieth century, the rise of quantitative and "behavioral" approaches and a focus on pluralism and politics as interest group behavior made discussions of the public interest seem passé and, worse, "metaphysical and unscientific." Critics assailed the public interest as unrealistic, impractical, imprecise, ambiguous, devoid of meaning, and even as the handmaiden to authoritarianism. In perhaps the best-known criticism of public interest theory, Glendon Schubert (1961, 348) observed that political realists "have put behind them childish myths which postulate any independent substantive content for such notions as 'the public will' and the 'public interest.'" Similarly, Frank Sorauf (1957, 638) concluded that "public interest theories . . . perpetuate a number of fables about the political process and contribute to the low prestige and esteem generally accorded to partisan political activity." In their standard-setting public administration textbook, Simon, Smithburg, and Thompson (1950, 551) devoted less than a page to the public interest, dismissing it as simply a rationale for one's private view of the world: "When one looks in a mirror, one sees one's own image. Responsiveness to public interest, so defined, is responsiveness to one's own values and attitudes toward social problems."

Ironically, the success of some modern governments may have contributed to a diminished interest in deliberations about the public interest. Whereas in past centuries the idea of the public interest was set against despotic governments and tyrants, many modern nations have managed to develop governments that more often act as a bulwark against tyranny than as a perpetrator. As societies and governments succeed in rendering life less fearful and capricious, social stability and predictability settle in. This stability enables and supports economies. As fully articulated economies develop, individuals begin to focus less on collective security and more on wealth accumulation. At the same time, societies previously focused on combating tyranny and attending to social and political fissures have the luxury of focusing on economic development and efficiency.

In contrast to public interest theory, economic individualism, with its emphasis on individual liberty and each person's role as a producer and consumer, has in recent decades grown in its influence. The emphasis on economic individualism (a concept described in detail later) is certainly not a new one in the United States or, indeed, in most nations with monetary systems and legal codes for property rights. Since its inception, the United States has provided fertile ground for market-based philosophies of human behavior and public policy. However, in recent times, market values have been elevated to a normative level perhaps unsurpassed in U.S. history. With China and Russia opening massive new markets and each being enamored of quasi-market approaches to policy and public management, there are nearly 2 billion people affected deeply by market criteria and norms who were only two decades ago largely and forcibly inured to them. Even the bastions of social and public values—Western European nations—have increasingly come to grips with market values, especially in the face of increasing financial burdens on the welfare state. Few outposts remain where policymakers confidently reject economic efficiency and growth as transcendent goals of public policy and its management.

Understandably, in our daily lives we more often attend to the practical embodiments of economic individualism than to its philosophical bases. But economic individualism is a set of ideas with a long, distinguished pedigree. Indeed, if we consider together economic individualism, public interest and public values, and, at least equally important, religion, then we have covered most of the terrain on which governments are built.

Due to the need to maintain some focus, this book does not give much emphasis to religious values, but in many cases religious values prove an even stronger competitor to secular public values than does economic individualism. To some extent, public values and economic values are commensurate. Both public values reasoning and economic reasoning are rooted more in analytical traditions. While there is certainly much analysis devoted to religion, it seems indisputable that faith necessarily plays a qualitatively different role in religion, even compared to the strong ideologies often produced through political and economic reasoning and argument. For these reasons, religious values receive limited attention here.

I consider in the following sections some of the philosophical foundations of economic individualism, a topic treated more comprehensively in chapter 3.

THE PHILOSOPHICAL FOUNDATIONS OF "ECONOMIC INDIVIDUALISM"

The definition of *economic individualism* is implicit in the two words of the term, and it can be defined it as "a philosophy emphasizing in matters economic the values and interests of the individual." Because definitions including the same terms on each side of the equation are not sufficiently edifying, let me elaborate. As a philosophy, economic individualism is based on three central principles. First, it is human centered. Values are based on the needs of humans, not society. Second, social and government institutions are, at best, a means to satisfying individual needs. If they do not satisfy individual needs (but focus on community needs, ideals, or transcendent values such as God or the state), they are inimical to individualism. The third premise is that the individual is of supreme value, not the society or the polity, and that all individuals are of equal moral value. Individualism assumes that the best society is one that permits the individual maximum freedom of choice, that each person is the best judge of his or her interests, and that there is no transitivity of interests. Society, then, is seen as a collection of self-contained individuals, with government as a means of providing for those few values that enable individual expression, including education, defense and security, and enforcement of contracts voluntarily entered.

We have all heard the best-known maxim of economic individualism, "the government that governs least governs best." The philosophy of economic individualism bears close kinship to classical liberalism and to libertarianism, stressing unfettered self-interest and implying that societies in which individuals pursue aggressively their unrestrained self-interest will best serve aggregate needs and desires.

Interestingly, the term *individualism* (as in political and economic individualism) was introduced by Alexis de Tocqueville (1965), the eighteenth-century French political philosopher who became the iconic observer of American society and political culture. Tocqueville described economic individualism as a philosophy of moderated selfishness in which one favors oneself and perhaps a small set of family and friends.

While individualism seems to have had its strongest roots in the United States, it emerged as a philosophy in England, spurred by the ideas of political economist Adam Smith and political philosopher Jeremy Bentham. Smith's doctrine of laissez-faire, based on the conviction that there is a "natural harmony of individual wills," is the strongest economic embodiment of individualism. Smith's "obvious and simple system of natural liberty" conceptualized competitive markets as the ideal system for achieving mutual advantage. A free market is the means by which to "maximize efficiency as well as freedom, secure for each participant the largest yield from his resources to be had without injury to others, and achieve a just distribution, meaning a sharing of the social product in proportion to individual contributions" (Smith 1976, 231–32).

In political philosophy, Bentham's utilitarianism, especially its principle of "each to count for one and none for more than one," articulates and codifies individualistic values. It is the foundation for one of the best-known approaches to public interest philosophy, an approach quite in harmony with economic individualism. While utilitarianism is compatible with many of the premises of economic individualism, it is important to note that utilitarianism is not coterminous with economic individualism, and indeed, it has led to some political outcomes clearly violating the maxim "the government that governs least governs best." The philosophy of utilitarianism, at least as initially espoused by Bentham, includes considerations of justice and equity. Indeed, utilitarianism was cited as a rationale for some of the earliest social policies in Great Britain, including the elimination of child labor, usury, and prison abuse (Piven and Cloward 1971). These are not, of course, the uses to which contemporary neoclassical economic thinkers have put utilitarianism.

MANIFESTATIONS OF ECONOMIC INDIVIDUALISM

In an era increasingly influenced by a philosophy of economic individualism, public leaders and the public at large oftentimes look first to markets for solutions and then to government and nonmarket institutions only in those instances where market approaches seem unworkable. Indeed, that is the exact prescription of "market failure theory." Market failure theory prescribes use of markets, not government or other organizing principles, unless the efficiency of markets has been undermined by such factors as monopoly, poor information to consumers, or the inability for providers of goods and services to protect against "free riders" (those who benefit from a good or service but do not for one reason or another pay for it).

Market failure theory receives considerable attention in chapter 3. For now, suffice it to note that market failure reasoning is a practical embodiment of the philosophy of economic individualism and that the theory treats government as a residual or a provider of last resort. That is, government should intervene only when we can identify some structural flaw in the market (e.g., monopoly, inability to set efficient prices) that undermines the ability of the private sector to provide needed goods and services.

Related to market failure reasoning is the idea that marketlike approaches are often the most useful way for governments to provide goods and services. In chapter 2 we review in some detail a few noteworthy manifestations of market-based policies, but let us consider just a few of the categories of approaches here.

Before the 1980s and the rise of the Reagan Revolution and Thatcherism, policymaking and public management were more often thought of as something done by governments. But in the past few decades, market-based governance mechanisms have proliferated. Following is a brief list of the market-oriented approaches to public policy and management:

- sale of public assets to private parties (Walker 1994);
- privatization and contracting out (Donahue 1991; Savas 2000);
- policies based on vouchers or saleable credits (Hausker 1992);

- tax credits (Bucy 1985);
- creation of hybrid organizations, part public and part private (Emmert and Crow 1988);
- managed competition (Marquis and Long 1999; Trubac 1995);
- government management of contractors (Hefetz and Warner 2004; Domberger and Jensen 1997; Hisrch 1995); and
- contractor management of government (Bozeman and Wilson 2004).

Market efficiency serves both as rationale for delivery of goods and services and as a rallying cry for businesslike, entrepreneurial, or market savvy government (Osborne and Plastrik 1997). As a result of changes in traditional assumptions about providers of goods and services, the very meaning of "publicness" (Bozeman 1987; Antonsen and Jørgensen 1997) is changing. On the one hand, public agencies strive to be more businesslike with such practices as managed competition and fee-for-services. On the other hand, private corporations increasingly perform public responsibilities (Kettl 1993; Rainey 2003). One cannot always identify the economic individualism bases of public policy and management simply by examining their rhetoric or surface rationales (Boyne 2006; Kelly 2005). Quite often, public policies rooted in economic individualism are promoted with the softer rhetoric of public value, progressivism, or populism. An obvious recent case is the rhetoric of "compassionate conservatism," which argues that conservatism and compassion together are the best methods for solving social problems. In the United States, compassionate conservatives cite immoral behavior and original sin as the root cause of social problems, leading them to propose policies based on religious values, traditional families, and individual responsibility. One apparent consequence of this approach, when taken up by candidates, was to broaden their appeal to women voters (Hutchings et al. 2004).

Many noteworthy instances of soft rhetoric and liberal mythology blunting the reality of economic individualism can be found in U.S. tax policy. In theory, income taxation is based on progressive principles. However, if one examines actual tax burdens, especially in light of recent massive revisions during President George Bush's first term (2000–2004), one would be hard-pressed to argue that U.S. taxes are redistributive in their nature. If we consider the *actual* percentage of wealth and income taxed for persons at different economic strata, the relaxation of dividends taxes, and especially the repeal of inheritance taxes, one might well conclude that the U.S. tax code is set up to either put brakes on or reverse the welfare state.

To some extent, the creation of the welfare state can be viewed as a repudiation of economic individualism, based on assumptions that are at odds with individualism: social achievement, a community of interests, social as well as economic interdependence, and most divergent, redistribution of wealth and resources to provide a social "safety net." In the United States, the welfare state was never as extensive as in most European countries. Economic individualism, while it has waxed and waned in importance in the United States, has during most eras of the nation's history been in the foreground of public policy deliberations and decisions.

The past decade's "welfare reform" policies in the United States and Western Europe (Offerman 1999) have used a variety of soft rhetorical covers, including egalitarianism (Boleyn-Fitzgerald 1999), to deliver a reformulated welfare state in which subsistence is no longer an entitlement but a right to be earned by the individual. While the jury is still out on the effectiveness of these so-called reforms on poverty abatement and economic opportunity (Mead 2004; Slack et al. 2003; Rose 2000), the new policies have clearly shifted the fundamental assumptions about welfare and welfare rights (Stoesz 1999).

As nations strive to apply scarce resources in an effort to meet the needs and rising expectations of citizens, it is no surprise that policy models based on ideas of scarcity come increasingly to the fore. As I discuss in chapter 4, the managerial reform known as the "New Public Management" (see Barzelay 2001 for a detailed description and theoretical analysis) has to some extent codified and prescribed governance approaches based on economic individualism and market mechanisms. That chapter also examines the older and more targeted concept, privatization, and the values implicit in its approaches. Unquestionably, markets and market-based policymaking do, indeed, provide a great many advantages and have important roles to play in public policy and management. However, to the extent that public values and public interest are crowded out, some rethinking, adjustment, and recalibration seems in order. This book seeks to provide a counterbalance to both the philosophical and the more practical aspects of economic individualism. The practical prescription "managing publicness," provided in the concluding chapter, is an alternative to privatization and New Public Management. Managing publicness takes public values as its starting point and public interest ideals as its objective. The philosophical prescriptions include a pragmatic approach to public interest theory as well as a model for understanding public values criteria. Why is it useful to disinter long-buried questions of public interest? I provide a provisional answer in the following section. But this answer depends in part on understanding the opposite number of the relation of economic individualism and market forces operating in public policy and management.

PUBLICNESS

We can think of policies and institutions in terms of their economic basis and roots in economic individualism. Similarly, we can consider the *public* roots of those same policies and institutions. According to the theory of "dimensional publicness" (Bozeman 1987, 2004), *publicness* is best defined not on the basis of the legal status of institutions or their ownership (i.e., government or business) but according to the degree of political authority constraints and endowments affecting the institution. Similarly, an institution's "privateness" may be viewed according to the degree of *market* authority constraints and endowments affecting the institution. According to this model, it is sensible to speak of some government institutions as "more public" (or "more private") than others and of firms as "more public" (or "more private") than others. Indeed, it may in some instances even be sensible to conclude that particular government institutions are "more private" than particular business institutions and, likewise, that particular business institutions are "more public" than some government institutions.

At first blush, it may seem a bit strange to speak of the publicness of institutions and policies. Referring to the publicness of public policies or of public organizations perhaps seems redundant. The idea that some public organizations might be "more public" or, particularly, that some private organizations might be in some respects "more public" than some public organizations perhaps may seem perplexing or even illogical. One intuits that there will be fundamental differences between public and private organizations. Several important studies have supported this theory by documenting differences in behavioral tendencies and in the composition of government and private organizations and institutions. In one of the most impressive sustained theory-building efforts in public administration or political science, Rainey and his colleagues not only have organized and interpreted the literature on these differences between private and public organizations (e.g., Rainey, Backoff, and Levine 1976; Perry and Rainey 1988; Rainey 1989, 2002) but also have for many years conducted studies demonstrating important sector-based differences in motivation, personnel selection, organizational procedures, and red tape, among a number of topics (e.g., Rainey, 1979, 1983; Lan and Rainey 1992; Rainey, Pandey, and Bozeman 1995; Chun and Rainey 2005).

Despite appearances there is neither a logical nor an empirical inconsistency in simultaneously asserting that there tend to be core differences between government-owned and private-owned organizations and that publicness is a dimensional property (for an extended argument to this effect, see Rainey and Bozeman 2000). The seeming inconsistency between the idea of fundamental differences according to sector and the idea that publicness is dimensional is owing to the conflation of "public" and "government." The "core" approach to comparing public and private organizations and institutions focuses on sector and legal status of organizations, whereas the dimensional approach focuses on sources and extent of political and economic authority. Both are important in explaining behaviors and outcomes (for an empirical demonstration, see Bozeman and Bretschneider 1994).

One of the first studies of publicness, at least conceived as the relative degree of external political and economic authority impinging on institutions, was my (Bozeman 1984) analysis of the origins and evolution of U.S. aerospace firms. The study showed that the level of publicness affecting aerospace policy and firms in the industry changed remarkably over the years but that one could track the degree to which political forces and market forces, respectively, shaped outcomes. At the very inception of the industry, U.S. government needs for mail services and passenger conveyance led to government contracts that forever shaped the industry. At other points and for particular firms, the reliance of the firms on government was sharply diminished, as was the degree of external political control. But at every point in the history of the aerospace industry a dynamic mix of external political and market forces shaped outcomes. One indicator of changes in degree of publicness—one among many but an especially obvious indicator—is the degree to which aerospace firms depended upon government contracts for their resources. At the time of the study the range was between 18 percent and 99 percent, and the study hypothesized that this variance in publicness would strongly affect the behaviors and composition of the respective firms.

Preliminary work on dimensional publicness has been extended in a number of studies using a wide variety of methods. In addition to general theoretical formulations (e.g., Boyne 2002; Antonsen and Jørgensen 1997; Emmert and Crow 1988; Haque 2001) applying a dimensional publicness approach, it has been used in connection with a wide variety of organizational and institutional studies focusing on such diverse topics as strategic management (e.g., Nutt and Backoff 1993), deployment of information technology (e.g., Bretschneider 1990), decision making (e.g., Coursey and Bozeman 1990; Jennings 1996; Nutt 2006), administrative procedures and government reform (Dutta and Heininger 1999), organizational networks (Isett and Provan 2005), ethics (Wittmer and Coursey 1996; Wheeler and Brady 1998), and even operations management (Goldstein and Naor 2005). In a distinctive application of the dimensional publicness model, Demortain (2004) argues that publicness can also be viewed as a symbol that official actors and other stakeholders, regardless of sector, seek to shape and exploit.

Most studies of dimensional publicness have focused on institutions, organizations, and their management. However, the model seems just as applicable to policies and policy implementation and has been used to understand the mix of economic and political authority in specific policy domains such as science and technology policy (Crow and Bozeman 1998), mass transit (Boschken 1992), and substance abuse (Heinrich and Fournier 2004). Indeed, we can think of almost any set of government policies (as well as, for that matter, firms' policies) as representing and responding to a distinctive mix of political and market forces.

In chapter 2 I consider some contemporary policies and assess their implications for this volatile mix of economic and political authority I have referred to as "publicness." There is no suggestion that policies that are "more public" are in some sense better or worse, but, as we shall see at various points in this book, understanding public interest and public values often requires some attention to the mix of political and economic authority.

NORMATIVE PUBLICNESS

To say that a policy or an institution is "more public" says only that it is more influenced by political authority. Standing alone, that is not in any sense a normative or value-based statement. In the context of public values, the degree of publicness (and privateness) of policies and institutions is of interest because of the belief that achieving public values, and ultimately achieving public interest, depends to such a large degree on bringing to bear the optimal mix of political and economic authority in pursuit of values (both individual and public).

While previous theories and research on publicness have focused on the political and economic dimensions of organizations, institutions, and most recently (e.g., Bozeman and Sarewitz 2005; Feeney and Bozeman 2007), policies, we can also think of publicness as a concept for guiding normative analysis. Arguably, a key issue in analysis of the publicness dimensions of institutions and policies is to help us understand the blend of political authority and economic authority most likely to serve common ends. "Normative publicness" presents us with a simple injunction: *we must understand the mix of political and economic authority of institutions and policies if we are to understand their potential to achieve public values and to work toward public interest ideals.* In this respect, the empirical and the normative come together. If one assumes that the evolution of policies and institutions is to a large extent owing to changes in their respective mix of economic and political (Dahl and Lindblom 1953), then it takes only a small step to assert that normative inquiry should include deliberation about the values implications of publicness.

One might not expect Nobel laureate James Buchanan (Buchanan and Tullock 1978, 364), one of the intellectual leaders of economic individualist approaches, to embrace this view, but as we see in the following commentary, there is at least common ground between economic individualism and public interest. That common ground is a concern for institutions: "Attempts must be made to modify institutions. . . . [T]he observed behavior of the modern American is excessively 'self-interested.' Rather than hope for a 'new morality,' I shall focus on the potential for institutional reform that may indirectly modify man's behavior toward his fellows. Institutions may have been allowed to develop and to persevere that exacerbate rather than mitigate man's ever present temptations to act as if he is an island, with others treated as his natural environment."

In later chapters, especially chapter 8, I return to the normative publicness concept and its relationship to public values and public interest. At this point, however, it is worth stating why it is important to revisit and perhaps reformulate public interest theory.

WHY RESURRECT PUBLIC INTEREST THEORY?

Clearly, one interested in institutional reform or policy change need not attend to any concept or theory of the public interest. It is possible to seek to achieve specific programs delivered by particular institutions with no reference to public interest theories. Nevertheless, there are several arguments for self-conscious consideration of public interest theory, especially a more pragmatic formulation of public interest. One reason to resurrect public interest theory is that if progress can be made in public interest theorizing, it should have payoff for a wide variety of value and policy domains. Moreover, even though public interest *theory* receives less attention now than fifty years ago, concern for "public interest," not the theory of public interest but its active incarnation in public policy and management, remains high. In part, this is because legislators continue making laws referring to the "public interest," regulators regulate in the "public interest," and courts rule in the "public interest." The term *public interest* appears again and again in statutes, generally as shorthand admonishing against full capture by organized economic and corporate interests and by other varieties of associational interest groups. No political campaign would be complete without opponents arguing that their respective policies, even if contradictory with one another, are in the "public interest." In short, the public remains interested in public interest.

As we see in later chapters, critics provide strong and in some cases valid indictments of public interest theory. Many such arguments attack the lack of analytical precision of public interest theory. But in some cases these attacks are overly zealous. While public interest theory seems unlikely to yield concepts and propositions that are as detailed and precise as those provided in formal economic theory, public interest theory need not be limited to generalities. Furthermore, just as economic theory has given rise to useful conceptual applications, the same is possible for public interest theory. Indeed, this book presents specific criteria for public values potentially useful within a public interest theory framework. The fact is that determining exactly the "public interest" is virtually impossible, at least doing so in any precise, axiomatic, or deductive way. The fact is that this is not a requirement for useful theories of public interest or for useful applications. The argument presented in chapter 6 suggests that a pragmatic approach to public interest theory, an approach based on empiricism and deliberation, is not only satisfactory but also more likely to lead to useful outcomes. A key difference between market theory, at least as embodied in market failure theory (chapter 3), and public interest theory (chapter 5) is that the former begins with an ideal (the perfectly competitive market) and proceeds to apply the idea to public policy and management issues, whereas the latter begins with the policy issue and, by systematic deliberation, develops a pragmatic operationalization of the public interest.

PUBLIC INTEREST DEFINED

Critics of public interest theories (e.g., Schubert 1961; Sorauf 1957) have lamented the fact that public interest concepts are almost always imprecise and expansive. These critics are not wrong, but they exaggerate the case against public interest theory, and in those instances where their criticism is entirely correct, they sometimes draw the wrong conclusions. If we follow political scientist James Fesler's (1990) argument that public interest theory is about an ideal rather than a scientifically instrumental construct, the criticisms about its imprecision prove less compelling. According to Fesler, public-interest-based theories are imprecise because the subject of these theories is an ideal rather than a discrete construct. Moreover, the imprecise, illusory nature of the public interest presents no greater theoretical or practical problems than other such ideal concepts.

A most important distinction between public interest and public values is that (at least as used in this book) "public interest" is an ideal, whereas "public values" have specific, identifiable content. *Public interest* is the more encompassing term and, as an ideal, the more elusive one. Following is a workable definition for present purposes: *In a particular context, the public interest refers to the outcomes best serving the long-run survival and well-being of a social collective construed as a "public."*

While this is a simple definition in some respects, its embedded assumptions touch off shock waves of implications and other assumptions. The focus is on *outcomes* not on policies, intentions, or specific actions. This focus is suitable for an ideal concept. The public interest concept cannot, then, endorse any specific policy or action, only the public interest ideal. However, specific policies and actions can be motivated (as they often are in real-world policymaking) as seeming to best serve public interest.

While the definition may seem to have much in common with utilitarian ("greatest good for the greatest number") theories of the public interest, it is not fundamentally utilitarian. The fact that survival is privileged in this definition undercuts some bases of utilitarianism. Similarly, the focus on the long run and on the social collective as a whole (rather than the majority) presents some departure from utilitarian theories.

As is the case for most theories of the public interest, this definition presents no sharp demarcation of "the public." Unlike some of the theories reviewed in chapter 3, the concept presented earlier requires that the public interest focus on the public (such as it is defined) as a whole rather than its constituent parts. Thus, while the public interest is situation dependent, it is not different for various groups or individuals. By the previously mentioned definition, it is not sensible to talk about individual or group public interest because the concept focuses on collective good (i.e., for the aggregate of groups and individuals). But determining "the public" can present problems here. However, those problems seem no greater than determining "the market" in market failure or "the interest" in interest group pluralism.

For literally hundreds of years, philosophers and others have debated whether the public interest is best viewed as general or specific to the case, contingent or immutable. An especially important aspect of the previous definition is that public interest is dynamic. By this definition, what is "in the public interest" changes not only case-by-case but also within the same case as time advances and conditions change. An example of the changing nature of the public interest ideal is the concept of "political freedom." In contemporary times, few would limit the ideal to educated, property-owning, white males, but at the nation's founding such a boundary for political freedom was taken for granted by most of the framers of the U.S. Constitution.

A concept of public-interest-as-changeable and situation dependent suggests the relevance of learning and empiricism, including (among other relevant forms), policy analysis and applied social science. As I discuss later in this book, the theory of public interest put forward here closely resembles philosopher John Dewey's (1927) approach. We can think of Dewey's approach as a "pragmatic idealism" (my term, not Dewey's). While this concept seems a contradiction in terms, it is better viewed as a conjoining of approaches. Pragmatic idealism consists of keeping in mind an ideal of the public interest, but without specific content, and then moving toward that ideal, making the ideal more concrete as one moves toward it.

For Dewey, the "public interest" cannot be known in any important sense in the absence of social inquiry and public discussion and debate. The public interest is an ideal that is given shape, on a case-by-case basis, by a public motivated to secure its common interests as a public. This commitment, in turn, encourages the preservation of the public by highlighting common interests and promoting dialogue among its members (Dewey 1927). In chapter 6 I explore Dewey's public interest theory in more detail.

PUBLIC VALUES

For the present, let us assume that *values* are complex personal judgments based on knowledge as well as an emotional reaction. This is just a "placeholder" definition; values concepts are explored in much more depth in chapter 7. Here we focus on *public* values. As used in this book, the term *public values* can be defined as follows: *A society's "public values" are those providing normative consensus about (a) the rights, benefits, and prerogatives to which citizens should (and should not) be entitled; (b) the obligations of citizens to society, the state, and one another; and (c) the principles on which governments and policies should be based.*

My chief concern here is with a society's or a nation's public values, and when I use the term *public values*, it is to these I refer. However, it is certainly the case that individuals hold public values, at least if by that one means individual values about things public. Thus, the individual's public values can be defined as follows: *Individual "public values" are the content-specific preferences of individuals concerning, on the one hand, the rights, obligations, and benefits to which citizens are entitled and, on the other hand, the obligations expected of citizens and their designated representatives.*

As we will see in other parts of the book, a key issue of public policy and management is identifying and assessing the best means of moving from disparate individual public values (deLeon 1995), relatively easily determined through opinion polls, votes, and sometimes even markets, to the society's public values. More difficult still is determining the best means of linking public values in specific action contexts (e.g., policymaking) to the public interest.

Whereas the public interest is an ideal to be pursued but not tied to any specific content, public values, even when they are quite general, have content and in many cases can be easily identified and (albeit less easily) measured and evaluated. To say that public values are held in common does not mean that they are universally embraced or that people agree on the exact nature or content of public values. Nor does it necessarily imply that public values reflect a munificent morality. Public values may include, for example, a consensus that all citizens should be provided ample sustenance as to maintain their health, that citizens should be equal before the law, or that government actions should be disinterested. But public values may in some instances draw sharp distinctions among people, their rights, and obligations. For example, it is possible for a society to be organized on the basis of the public value of racial purity or gender preference. Moreover, there is no requirement that all public values be viewed as positive by all persons in a society, especially if a predominant public value diminishes their rights or benefits.

How are public values different from public opinion? The line may not always be clear, because public opinions are often opinions *about* public values. But the distinction is one of temporal duration. Whereas public opinion is highly volatile, both in its concerns and in its directions, public values are much more stable. New public values may enter and old ones may exit but generally only after great social change and the passing of generations. Thus, universal adult suffrage is now taken for granted in many nations, but in those same nations minorities fought for decades to transform societies and their public values.

How are public values different from public goods? A familiar concept in economics, a public good is one that does not provide the producer with efficient profits because benefits can be enjoyed by persons who do not pay for the good. The extra benefits are referred to as "externalities," and these are one of the major categories of market failure. One formal definition of a public good (Breton 1965, 175–187) tells us this is a good (including a service or commodity) that "though not available equally to all, has the property that the amount available to one individual does not reduce that available to others by an equal amount."

A classic example of a public good is national defense; if it is supplied at all it is available to all citizens. Thus national defense is generally viewed as a type of good and service that should be provided by government because of the market failures inherent in its production (Klein 1987; Olson 1971; Rhoads 1985). We shall consider public goods in other sections of this book, but for present purposes it is sufficient to note that public goods do not necessarily relate at all to the question of public values. Public goods pertain to pricing efficiency. Pricing efficiency simply is not a consideration for public values. The key question for public goods: "Is it possible to exclude those who do not pay for the good?" The key question in public values: "Have those public values endorsed by the social collective been provided or guaranteed?"

Where does one look for public values? I consider this question in later chapters, but for now let us identify some common sources. A nation's more fundamental laws and, if there is one, its constitution provide good starting points for identifying public values, though public law is best viewed as reflecting public values, not as establishing them. In nations where governments are tyrannical or even benign but not representative, there is no reason to assume that laws will reflect public values. In any nation, it is useful to remember that laws may not evolve at the same pace as public values. Public values can be found in the fundamental myths of nations. Such myths as "the land of opportunity" often contain several broad public values. In some nations public values are closely reflected in policy and politics, but in other nations these are not so closely related. As political scientists Almond and Verba (1963, 243) noted in their classic book *Civic Culture:* "The 'modern' political system has within it the seeds of great fragmentation—among political structures, along partisan lines, between polity and society. But in Britain and the United States this fragmentation is impeded by the force of shared social values and attitudes, which permeate all aspects of society."

In nations with a strong judiciary, the high courts are an excellent viewing point for public values. Many high court decisions are, essentially, renderings and interpretations of public values. The public speeches of national and sometimes subnational public officials are often laced with public values. In the United States, the president's annual State of the Union message often is a chronicle of public values. The mission statements of public agencies provide another excellent source of public values. Elections often are about public values. Although even the most important elections can turn on highly idiosyncratic events or on small personal characteristics of candidates, most national and regional elections highlight public values.

In many cases, the scholarly literature of public policy, political science, public administration, and often many other fields deal directly or indirectly with public values, and, thus, public values can be distilled from the literature. Elsewhere the author and a colleague (Jørgensen and Bozeman 2007) developed an inventory of public values. This inventory was based chiefly on a review of the literature, but also on case studies (Jørgensen and Bozeman 2002), and identified public values such as transparency, accountability, equity, and political participation. The list included more than one hundred fundamental values that others had identified as *public* values. Even though extensive, it seems unlikely that the list is exhaustive inasmuch as public values differ among societies and political cultures, as well as across time.

PUBLIC VALUES CRITERIA

Markets fail; can public values "fail"? From one perspective it is not possible for public values to fail; they simply change. But if we consider a public value about which there is consensus and observe that the value is not being obtained, then perhaps it can be said to have failed. For example, if there is a public value that holds that all citizens should be equal before the law and policies or government actions violate this public value, then this can be said to be a public values failure, that is, a failure in a society's provision of a public value. Likewise, a public policy that condones or enhances gender discrimination in a society where gender equality is a public value could be said to be a public value failure. In the first example, the failure is one of omission and in the second, one of commission. In general, "public values failure" occurs when neither the market nor the public sector provides goods and services required to achieve public values.

In order to make judgments about the status of public values, it seems useful to identify public values criteria. Chapter 8 presents a Public Value Mapping model that establishes criteria for helping determine the degree to which particular public values are succeeding or failing. Chapter 9 provides an application of the Public Value Mapping model to the case of genetically modified crops.

It should be noted that the term *public value* should not be equated with government responsibility. To say that a public value is held says nothing about responsibilities for providing for the public value. Thus, if there is a public value for universal, high-quality health care, and all health care is privately provided and is, indeed, effective, affordable, and universal, then there is no public values failure. By the same token, if there is government-provided heath care and it is either not universal or not of sufficient quality, then the public value of universal, high-quality health care can be said to have failed.

Just as we can distinguish between public interest and public interest *theory*, we can delineate public value and public value theory. As we shall see in chapter 4, many theories of public interest have been provided, but few theories of public value have thus far been developed. Much of the remainder of this book deals with public values. What are they? How do we know them? What is the relationship among them? What is their relationship to public interest? How might they be codified?

A CONCEPTUAL SUMMARY

The content of this book requires that we deal with a number of core "public concepts" that have diverse meanings in various academic disciplines. Public interest, public goods, and public value are perhaps just a bit too close, terminologically, for comfort. With this in mind, and at the risk of repetition, I provide a conceptual summary. The idea behind this conceptual summary is to give the terminological usages employed here. There is no argument that other uses are invalid. Indeed, the careful reader will see that it is necessary, in some cases, to reckon with multiple uses even while establishing a lexicon for this book's treatment of these terms. This conceptual summary is not an attempt to either establish a canonical set of conceptual definitions or preempt others' concepts. It is simply to provide a basis for understanding the use of fundamental terms in this book's lexicon.

Table 1.1 provides a makeshift glossary (makeshift because these terms will receive more careful attention elsewhere in the book).

Table 1.1   Definitions of Public Concepts

Key Term	Provisional Definition	Comment
Public interest	An ideal public interest refers to those outcomes best serving the long-run survival and well-being of a social collective construed as a "public."	This is examined in detail in chapter 4, including a more elaborate definition.
Public values	A society's "public values" are those providing normative consensus about (a) the rights, benefits, and prerogatives to which citizens should (and should not) be entitled; (b) the obligations of citizens to society, the state, and one another; and (c) the principles on which governments and policies should be based.	Chapter 7 examines public values in great detail, contrasting public values and economic values.
Economic value	The exchange value of goods and services, usually based on socially sanctioned indices, especially monetary units.	By this definition, economic value is, explicitly, instrumental rather than prime (or end state) value.
Market failure	According to Donahue (1991, 18), market failure occurs when "prices lie—that is, when the prices of goods and services give false signals about their real value, confounding the communication between consumers and producers."	More detail is provided in chapter 3. Typically market failure is judged by standard criteria including presence of monopoly providers, market information deficits, and "spill-overs" (i.e., some receive value without paying for it).

(continued)

Table 1.1,   *(continued)*

Key Term	Provisional Definition	Comment
Public value criteria	Public value criteria are used to investigate the extent to which public values seemed to have been achieved. "Public values failure" occurs when neither the market nor public sector provides goods and services required to achieve public values.	Chapter 7 examines public values and criteria for the failure and success of public values. These public values diagnostic criteria, include, for example, short time horizons, imperfect monopolies (for goods and services where monopoly is preferred), and benefit hoarding.
Publicness	"An organization is 'public' to the extent that it exerts or is constrained by political authority." . . . "An organization is 'private' to the extent that it exerts or is constrained by economic authority" (Bozeman 1987, 84–85).	Chapter 2 elaborates the mix of economic and political authority in many contemporary policies.
Normative publicness	An approach to values analysis assuming that a knowledge of the mix of political and economic authority of institutions and policies is a prerequisite of understanding the potential of institutions and policies to achieve public values and to work toward public interest ideals.	While chapter 2 illustrates the ways in which the publicness of institutions and policies can affect public values, chapter 8 fleshes out the significance and uses of normative publicness.
Public goods	One of the most ubiquitous terms in policy analysis and public economics; one of the leading textbooks defines public goods as those goods that are, "in varying degrees, *nonrivalrous* in consumption, *nonexcludable* in use, or *both*" (Weimer and Vining 1999, 72). These same authors note that rivalrous consumption means that if one person consumes the good, it is not available to another. Excludable ownership means that one individual or group has control over its use.	We make note of this term here not because it is central to the views or coverage of this book, but because public goods reasoning is pervasive and because the term is easily confused with terms used here (e.g., public value).

THE BOOK'S OBJECTIVE: NORMATIVE PUBLICNESS

It is easy enough to state the primary objective of this book, but some discussion is required to understand the importance of the objective. The book's objective is *to address the imbalance of theoretical bases between, respectively, market-based and public values approaches to policy and management.* It seeks to advance public interest and public value theories, together referred to as normative publicness, by developing some new approaches and arguing the continued relevance of some old ones.

A fundamental assumption of this book is that the ability to provide strong theoretical rationales for approaches to public policy and management greatly enhances the ability to influence policy agendas and choices and, ultimately, advances normative publicness. Not everyone will agree with this assumption.

At first glance, little in the messy, rushed, frenetic realm of policymaking and management seems guided by theory. Indeed, we must start by acknowledging that in many cases public policy and management practice have little to do with theoretical rationales. Such factors as manifest necessity, social consensus, and political will almost always best strong theory—at least in the short term. Likewise, strong moral or religious conviction, especially when it is well organized, often triumphs over theory, analysis, and evidence-based information, which the faithful may perceive as essentially irrelevant. Stem cell research policies come to mind. So do policies pertaining to the rights of homosexuals. Perhaps the best example, though, is the Israeli–Palestinian conflict. Neither economics nor secular public values carry much weight when disputants believe that God has ordained that the land belongs to them.

In policy environments characterized by partisanship, opportunism, competing interests, and religion-based political activism, it may seem naïve or hyperrational to fret about shortcomings of theory. But the skeptic who completely dismisses the role of theory in public policy may be viewing its influence from too narrow a lens. If we consider the impact of theory based solely upon its explanatory power, then it may seem to have a modest role in real-world policymaking. It seems unlikely that many elected officials or bureaucrats reflect upon the ideas of economist Milton Friedman or philosopher John Dewey (much less Aristotle or John Stuart Mill) as they seek to forge or implement public policy. But theory is socially enacted and includes not only sets of ideas but also interpretations, applications, rhetoric, and symbols. In many instances, people who may have never read about or even heard of a particular theorist or theory may nonetheless be influenced by popularizations and other secondary uses of the theory. Related, and just as important, if theories produce useful analytical tools (as has certainly been the case with microeconomics), one need not read or fully understand theory in order to employ, and be strongly influenced by, the tool that has issued from it.

Another hazard to understanding the power of theory in public deliberation is placing too tight a temporal coupling between theory and decision. If one focuses on particular decisions one rarely sees a major role played by theory (judicial policymaking being a partial exception). However, theories often have their strongest influence not in helping us decide among choices but in helping identify the set of choices we will ultimately decide among. Because theories and assumptions shape ways of thinking, they often have their strongest influence in framing the choice set. To take a simple but relevant example, if one begins with the assumption that markets are more efficient than governments, then the set of policies identified and the ultimate choice among them is greatly constrained by that initial assumption. While public policy and management practice rarely include direct and deeply informed applications of theory, there are many instances of "theory creep" whereby theories and, more often, the knowledge accoutrement of theories, find their way into the premises and substance of public policy and management (Lindblom and Cohen 1979).

In the same direct and indirect ways that market-oriented theories support the march toward market-oriented policy and management, there is a potential for theories of public interest and public value to exert influence. However, the relative undersupply of such theories lessens the likelihood that policy choices will be premised on public values. We come back again to the idea of counterbalance. Those who argue for a market-based approach to policy or public management have at their disposal, among other possibilities, market failure theory, public goods theory, proprietary property rights theory, principle-agent theory, and a large kit bag of analytical tools (such as cost–benefit analysis) flowing from these theories. (For a more detailed account, see Furubotn and Richter 2005.)

By contrast, one advancing public values and the public interest commands little theory, except of the broadest sort. Typically, public values arguments appeal to the particular merits of the case (important, but also available to those advancing market values) and to abstract theories of public interest, theories too general and too ambiguous to provide much traction. The result is that parties interested in those public values find themselves with little analytical support, no matter how strong their moral, political, or contextual case.

The goal of redressing the imbalance of theoretical bases between, respectively, market-based and public values approaches to policy and management seems an inordinately ambitious goal, especially given the huge gap between economic theory and public interest theory. However, the objective here is not parity but simply some increased attention to systematic thinking and theorizing about public values and the public interest. By resurrecting public interest theory and suggesting some new ways of thinking about public value, perhaps it is possible to elevate the power of public value discourse and thereby the impact of these values in public policy and public management.

One of the new ways of thinking about public values is the "public value mapping" model identifying public value criteria potentially useful for policy deliberation (see chapters 8 and 9). These criteria are in some respects similar to the familiar and widely used market failure criteria referred to earlier. The "something old" is a pragmatic theory of the public interest similar to that espoused by philosopher John Dewey (1927). The book argues that Dewey's pragmatic approach potentially resolves many of the alleged weaknesses of public interest theories and gives guideposts for public policy deliberations.

CHAPTER 2: THE BASE CASES

As the preceding discussion makes apparent, this book is about theory not about specific policies or particular problems in management. The book may test many readers' commitment to theory, moving as it does from public interest theory to economic theory to moral theory and then back again. There is even a bit of theory of knowledge and epistemology thrown in the mix.

Despite the theoretical aims of the book, there is some effort to develop policy hooks for the sundry theory hats. One of the best ways to diminish theory is to strip it of its context. This does not mean that it is necessary to provide detailed real-world illustrations for each point developed here, but it does require some attention to policy realities that help make the case and, it is hoped, make it clearer. While simple illustrations are used throughout the book and one chapter is devoted to a single policy case and application (chapter 9 focuses on genetically modified seeds), I also use the approach referred to as "base cases." Chapter 2 presents several extended cases of recent policy issues that show the shifting landscape of "public" and "private." One objective for chapter 2 is simply to underscore a point made in this chapter—that economic individualism and market-based approaches are even more prominent today than in decades past, and, similarly, their manifestations sometimes run counter to expectations one might have from political economy theory or pluralistic political science. A second purpose of chapter 2 is to provide several base cases that can be cross-referenced throughout the book. Many of the arguments developed in the book will refer to these cases.

ECONOMIC INDIVIDUALISM AND THE "PUBLICNESS" OF POLICIES:

CASES AND CONTROVERSIES

Every good cause is worth some inefficiency.

—PAUL SAMUELSON (Lohr 2004)

Is economic individualism sweeping the world? In the words of economist Robert Kuttner (1997), is "everything for sale"? Do we serve "one market under God," with market populism being "the New American consensus" (Frank 2004, xv)? Or perhaps public policies and public management are proceeding more as less as usual, the cyclical shifts in public and economic forces occurring well with normal range? One might well argue that in the United States not much of consequence has changed. There is still a "social safety net," albeit one that seems to be shrinking, and the New Deal compact forged by Roosevelt is still in place, if a bit shaken.

This book cannot provide a good answer to the "have things *really* changed" question, and, fortunately, its justification does not depend on any particular answer to that question. Policy and public management history is always about the ebb and flow of political and economic forces and the values they represent. Ideas pertaining to those values have perennial importance. This chapter emphasizes policies and government reforms arising from the shifts to market-based policies and governance, but less because of an inexorable march toward market-based policies than because there will always be market (and political) forces in democratically conceived governance.

"COUNTERBALANCING"?

Note the book's subtitle: "*Counterbalancing* Economic Individualism." This subtitle does not imply that policy-theories-based assumptions of economics or economic individualism are harmful, wrong, or of little practical use. Indeed, economics-based policy theories and ideas often contribute enormously to policy deliberation, formulation, implementation, and, especially, analysis. Nor should the subtitle be taken as a rallying cry to more centralized policies emphasizing political control. Rather, the need for counterbalance owes more to shortcomings of ideas and theories pertaining to public interest and public values. These theories are generally not as well developed, not as precise, and rarely have accompanying analytical tools. Microeconomics-based policy theories have succeeded so well that they have in some instances driven competing policy theories, including theories of public interest and public value, from the intellectual playing fields.

An assumption I make in this book, one not easily proved, is that the analytical power, including theory and tools of application, of contemporary microeconomics has helped lend force and persuasiveness to policies based on economic individualism. There are, of course, a great many forces in play that affect the ebb and flow of public policies and government reforms, and many of these (e.g., changing demographics, cross-national conflicts) have nothing to do with formally expressed ideas. But there is no claim here that economic individualism is the *only* factor affecting changes in public policy and management but rather that it seems to be making headway against public interest and public values influences.

THE PUBLICNESS OF POLICIES: WHAT HAPPENS WHEN THE MIX OF ECONOMIC AND POLITICAL AUTHORITY CHANGES?

Regardless of how one feels about the relative importance of ideas as an ingredient of policy change, there is the *fact* of change awaiting explanation. Is there an imbalance not only in formal ideas, theories, and analytical tools but also in policies themselves? The answer to this question is that there is no answer, at least not apart from one's values. What does "imbalance" mean with respect to policies? Another way to think about the question of policy change is this: Has the mix of market and political control of public policies changed? Are there changes in the relative publicness (Bozeman 1987) of policies and institutions?

As suggested in chapter 1, we can think of almost any set of policies (as well as most sets of industrial firms and government agencies) as representing and responding to a distinctive mix of political and market forces. In this chapter we consider some contemporary policies by gauging their implications for this volatile aspect we have referred to as "publicness." The implicit question for each policy is this: Has the mix of economic and political authority represented by these policy domains shifted from earlier periods? The answers to these questions are rarely straightforward.

In this chapter we examine privatization cases, ones in which the mix of economic authority has changed such that publicness has diminished. These policies are not representative of the degree of publicness (or privateness) in contemporary policies. Indeed, they were chosen as examples of the different ways in which market-oriented approaches can be deployed in the public agencies. Each of these cases is an example of diminished publicness. However, we will see that the injection of market thinking into policies that have a history of "high publicness" policies has affected these respective policy domains, sometimes unpredictably and sometimes perversely. For example, in one case, we will see that national defense policy, the classic illustration for policies that have a "pure public goods" character, seems inconsistent with both the expectations and prescriptions of economic theorists. In another case, prison policy, we see some of the unexpected results of privatization of a policy realm that, perhaps more than any other, embodies the coercive side of political authority. In all the cases examined in the following sections, we see a rethinking publicness, a change in the historical mix of economic and political authority.

ECONOMIC INDIVIDUALISM IN PUBLIC POLICY

In the following sections we consider illustrative cases of increased privatization in five public policy domains: Social Security, national defense, water, prisons, and local government. The cases suggest not only the scope and breadth of influence of economic individualism but also the ways in which citizens, policy clients, and stakeholders are affected by changes in the degree of publicness of policies. Each of the cases is sufficiently rich and suffused with controversy to permit multiple interpretations and multiple lessons. Notwithstanding the multiple possibilities, each case is used to highlight one major point about the mix of political and economic authority.

Social Security Privatization

It has long been recognized as an inescapable obligation of a democratic society to provide for every individual some measure of basic protection from hardship and want caused by factors beyond his control. In our own country, the obligation of the Federal Government in this respect has been recognized by the establishment of our Social Security system. . . . The passage of the Social Security Act in 1935 marked a great advance in our concept of the means by which our citizens, through their Government, can provide against common economic risks.

—Harry S. Truman, May 24, 1948

The classic American social policy, the first on most any list, is Social Security. But there is a widely embraced but not yet authoritative alternative version— Social Security investment accounts. At the close of 2005, the centerpiece of the Bush administration's legislative agenda, privatized Social Security, was narrowly defeated in the U.S. Congress.

Social Security in the United States was first established in 1935 as part of Franklin D. Roosevelt's post-Depression New Deal reforms. Similar to nations around the world, the United States is facing the challenge of caring for an expanding aging population with the contributions of a declining workforce. Today, there are more than 47 million Americans defined as Old Age, Survivor, and Disabled Individuals (OASDI), qualifying them to receive Social Security benefits (Social Security Administration 2005a). According to the Social Security Administration, seniors make up 20 percent of the voting public in the United States and will continue to increase in number, making up approximately one-fourth of the voting population by 2018 (Hertzberg 2005a).

The U.S. Social Security system has many features that are typical of social insurance programs throughout the world. Participation is compulsory and not means-tested (all citizens are eligible for benefits regardless of need), eligibility and benefit levels depend on contributions made by workers, and payments begin with some occurrence such as illness, disability, retirement, or unemployment. Social Security is the largest domestic spending program in the United States (OASDI expenditures were approximately $501 billion in 2004) and operates as a pay-as-you-go system—benefits to current retirees are supported by payments from current workers. Individuals pay into the system throughout their working lives and upon retirement, unemployment, or injury receive a fixed annual benefit for as long as they live, thus insuring against the possibility that one will outlive one's savings. The current Social Security system mandates that individuals insure themselves and distributes income to elderly and disabled citizens who lack the ability to support themselves.

In 1983, as a result of the impending retirement of the post–World War II baby boomers, the Social Security Trust Fund was established, making the Social Security system a partially funded system, with the Social Security Trust Fund supplementing Social Security payments in the future when the contributions of workers alone no longer meet the needs of retirees.

Today, Social Security payroll taxes exceed benefits and will continue to do so through at least 2028, if not longer (Hertzberg 2005a). For example, a net increase of $156 million was reported for OASDI for fiscal year 2003–4 and a year end amount of $1.6 trillion (Social Security Administration 2005b). These surpluses are invested in the Social Security Trust Fund in the form of government savings bonds and are typically used to fund other government programs. The nonpartisan Congressional Budget Office predicts that the Social Security Trust Fund will be exhausted by 2052 (Hertzberg 2005a). In response to the threat of the demise of the Social Security Trust Fund, U.S. policymakers and academics are seeking to reform the system. For example, by 2022, the retirement age for American workers will shift from the age of sixty-five, with the options of retiring at sixty-two and receiving reduced benefits or delaying retirement until age sixty-seven and receiving increased benefits.

One of the most popular contemporary reforms calls for privatization of the Social Security system by earmarking individual contributions to be saved for each individual worker. Workers and employers would continue to make required contributions to Social Security, but those contributions would go to individualized accounts. At the end of one's work life, retirement would be financed out of personal savings, not pooled contributions of current workers. The advantages of this privatized system would include, first, the decrease of taxes on the current work force and, second, the possible advantage that individuals could invest retirement savings in the private market and hopefully increase their rates of return and enjoy larger benefits upon retirement.

In his 2005 State of the Union address President George W. Bush proposed to overhaul Social Security and establish private investment accounts. The Bush proposal included the individualization of retirement savings and the elimination of the Social Security Trust Fund. The plan was hotly debated but eventually reached its demise in fall 2005, when Democrats fiercely opposed Bush's proposal (Toner, Schemo, and Pear 2006). Despite the failure to gain congressional support for the privatization of Social Security, Bush resurrected his efforts in the 2006 State of the Union address by proposing the creation of a bipartisan commission to reform Social Security and Medicare (Toner, Schemo, and Pear 2006).

Personal Financial Risk. The privatization of Social Security would force individuals to take on the personal financial risk of saving for retirement and would leave individuals in the precarious situation of predicting their retirement needs and life expectancy. Furthermore, if individuals are required to save for their own retirement through government-approved investments, it follows that one's retirement wealth will be dictated by the wealth one started with, assuming one's investments do not go bad. That is, the rich are guaranteed a rich retirement, and everyone else is left to either work through old age or retire very poor (Hertzberg 2005b).

Research indicates that some individuals may not be capable of managing their own savings and retirement accounts because of limited understanding of investment funds or even of simple aspects of investments, such as fees and charges for various investments (Hulbert 2006). In a recent study of undergraduate and graduate students at Harvard and the Wharton School of Business (University of Pennsylvania), researchers found that students were unable to select the lowest cost index fund for their portfolios, even when the lowest cost options were made "obvious" (Choi, Laibson, and Madrian 2006). Students required detailed guidance in order to invest their money in low-cost index funds. This study points to the increased administrative assistance that would be required to ensure that American workers do not assume inappropriate risk with privatized accounts (Hulbert 2006).

In addition to the risk of losing one's investments, an individual would be required to predict her own retirement needs and life expectancy because she would no longer be guaranteed benefits from retirement to death. One of the benefits of the current Social Security system and its collective savings pool and trust fund is that benefits are paid through death, ensuring that one who lives beyond life expectancy and savings will not be left destitute. The costs of benefits for individuals who live to ninety-five are offset by the earlier passing of other retirees. For example, imagine that Paul Smith, age sixty-five, has $150,000 in savings. How much does Paul need to live through retirement? His response could vary from $1,250 per month, if he lives for ten years, to $625 per month, if he lives to be eighty-five. If Paul has the misfortune of living to ninety-five years of age, he would be forced to allocate himself a monthly stipend of $416 and hope that he never falls ill or requires expensive medical care. How can we, as a society, expect individual pensioners to predict their life expectancies and financial needs? And when their predictions fall short, who will bear the cost?

Administrative Costs. Critics argue that reforms to privatize Social Security will increase administrative costs. For example, the Chilean retirement system, one of the best-known privatized Social Security systems, has greatly raised administrative costs because every worker and investment fund requires a manager, and government regulatory oversight of the program is extensive and expensive (Diamond 1996). Today, the administrative costs for OASDI hover around $4.6 billion and are drawn from the payroll and income tax contributions of workers. According to Bush, workers would need help managing their personalized Social Security investments, though it is unclear who would pay for this management and how (Rosen 2006).

Loss of the Social Security Trust Fund. In addition to ensuring direct disbursement to approximately 50 million retirees and disabled individuals, the government bonds in the Social Security Trust Fund provide a substantial source of funding for government loans and federal programs and help to finance the federal deficit. For example, the trust fund played a critical role in lowering the federal budget deficit from 1998 to 2001 and lowered the 2005 budget deficit by approximately $151 billion (Hertzberg 2005b).

As of 2005 the trust fund had nearly $1.7 trillion in U.S. Treasury bonds, which are a stable, secure source of income because they do not fluctuate in value and cannot be traded on Wall Street (Social Security Administration 2005a). With the elimination of the trust fund, government bonds would be sold to private investors, shifting this source of government funding from a public trust to private security (or insecurity) and leaving the government reliant on more volatile, high-risk private investments.

The Collective Good. In classic economic and public finance terms, social insurance is justified on the basis of adverse selection, decision-making costs, income distribution, paternalism, and public good. The proposal to privatize Social Security leaves the decision-making costs and risks to individuals. In addition to leaving the citizens reliant on their ability to predict future needs when they are thirty years old, it also leaves little room for the provision of insurance to the disabled and the dependent. President Bush and David Walker, the comptroller general of the United States, admit that that the problem of Social Security's solvency and the increasing demands of caring for the elderly will not be solved by private investment accounts (Hertzberg 2005a).

According to columnist Henrik Hertzberg, "Social Security—like the public-school system, the progressive income tax, the neighborhood public library, the subways and buses, food stamps, and a host of other socialistic schemes—runs counter to the narrow economic interests of the rich, because they generally have to put more money into it than they get out" (2005b). Still, though the tangible benefits of Social Security pass to the poorer, the intangible benefits of peace, decency, and public good pass to the entire society. Hertzberg writes about the tension between economic individualism and public value, as it pertains to Social Security and, unlike some observers (e.g., White House 2005; Beach et al. 2004), comes down firmly on the side of public value.

> Yes, self-reliance is good; but solidarity is good, too. Looking after yourself is good, but making a firm social decision to banish indigence among the old is also good. Market discipline is good, but it is also good for there to be places where the tyranny of winning and losing does not dominate. Individual choice is good. But making the well-being of the old dependent on the luck or skill of their stock picks or mutual-fund choices is not so good. The idea behind Social Security is not just that old folks should be entitled to comfort regardless of their personal merits. It is that none of us, of any age, should be obliged to live in a society where minimal dignity and the minimal decencies are denied to any of our fellow-citizens at the end of life. (Hertzberg 2005a)

Implications: Publicness and Social Security. A great many perspectives can and have been brought to the issue of Social Security privatization. For now, let us consider implications for the publicness of policies and for the influence of economic individualism.

In the first place, we can observe that Social Security is perhaps the foremost example of a public policy in the United States that defies the idea that the political culture of the nation is predominantly based on economic individualism. One possible interpretation of the move to privatize Social Security is that there has, indeed, been a fundamental change, at least in the United States, in the mix of public and economic authority underpinning core public policies. One reaction to this is the following: If Social Security, the prototype collective welfare policy, goes private, is any policy exempt from the dominance of economic individualism? But another reading is that the *failure* (thus far) to privatize Social Security shows that there is a bottom to economic individualism and market-based policies and, perhaps, that Social Security defines that bottom.

One implication of the case, one not quite so straightforward, is that Social Security privatization can be viewed as demonstrating that during times of crisis (i.e., the impending bankruptcy of the Social Security Trust Fund) policymakers struggle to develop solutions to crisis, and, almost inexorably, those struggles lead to a reexamination of the political and economic authority bases of public policy. Related to this, the publicness recombination that so often occurs in crises can be especially useful for helping us plumb the fundamental public and private values in society and society's expressed normative boundaries for the uses of economic and political authority, respectively.

The following case considers how crisis has changed public policy in a different way and in pursuit of different objectives, but again with a shake-up in the historical mix of political and economic authority. The Iraq War has by most any measure been the most "privatized" large-scale war ever waged.

Contracting Out National Defense

The national defense is one of the cardinal duties of a statesman.

—JOHN ADAMS (Mills 1966)

Discussions of political economy theory often cite national defense as the classic case of a public good (i.e., a good whose provision to some persons implies its provision to all). For example, *The Concise Encyclopedia of Economics* tells us: "Most economic arguments for government intervention are based on the idea that the marketplace cannot provide public goods or handle externalities. Public health and welfare programs, education, roads, research and development, national and domestic security, and a clean environment all have been labeled public goods" (Cowen 2006). Consistent with this expectation, national defense is financed almost entirely by tax dollars. However, the national defense effort in the United States has for quite some time been supported extensively by private contractors, and this trend accelerated sharply during the Iraq War.

Even as early as World War I, contracting out military services was commonplace. Such companies as the American Sugar Refining Company, the International Nickel Company, and United States Steel were among the most active in providing goods and services for the military in World War I. However, the widespread use of sole-source and no-bid contracts and the placement of private contractors on the ground in Iraq are new developments. The private role in Iraq has been quite controversial, not so much because of the use of private firms per se as because billions of dollars' worth of contracts have been awarded and administered without competitive bidding. In 2003, the United States estimated that there would be more than $18 billion in reconstruction contracts in Iraq (Associated Press 2003). That same year, the U.S. Agency for International Development (USAID) asked a select group of firms to bid for approximately $900 million in government contracts to repair and reconstruct Iraqi infrastructure including water systems, schools, hospitals, and roads and bridges. The largest recipients of these contracts included Halliburton, whose former chief executive, Dick Cheney, is the current vice president; Bechtel Group Inc.; Fluor Corporation; Louis Berger Group Inc.; Parsons Corporation; and Washington Group International Inc.

Though there are numerous issues associated with the widespread contracting out of military services and the reconstruction in Iraq, this chapter highlights three primary problems. First, U.S. policies favoring particular American firms and reducing competition by relying on no-bid contracts are widely believed to have led to corruption and waste. Second, the inability of the U.S. government and military to monitor private contractors has reduced transparency, accountability, and responsibility for government action as private contractors often are perceived as an extension of the military. Third, the military's reliance on American private contractors has reduced our ability to mount a coordinated effort to address the problems of Iraqi civilians.

In addition to placing responsibility for most Iraqi rebuilding efforts into private hands, U.S. policies have favored American private firms at the expense of increasing competition and ensuring that contractors provide the best services at the lowest costs to American taxpayers. In 2003 President Bush announced a policy that would ban companies from those countries who opposed the invasion of Iraq, including France, Germany, Canada, and Russia, from bidding on reconstruction contracts funded by U.S. tax dollars (Associated Press 2003). Companies from antiwar countries were eligible to bid on more than $13 billion worth of contracts from an international fund, could serve as subcontractors to U.S. companies, and could bid on contracts managed by Great Britain, who, though it supported the United States' right to determine how it will spend its tax dollars, would award contracts solely on merit (Associated Press 2003).

One of the primary justifications for privatizing government services is to create competitive markets for public goods. In this case, military services and reconstruction efforts in Iraq have been outsourced to increase cost efficiency and expedite the rebuilding of Iraq. However, because the majority of Iraqi contracts were no-bid contracts, there was no obvious incentive for private companies to reduce costs in order to win contracts. Furthermore, because USAID excluded Iraqi companies, humanitarian organizations, the United Nations, and many non-U.S.-based businesses and organizations from bidding for contracts, the argument that outsourcing brings the free market to public services, in this case, is undercut. For more than three years private firms were not allowed to compete for contracts in Iraq, resulting in many contracts going to only six firms, each with a strong connection to the administration.

Five years after the initial invasion of Iraq, auditors have uncovered confusion, waste, unfinished work, and a general lack of accountability in their assessment of Iraqi rebuilding contracts (Glanz 2006b). A U.S. Justice Department investigation found that Halliburton had made approximately $2.7 billion in errors, such as failing to report canceled subcontracts to contract managers and overcharging for food services and petrol. Additional audits have disputed costs on no-bid contracts for food and oil equipment repairs including accusations that a Halliburton subsidiary, Kellogg Brown and Root (KBP) charged the army three times what others were charging for fuel deliveries. Rhonda James, a Dallas-based spokeswoman for the U.S. Army Corps of Engineers, notes that the demand for haste and the dangers of war warrant excessive costs and that under some no-bid contractors are "not required to perform perfectly to be entitled to reimbursement" because the army places "more emphasis on timely mission accomplishment than on cost control and paperwork" (Glanz 2006a).

Accusations of contract abuse abound. In 2005 the Justice Department filed a criminal corruption case against Robert J. Stein Jr., who while working for the Coalition Provisional Authority in Iraq accepted $546,000 in llegal payments in exchange for directing contracts to Philip H. Bloom, an American businessman who ran several companies in Romania. In addition to the case of conspiracy, fraud, and money-laundering against these two men, the Justice Department is investigating more than fifty other criminal cases related to contracts in Iraq (Babcock and Renaee 2005). It was not till July 2006 that, in the interest of saving money, the Pentagon decided to alter its method for awarding multibillion-dollar contracts in Iraq to a competitive process instead of giving them exclusively to Halliburton (Burnett 2003, 2006).

The second problem with the privatization of military services is the loss of transparency and public accountability. The large population of private contractors in Iraq operates as an extension of the military—an extension that is less accountable to military commanders, omitted from the body count of soldiers, omitted from calculations of the financial cost of war, and hidden from the oversight of public officials and public opinion. Private contractors have many of the same duties as soldiers, but lack the training and oversight of the armed forces.

Private contractors working as cooks, mail deliverers, and cleaning crews have freed the ever shrinking U.S. Army, down from 2.1 million in 1990 to 1.4 million in 2003, to fight on the front lines (Krane 2003). Still, contractors run high risks working in Iraq and often are killed while providing services to the U.S. military or Iraqi civilians. However, there is no official count of the number of private contractors who have been killed, or even of those who work in Iraq (estimated at more than 20,000 in 2003; Krane 2003). Unfortunately, with such little oversight over private contractors, the second largest coalition partner in Iraq, it is difficult for the public and Congress to evaluate the success of American efforts in Iraq.

The use of private contractors can often result in no one being responsible for incomplete projects. For example, in May 2006 the Army Corps of Engineers canceled the remainder of a $70 million contract to refurbish twenty Iraqi hospitals when Parsons, the contractor, was unable to finish eight of the hospitals on time. Brigadier General William H. McCoy Jr., commander of the corps division that administered the contracts, noted that though he was responsible for overseeing the contracts, he could not have prevented Parsons' poor workmanship and cost overruns. McCoy noted, "I'm responsible for construction in Iraq," but "this contractor was not performing, and we took aggressive action" (Glantz 2006b). Parsons officials countered that the Corps was responsible for delays and inefficiencies because the Corps inspectors were not approving the work, funded from multiple contracts, quickly enough to ensure adequate implementation. This case illustrates how accountability and responsibility can be unclear when contractors and military contract managers pass the buck back and forth.

The lack of oversight in managing contractors in Iraq has led to widespread concerns regarding both the responsibility of the U.S. military to know what is happening on the ground in Iraq and the responsibility of U.S. leadership to manage taxpayer monies. According to Representative Henry A. Waxman (D-Calif), before the war the Republican-controlled Congress held thirteen hearings on the UN oil-for-food program in Iraq but since the invasion of Iraq has held only one hearing on the spending and management of reconstruction funds. It seems that Congress has abdicated all oversight responsibility to contract managers and private firms while private firms such as Halliburton have "gouged the taxpayer" with little to no reaction from Congress (Glanz 2006a).

Finally, the widespread use of American contractors in Iraq has reduced the capacity of the U.S. military and political leadership to protect both the interests of Iraqis as they work to rebuild the country and the interests of Americans who are footing the bill for that work. First, the use of American-based private contractors has reduced the inclusion of local Iraqi firms and interests in rebuilding the country, making it more difficult for the United States to withdraw from Iraq. Second, contractors have been reluctant to consult with qualified Iraqis who are more familiar with the region and more adept at dealing with the insecure climate instead relying on Western contractors to work in Iraq without the language or cultural understanding of how to best meet the needs of the local communities.

In a recent report reviewing thirteen hospitals in Iraq and a testimony at the World Tribunal, journalist Dahr Jamail documented the challenges facing the use of private contractors to manage health and medical facilities in Iraq. Jamail concludes that the medical system is suffering more under the occupation than it did under the sanctions against Iraq. According to Deputy Minister of Health Dr. Amer Al Khuzaie, in June 2004 USAID awarded Bechtel $1 billion to rebuild and repair hospitals in Iraq, with $300 million of that allocation going directly to the Ministry of Health. Khuzaie reports that, because of security issues, Bechtel has not maintained the medical infrastructure (Jamail 2005a, 23).

There is no necessary reason to expect that the private sector providers of Iraq War goods and services have performed worse than civilian, Defense Department, or military providers would have. However, because it is an arm of the government, when the military acts inappropriately, elected officials and citizens can investigate the actions of the military. When private contractors behave inappropriately, they are not subject to the same level of public scrutiny because they are protected by privacy laws and regulations.

The case of Iraq War contracting presents little of value concerning the appropriate mix of economic and political authority but holds useful lessons about the appropriate relationship between these bases of policy. The classic argument for market-based policy is the use of market competition to achieve efficiency (chapter 3 explores this argument in some detail). But this argument is largely irrelevant in instances where there is no competition, such as the no-bid contracts common in the privatization of the Iraq War. If there is a single publicness lesson to be learned from the Iraq War contracting case, perhaps it is the harm that can occur when political authority is bent to the needs of individuals rather than the needs of the public or even of the competitive market. In this case, political authority seems, in a great many instances, to be deployed to expand the economic authority domains of a relatively small number of interests and actors, resulting in arguably the most poisonous mix of political and economic authority possible. Whether or not one views the provision of no-bid contracts to politically influential economic interests as corruption per se, it takes little imagination to see how such a means of policy delivery can result in a series of discrete instances of corruption.

A major implication in the Iraq War contracting case is the hazard of using political authority to advance private values. The Iraq War contracting case seems especially pernicious in that it involves narrow-gauged economic individualism cloaked in the rhetoric of private sector performance efficiency. Perhaps it is inevitable that those in power will sometimes advance their own interests and those of their associates at the expense of public interest. But the threats of the private misuse of the public sector are especially great during periods of crisis, in cases where the level of effort is massive and when public accountability mechanisms are diminished.

Politics, Markets, and Sustaining Life: Water

Human beings must have food and drink, clothing and shelter, first of all, before they can interest themselves in politics, science, art, religion, and the like.
—FRIEDRICH ENGELS, Funeral oration for Karl Marx, March 17, 1883

In most of the developed world and in many developing nations local water supplies are delivered by publicly owned water agencies. Water has typically been treated as an inexhaustible resource and a public good, available to everyone at little to no cost. However, in many of the poorest nations, access to clean, safe drinking water is limited, expensive, and certainly not guaranteed. Around the world we are becoming increasingly aware that water is not inexhaustible.

As demand for water outstrips supply, governments, interest groups, and private companies are calling for the creation of economic markets to manage water. Where public waterworks systems exist, they have become a popular target for privatization and contracting, sometimes enhancing efficiency (e.g., Short 1997), sometimes giving rise to disastrous consequences (e.g., Jørgensen and Bozeman 2002). Where public waterworks systems are nonexistent, private companies have moved in to create and manage water systems.

Worldwide, more than a billion people lack access to safe drinking water, and 2.4 billion people do not have adequately sanitized water, resulting in widespread disease and the death of nearly 12 million people annually (Segerfeldt 2005; UNEP 2002). According to Fredrik Segerfeldt, a Swedish activist and author, the very poor, who are not connected to strong water markets, pay more than twelve times the average price for clean water. Most illness and death associated with water occurs in poorer countries where 97 percent of water distribution is managed by weak public providers (Segerfeldt 2005). Approximately 30 to 40 percent of clean water in the world is lost through illegal tapping and leaks (UNWWDR 2006).

Proponents of water privatization argue that access to private markets can help to dramatically reduce the high cost of water for the poor, as exemplified in privatization efforts in Argentina, the Philippines, Cambodia, and Morocco, where private investments help to manage and distribute water resources (Segerfeldt 2005). According to Inter-American Development Bank president Luis Alberto Moreno, private companies serve water customers throughout Latin America, including those in Brazil, Honduras, Peru, Chile, Paraguay, Bolivia, Ecuador, and Colombia (*Wall Street Journal* March 10, 2006, p. 8, "A Home-grown Solution for Latin America's Water Crisis"). Water systems have also been privatized in Puerto Rico, the Gaza Strip, Australia, New Zealand, ten countries in Asia, ten in Africa, three in North America, two in the Caribbean, three in the Middle East, and eighteen European nations (ICIJ 2003).

Though private investment and public-private partnerships have improved water sanitation and access in some communities, Moreno notes, "Private investment is not a panacea for Latin America's sanitation problems" (*Wall Street Journal* March 10, 2006, p. 8), as more than 90 percent of the population in Latin America remains dependent on public utilities. Moreover, the 2005 UN World Water Report notes that water policies around the world continue to fail in their Millennium Development Goal of providing adequate access to clean, safe drinking water around the world.

The United Nations and the Sustainable Development Network, a group of thirty nongovernmental organizations, continues to blame governments and heavy regulations for the failure to provide drinking water to the world's population while private companies continue to fill in the gaps where governments have failed (Okonski 2006). Kendra Okonski, director of the U.K.-based International Policy Network, claims that we need to manage water with markets, property rights, and laws in order to ensure that people use water more effectively (Kinver 2006). In contrast, Peter Hardstaff of the World Development Movement argues that, overall, efforts to privatize water have failed. Hardstaff contends that even the largest firms lack the money required to effectively manage water systems around the world and argues that the best way to manage and provide clean water is through the investment of public infrastructure. Mary Ann Manahan, a researcher with Focus on the Global South, argues that because water is a basic need and access to water is a basic right, water should be community owned and managed (Netto 2005).

Over the last ten years, private management of water systems has grown around the world, in both developing and developed countries. Recently, water companies have expanded into the United States, a lucrative water market with more than 150 million customers. According to an investigation by the International Consortium of Investigative Journalists (ICIJ), three European private water companies—Suez and Vivendi Environnement in France and British-based Thames Water, owned by Germany's RWE AG—currently control about 5 percent of the water in the world and are working closely with the World Bank and other international trade organizations to expand their ownership of water (Marsden 2003). Between 1990 and 2002 the five largest water companies in the world expanded their water distribution networks from twelve countries to fifty-six countries and two territories, expanding the private provision of water from 51 million people to more than 300 million people worldwide.

According to Riccardo Petrella, advisor to the European Union on Science and Technology and a professor at the Catholic University in Louvain, Belgium, "Water has become important for capital because water is increasingly characterized by a crisis of scarcity . . . [a]nd scarcity is the basis of modern capitalism" (Marsden 2003). Though private companies insist that water should not be free, they face opposition because water is vital to human survival. An example of this opposition is the 1999 case of privatizing water markets in Cochabamba, Bolivia. When awarded a no-bid contract for the public waterworks in Bolivia, Aguas del Tunari, a consortium owned by Bechtel and United Utilities, raised water rates up to 150 percent. When Aguas del Tunari threatened to cut off wells and groundwater to those who did not meet their payments, citizens participated in widespread protests resulting in two deaths and approximately $25 million in police and security costs.

According to Gerard Payen, vice president of the France-based Suez Lyonnaise des Eaux, "Water is not a commodity. It is a public good. It is also a social good. It is essential for life" (Marsden 2003). Peter Spillett, a senior executive of British-based Thames Water, contends that "water is both a commodity and a [public] service," because, though it falls from the sky, companies add value to the public good when they clean, bottle, and ship it (Marsden 2003). Many companies do not claim to privatize water, but instead argue that they work with government to manage water and produce a better end product. Privatization advocates argue that water markets may help to recoup some of the large costs of sanitizing water and maintaining waterworks infrastructure and reduce the tendency to waste water when it is underpriced. Because water is a limited resource, by selling it on markets, companies help to reduce waste and increase conservation.

Davis Boys of Public Services International, a global federation of more than six hundred public sector trade unions delivering public services in 160 countries, argues that water is indeed a public good. He argues, "We must be extremely careful not to impose market forces on water because there are many more decisions that go into managing water—there are environmental decisions, social-culture decisions" (Marsden 2003).

In most instances, modern governments' provision of water increases the likelihood that the high costs of sanitizing and maintaining access to water is shared by all citizens, while distributing the benefits of clean water and public health to everyone. Under government provision, there is collective responsibility for the collective good, which ensures that when water resources are inappropriately managed, priced, or conserved, the public is able to engage in the water debate through social, economic, and political mechanisms. By contrast, when private companies manage water resources, the public has only consumer mechanisms for altering water management policies.

But the case for government provision is not so clear-cut. Not all governments are "modern" (i.e., have adequate service delivery capabilities), and many governments are corrupt. Unfortunately, private provision of water provides no assurance of effective, efficient, or noncorrupt provision of water and may increase the likelihood of distributional inequity.

In chapter 1 I defined "public value" in terms of a society's "consensus about (a) the rights, benefits, and prerogatives to which citizens should (and should not) be entitled; (b) the obligations of citizens to society, the state, and one another; and (c) the principles on which governments and policies should be based." Public values differ from one society to the next, and, for any particular value, the extent to which it is embraced likewise varies both across and within societies. But those values that relate directly to human existence and the prerequisites for sustaining life are perhaps least variant. Even in highly stratified and chaotic societies, there is often a commitment to providing the literal necessities of life. One lesson regarding the publicness of water and water services is that some resources are simply too important to support ideological or even theoretical presumptions about their provision. Some guarantee of foundational public values is required in order to hold a society together, and thus, such foundational values, those pertaining to survival, have a special status even among public values.

The Prison Business

Bureau of Prisons Mission Statement
It is the mission of the Federal Bureau of Prisons to protect society by confining offenders in the controlled environments of prisons and community-based facilities that are safe, humane, cost-efficient, and appropriately secure, and that provide work and other self-improvement opportunities to assist offenders in becoming law-abiding citizens.

Bureau of Prisons Vision Statement
The Federal Bureau of Prisons, judged by any standard, is widely and consistently regarded as a model of outstanding public administration, and as the best value provider of efficient, safe and humane correctional services and programs in America.

—Federal Bureau of Prisons, www.bop.gov/about/mission.jsp
(downloaded October 30, 2006)

Prisons are a policy institution where just a few years ago there was near universal government service delivery. At the present time, prison populations in the United States are predicted to grow annually at 3 to 5 percent (Ghosh 2006), with states buckling under the pressure of "three-strikes-and-you're out" policies. Increasingly, the government monopoly on prison services has been replaced by a thriving (albeit often financially unsuccessful) private sector prison management industry, including prison operators such as the Corrections Corporation of America and the Geo Group. Contractors contend that they can run prisons at a lower cost than the government, while critics of privatization argue that there is little evidence to support these claims.

The trend toward outsourcing prison services and management began accelerating in the 1990s but was common even a decade before. By November 1990 approximately twenty-four government agencies planned to or already had contracted out prison and jail space for their adult inmates in order to reduce overcrowding and provide prison space at lower costs (U.S. GAO 1991). Though counts vary, by 2005 private corporations managed the beds of approximately 122,900 inmates (Yeoman 2000) and were responsible for 65,160 inmates in 140 private jails and prisons in 31 states, accounting for 2 to 5 percent of the total inmate population in the United States (Austin and Coventry 2001). The privatization of prisons has become especially popular in Florida, the state with the largest prison system; California, the state with the largest prison population; and Texas and New Mexico, states with growing prison populations (Talvi 2006). According to a Government Accountability Office (GAO) report analyzing five existing studies that compare public and private correctional facilities between 1991 and 1996, overall there is little to no difference in costs between public and private correctional facilities, but there are variations in quality (U.S. GAO 1996).

One of the most widely known cases of the negative outcomes of prison privatization is the Northeast Ohio Correctional Center in Youngstown, Ohio. Faced with economic depression and high unemployment rates following the closure of local steel mills, Youngstown was eager to attract new building projects, employment opportunities, and tax revenue. Elected officials, searching for projects to boost the local economy, contracted with the Corrections Corporation of America (CCA), a multinational company based in Nashville, Tennessee, to manage the for-profit Youngstown facility. In exchange for tax breaks and water and sewer hookups, CCA promised to employ 350 locals, providing incomes of about $25,000 per year.

Between May and October 1997, the CCA collected $182 million for importing 1,700 violent inmates from Washington, D.C., to the medium-security facility (U.S. GAO 2000). The impacts of the influx of violent criminals to this facility were exacerbated by the fact that CCA staffed the facility with guards who had little or no experience in corrections. Furthermore, the CCA staff did not take basic security measures at the Youngstown facility such as preventing inmates' access to metal equipment, resulting in twenty prisoner stabbings and two murders. The staff provided minimal medical treatment to prisoners and was accused of using tear gas and humiliation tactics to maintain order among inmates (Yeoman 2000). In 1999 Youngstown prisoners were awarded $1.65 million in a class-action suit against the CCA. The prisoners cited ill treatment, including being forced to strip, being shackled or handcuffed in the nude, being ordered not to move or speak, being probed by prison employees, being denied access to religious materials, and being inappropriately sprayed with tear gas and pepper spray.

The frustrations at Youngstown continued. In 1998 two inmates were stabbed to death, and in 2000 the problems at Youngstown peaked with the escape of six inmates. According to the D.C. corrections trustee who monitors the prison, in this latter case a metal detector and a motion detector broke, and the area outside the prison was unmonitored for forty minutes because the staff member responsible for the detector was playing table tennis (Yeoman 2000). The prison break was bad enough, but the inmates had a head start on the local and state police because the company waited more than thirty minutes to notify local authorities.

Though the CCA was criticized for its poor maintenance of the Youngstown facility, no fines or penalties were levied, and CCA kept the profits it had earned. Indeed, the CCA dominion was expanded. More than five hundred beds were added to the prison, two more facilities were built for an additional five thousand prisoners, with the rationale that this would add fourteen hundred jobs and approximately $200 million in taxes. Some argue that the CCA's cost-cutting efforts have made prisoners, guards, and neighboring communities less secure (Yeoman 2000).

One of the most significant outcomes of privatizing the Youngstown facility was that, after the lawsuit, murders, and escapes, the community had little to no power to control the CCA's actions. The mayor of Youngstown, George McKelvey, noted, "Knowing what I know now . . . I would never have allowed CCA to build a prison here" (Yeoman 2000).

Though the GAO has investigated the cost-effectiveness of private prisons (U.S. GAO 1996) and made recommendations to reform the contractual procedures designed to hold private firms responsible for noncompliance (U.S. GAO 2000), there has been relatively little discussion of the ethical implications of turning over incarceration, punishment, rehabilitation, and the protection of civil society to the private sector. Nor is there any clear role for private citizens or elected officials to gain information about private prison maintenance or to alter prison policies once they are contracted to private firms.

There is one important respect in which policies pertaining to prisoners are distinctly different from those pertaining to other disadvantaged citizens. By law, prisoners in the United States forfeit some of their political rights. Their individual political authority is diminished in several important ways. Obviously, much of the Bill of Rights does not pertain to them (e.g., freedom of assembly, right to bear arms), nor do the usual statutory protections for privacy. While prisoners have some limited rights to petition political authorities, they do not have full civil rights, and of course, convicted felons cannot vote. Prisoners are in a very real sense lesser citizens with abridged rights. Some of these abridged rights pertain to political authority, but there are limits as well on prisoners' ability to participate in the market (e.g., limits on money to which prisoners have access, limits on commercial enterprise in prison, and in some cases, limits on the ability to profit from the publicity and notoriety of their crimes). In some U.S. states prisoners who have committed capital offenses undergo the ultimate loss of authority—their lives are forfeit.

There are many aspects of public policies of a great many nations that could be said to be variously regressive, upwardly redistributive, or elitist. Some may find such policies abhorrent, but in a democratic, pluralistic society there are means to address, say, unfair taxes or environmental injustice. Such policies may be undesirable from some perspectives, but they tell us little about the nature of political and economic authority other than they are operating in accustomed ways.

The case of prisoners seems to have different implications for publicness and the uses of political and economic authority. To be sure, virtually every civil society in the world has concluded that it is permissible to use legitimate political authority against those who have committed egregious offenses against society. That does not seem, however, to justify an extension of the use of political authority to diminish further the protections of those who have few or no individual political or economic rights merely to secure economic benefits to fully entitled citizens. Job creation and tax revenues have been used as rationalizations for most prison privatizations, but perhaps this is a category for the exercise of political authority that by its very nature undermines public interest by its effects on not only diminished citizens but also fully entitled citizens. This is not only a matter of publicness. The rule espoused earlier does not imply that prisons must be run by governments and certainly does not imply that prisons run by government will be humane (consider only the Attica riots or the Abu Ghraib Iraq prison scandal to underscore this point). Rather, it suggests that in realms where diminished citizens' protections are concerned, the deployment of political authority should not be chiefly about efficiency or economic gain. Later in this book I discuss further the philosophy of utilitarianism and other "consequentialism" approaches to values (ones arguing that values must be judged by the consequences of outcomes). Privatized prisons, when rationalized on the basis of economic gains, are a nearly perfect embodiment of utilitarianism and a powerful argument against it.

"Lock the Door to City Hall on the Way Out": Sandy Springs' Attempt to Privatize Everything

Power that controls the economy should be in the hands of elected representatives of the people, not in the hands of an industrial oligarchy.

WILLIAM O. DOUGLAS, Dissent, *U.S. v. Columbia Steel Co.*, 334 U.S. 495

Considering the extent to which national defense, security, and, yes, war can be privatized, one is perhaps now ready for the ultimate question: Is it possible to, essentially, abandon government and live within jurisdiction and authority of a fully privatized "government" institution? That question is now being put to the test in small- and medium-sized U.S. cities. One conspicuous example is the new, but hardly tiny, city of Sandy Springs, Georgia.

Until December 2005, Sandy Springs was part of unincorporated Fulton County.[1] For many years this growing entity (population 85,781 in 2000 and now at about 100,000 residents) obtained its government services from the county. But the marriage was becoming an unhappy one. Fulton County, which includes the city of Atlanta and, increasingly, little else, found itself dependent on the revenues of this affluent suburb. Sandy Springs, with its young, educated (median age thirty-three; 94 percent have a high school education or above, with 60 percent holding bachelors degrees), predominantly white (73 percent in 2000), affluent residents (median household income $60,428, median income per capita $52,484, more than double the U.S. average for the year 2000) and its significantly above-average median house value ($345,200 in 2000) was, indeed, a Fulton County cash cow and did, as is the case with so many affluent communities, essentially subsidize services in poorer parts of Fulton County.

On one side, many Sandy Springs residents felt detached from Fulton County and believed they were paying more than they should for what many perceived as substandard services. On the other side, Fulton County officials, among others, were quick to point out that the majority of Sandy Springs residents worked in Atlanta, not Sandy Springs, and that it was only fair that they help subsidize the infrastructure, transit, and other aspects of Atlanta upon which the region's commerce depends. But this story is not chiefly about home rule, annexing, or intergovernmental relations. The basic point is that after years of legal skirmishing, in 2005, when the Republican Party gained a majority in both houses of the Georgia General Assembly and repealed a requirement that new cities be at least three miles from existing cities (Sandy Springs shares its borders with two Georgia cities, Roswell and Atlanta), Sandy Springs was granted a divorce. In June 2005, a referendum open to Fulton County residents within the proposed Sandy Springs area but closed to other Fulton County residents was held. Ninety-four percent of Sandy Springs–area residents voted for incorporation, resulting in the creation of the seventh largest city in Georgia.

Having for years so many citizens dissatisfied with the services provided by Fulton County, the new, incorporated Sandy Springs thought it could increase service quality by reducing government to virtually nothing. The city hired Colorado-based CH2M Hill, one of the largest U.S. firms devoted to environmental and engineering consulting which currently provides services to more than sixty government clients in Georgia, with $3.2 billion in revenue and eighteen thousand employees, to essentially *be* the government (Nurse 2006a).

To further aid the efforts of Sandy Spring residents, the Georgia General Assembly repealed a 1995 law requiring all cities to provide at least three municipal services, thus enabling the city to move forward with a leaner city administration, totaling four city employees, including a city manager who, of course, devotes most of his time to contract management of all services except public safety personnel. For about $30 million for the 2007 fiscal year, Sandy Springs contracted CH2M Hill to staff all city offices and provide all services, excepting fire, police, and municipal courts. The consulting firm dedicated 190 employees to provide city services, including human resources, park management, customer service and purchasing, planning, zoning, transportation, and traffic management (Nurse 2006a).

Does this "privatization of everything" work? In the case of Sandy Springs it is too early to say. But, in the longer run, the answer to that question, as in any instance of privatization, contracting out, or outsourcing, will depend on what one means by "work." Certainly Sandy Springs has reduced the number of government employees. If that is a goal, then we can already say it works. Not surprisingly, the CH2M Hill staff is buoyant about this sweeping privatization. The program director, Rick Hirsekorn, contends that management by a single firm reduces the likelihood of fragmented work and turf wars one sometimes finds in public management: "Some governments take each department and build stovepipes and people turfs. As a privately held company, employee-owned, it behooves everyone in the company to help somebody else" (Dorrell 2006, 1). No less surprising is the reaction of Kerry Korpi, an official with the major government employees' union, American Federation of State, County, and Municipal Employees, who argues, "Contractors aren't subject to the same kind of open-records and open-meetings laws as public employees are. You end up with a shadow government," where the government workforce is minimal but the number of people doing government work expands through contracts (Guttman 1976; Smith and Lipsky 1993).

The early results indicate that CH2M Hill employees are more vigilant than the Fulton County employees they replaced, at least more vigilant with respect to enforcement and in searching for revenue sources. With respect to the former, uniformed code enforcement agents from CH2M Hill seem omnipresent, enforcing building codes, replacing signs, and making sure that residents park in designated places, not on the grass. Residents are also happy to have CH2M Hill's twenty-four-hour hotline that guarantees a real person will answer each telephone call to city hall (Nurse 2006c). They have also changed out inefficient traffic lightbulbs and replaced them with newer, higher efficiency bulbs. On the revenue side, they are using new computer mapping software to identify businesses whose license fees have not been paid or have lapsed. The company receives a 22 to 30 percent commission for each new business license it brings in. They are collecting more parking fines and ticketing residences not meeting grass-cutting standards. Interestingly, Sandy Springs seems to be getting more "government" services from CH2M Hill than they received from Fulton County. It remains to be seen whether they will get more than they want. As one parking miscreant noted after being cited for parking on the grass, "They're doing their jobs, but c'mon, I had my car there for 20 minutes."

The privatization of Sandy Springs has not been without controversy. One of the first problems to arise on the agenda was the management of public land, in this case, parks and recreation centers. State law prohibits counties from operating parks in cities of more than five thousand residents, thus requiring Fulton County to dispose of its parklands in the newly incorporated Sandy Springs. In July 2006 the Fulton County Commission voted 4 to 3 to sell six parks and recreation centers in Sandy Springs, valued at $27.6 million, on the open market (Gest 2006). Following the vote Sandy Springs residents filed numerous complaints, outraged that the seventy-four acres of public parks would be available for sale and possible development. Following the public outcry, within the week Commissioner at Large Rob Pitts amended his pro-park sale vote and clarified that the parklands would not be sold for development, because under state law the county cannot legally give the parks away, nor can they be sold for development. However, the county can sell them to Sandy Springs, though Sandy Springs officials and residents have argued that Sandy Springs taxpayers as Fulton County residents had already paid for those parks and should receive the parkland as part of their incorporation. By August 2006, the issue was finally resolved, with the Fulton County Commission voting 4 to 3 to sell the parklands to Sandy Springs for $100 per acre with a $1,000 minimum, for a total of $16,000. Now Sandy Springs is searching for the best way to privatize park management without "selling" the public land. Sandy Springs plans to lease the parks to private companies, though one wonders how a private company will find maintaining a city park sufficiently profitable.

Another issue arising in the new city of Sandy Springs is the responsibility of addressing the needs of their homeless population. Though Atlanta is infamous for its large homeless population, neighboring Sandy Springs has an unknown number of homeless among its shady parks and million-dollar homes. Municipal Court Solicitor Bill Riley notes that the court has heard nearly sixty homeless cases in the first eight months of its existence (Daniels 2006). Brandie Haywood, associate director for Pathways, a nonprofit organization that helps to count homeless populations, notes, "Government reps in North Fulton had been working with groups who were reporting on a regular basis that they were serving several dozen [homeless individuals]" (Daniels 2006).

Though Sandy Springs mayor Eva Galambos says that homelessness is not on the city's agenda, it is on the agenda of residents, business owners, and community advocates who have started a homelessness task force (Daniels 2006). The city seems to be waiting for the homeless to move to metro Atlanta for services or for private and nonprofit organizations in Sandy Springs to take care of the homeless. Tamara Carrera, executive director of the Community Action Center, an organization that provides assistance and services to Sandy Springs households, argues this point: "Now that we're a city, I think we have the same obligation that all cities have," Carrera said. "We can't just send people who are here to the next city over. . . . We have to take care of whoever is here in this city for whatever reason" (Daniels 2006).

It is too early to measure the successes of Sandy Springs and its model of privatized city management. However, it is not too early to notice the emerging challenges of relying on private markets for managing public goods, such as parks, and social goods, such as assisting the homeless. It is not clear whether the city will be able to contract out the management of city parks and recreation centers, where profits are minimal and all citizens should have access (regardless of their ability to pay). It is also not clear whether the city will be able to, or be willing to, take on the provision of social services, such as caring for the homeless, in the interest of both homeless individuals and Sandy Springs residents.

In addition, there is little precedent for predicting how CH2M Hill will respond to demands for transparency and public oversight of their management techniques. Already local reporters at the *Atlanta Journal-Constitution* have had difficulty getting access to CH2M Hill's compilation of city records, which should be public information (Nurse 2006c). For example, in April 2006 the company removed a public works director, though the city council has no idea why (Nurse 2006c). It is uncertain how the city council or individual citizens will be able to hold private managers accountable to public values, maintain oversight of company profits that are earned at the expense of taxpayers, or ensure that corruption and patronage do not overwhelm the process of selling city services. Though Sandy Springs has the option of canceling its contract with CH2M Hill, it is not evident whether they are able to tweak or monitor the contract.

After providing the up-front funding to get Sandy Springs running, CH2M Hill was awarded a $30 million annual renewable contract to manage Sandy Springs. But this contract is just a small portion of CH2M Hill's annual earnings, at more than $3.7 billion in 2005. In addition to private engineering services, CH2M Hill manages nearly sixty government projects around the country, but its venture into city management offers a new, low-risk, stable investment that requires no land purchase and little capital outlays. The incentives for firms to manage cities and for cities to outsource management seem to converge nicely in this case. As other cities around Georgia, including John's Creek and Milton, begin to follow the Sandy Springs model by hiring the same private company to run their cities, it will become increasingly important that citizens monitor the ability of private companies to manage their cities not only with cost efficiency in mind but also with the values of equality, effectiveness, and the public interest in mind.

The Sandy Springs case does not yet tell us much of value about the wisdom of privatization but it does speak volumes about the limits of privatization. What it shows us is that there are virtually no limits.

The city has a handful of public employees responsible for negotiating and overseeing the contract. Significantly, the city has thus far chosen to maintain its public safety employees, even if altering the terms and conditions of work. Sandy Springs still has elected officials answerable to the citizens of this new jurisdiction. The city does not define the theoretical extreme of private authority exercised to public purpose. But developments in this new "corporate" city do seem to suggest that previous ideas about what is within the public domain and what is in the private domain may need some revision. It is easy to see how Sandy Springs, with just a few changes in service personnel and in its contracting, could exhibit the maximum skewness and the minimum tie between political and economic authority. Can "everything" be privatized? Perhaps not everything. If the city of Sandy Springs were simply sold, it would not be "privatized," it would be private. With one important exception there is literally no good or service that cannot be delivered by private agents. The only theoretical limit to the universal exercise of economic authority on behalf of public purpose is whatever slender thread of political accountability is required to forge the contract.

POLITICAL AUTHORITY, ECONOMIC AUTHORITY, AND NORMATIVE PUBLICNESS

Considering the previously described cases, let us briefly reexamine the public interest concept outlined in chapter 1. The provision of Social Security, national security, water, prisons, and city government and management in the United States has typically been the responsibility of governments. When the government fails to provide these goods and services, citizens have the option of voting for new representatives, engaging in public protests, or lobbying for policy change. In the traditional model of market failure and economic individualism, when citizens are unsatisfied with the goods and services provided by the market, they have the option of altering their consumer choices.

In the case of privatizing prisons, in particular the case of the Youngstown facility, we see how the economic interests of the CCA displaced the public interest for safety in Youngstown. Prison policies, including importing violent criminals from Washington, D.C., and managing inmates within the facility, were dictated by CCA's interest in increased profits. In the traditional economic model, when dissatisfied with services, consumers make purchasing choices to alter the behavior of the provider. In this case, how exactly were neighbors and Youngstown citizens, now defined as consumers, expected to affect CCA's behavior? The market for the Youngstown prison was not dictated by local resident views or the public interest.

Similar to the displacement of public opinion in Youngstown, it is unclear what the role of elections, citizens, and public opinion will be in driving the management of Sandy Springs, now under the purchased leadership of CH2M Hill, and more important, how the interests and rights of disadvantaged populations will be protected under this new "private government." In the case of privatizing national security, we see private contractors connected to political leadership becoming increasingly responsible for providing national defense, a public good. How do privatized military services respond to the interests of Iraqi citizens, American citizens, or American servicemen and women in Iraq? Public interest ideals are outside the purview of the traditional economic model of market failure. As demonstrated by these few examples, when we move the government's provision of public goods and the public interest to the private market, any efficiency gains must be weighted against the different nature of corporations' obligations to citizens. Specifically, those obligations are legal and contractual. If public values are ensured in contracts, the privatization may prove to be in the public interest. But in those cases where public values and public interest do not seem to be well served by the exercise of greater economic authority, the rights to information and the ability to redress adverse outcomes are generally lessened. If citizens are, indeed, customers, it is possible that they will be well served, but it is also likely that if they are not well served their rights as consumers will prove inferior or at least quite different than the traditional rights of citizens.

The normative publicness model introduced in chapter 1 does not require that public policies choose between the outcomes of public interests and individual interests. The two are neither discrete nor mutually exclusive. In fact, one could argue that attending to public values and public interest helps to strengthen and protect the ability of markets to effectively and efficiently provide for individual interests. Studies of business location decisions and economic development consistently show that quality public education, public transportation, and public infrastructure are vitally important to those making decisions pertaining to the creation of private wealth. As we see from a dimensional view of publicness, public values can be obtained with a great variety of mixtures of political and economic authority, and when public values are realized they often benefit individual economic interests while advancing public interest ideals. When all citizens have abundant clean water, the resultant health and productivity outcomes are universally enjoyed. There is no one best means, no fixed blend of economic and political authority, for guaranteeing the provision of abundant clean water. But there is a public interest in doing so and a legitimate expectation that political authority will be exercised to advance this public interest. Unlike political authority, the basis of economic authority is not the legitimate consent of the governed (Bozeman 1987) but the power of wealth and individual or corporate resources. Economic authority carries with it no necessary expectation of specific public values or of public interest ideals.

NOTE

This chapter was coauthored with Mary Feeney.

1. In the United States, a county is the unit of government organization immediately below the state and above the municipality or township. Land, businesses, and residences outside of city limits (unincorporated areas) fall under the jurisdiction of county government. Counties are the largest territorial division for local government within a state in the United States.

CHAPTER THREE
ECONOMIC INDIVIDUALISM
IN PUBLIC POLICY

In the ownership society, the more people own, the bigger the stake they have in society.

—GEORGE W. BUSH, 2005

Chapter 1 argued that economic individualism has become increasingly influential in public policy and management, and chapter 2 illustrated some particular instances of economic individualism's impacts on policy, including in some cases quite unfortunate impacts. This chapter considers some of the pathways by which economic individualism has influenced public policy, focusing particularly on the ideas supporting both economic individualism and economics-based models of the government and private-sector roles in public policy. The following chapter considers how these ideas have influenced public management. This is a bit of an artificial distinction because public policy and public management have soft boundaries and inevitably meld. However, it is a useful distinction, even if somewhat unrealistic, in that it reflects two largely separate literatures: one emphasizing the development and analysis of policy and the other emphasizing the implementation and management of public policies and the institutions created by them.

After presenting a brief discussion of the reasons why economic individualism has such a strong and long-standing grip in American political culture, I focus on some of the manifestations of economic individualism in public policy. Each of the brief case studies presented in this section illustrates that policies develop as a dynamic interplay between economic values and desiderata and public ones. Most of the chapter is devoted to the ideas underpinning economic theories of public policy, in line with a prime thesis of this book that theories of public interest and public value have not generally kept pace with the development of policy and management theories based on economic premises. It may not be entirely clear why this is important, as there is so little obvious evidence of theoretical reasoning in day-to-day policymaking. Thus, before presenting a synoptic overview of some of the best-known general

47

economic models for policy analysis and prescription, I make a brief detour into the sociology of knowledge whereupon I consider just why ideas can be so important in a policy world that so often seems to eschew ideas, especially models, in favor of either urgency, venality, or uncertainty reduction. The basic point of this section is to show that ideas diffuse in ways that allow them to creep into policy and, over long periods of time, exert considerable influence by helping frame policy discourse. I then turn to the primary focus of the chapter, outlining three major intellectual structures supporting economic individualism in public policy—market failure, property rights theory, and principal–agent theory. Readers already familiar with these models will learn nothing new. However, the focus of the book necessitates an introduction to these models. The book responds to the felt need to counterbalance these influential and, in many respects, powerful economic models with analytical structures that more easily accommodate thinking about public values and public interest. Judgments about the utility of public values models require some passing knowledge of the "other" that the public values models seek to redress.

ECONOMIC INDIVIDUALISM IN AMERICAN POLITICAL CULTURE

In his oft-quoted and sometimes misunderstood assessment of eighteenth-century Americans, Tocqueville (1965, 611) observed that "enlightened self-love continually leads them to help one another and inclines them to devote freely a part of their time and wealth to the welfare of the state." Tocqueville recognized both the morality and the greed pervading American political culture and believed one of the great strengths of America was holding the two in balance. The greed was manifested in economic individualism, balanced by recognition of the common good.

In many nations the focus on market theories and approaches to government can be explained by the imperatives of economic development. But in the United States, it is in part due to the close match of economic reasoning and the economic values at the core of American political culture. In the absence of a unifying or compelling American idea of the public interest, economic individualism has emerged as a galvanizing policy philosophy of social action and, at the same time, social constraint. Certainly, economic individualism is the most important policy philosophy if we mean by "important" either influential or widely embraced. Public policymaking and public management in the United States, but not only in the United States, are pervaded by the reasoning and rhetoric of economic individualism.

Why has economic individualism proved so popular in the United States? There are many reasons and the reasons vary according to the particular aspect or application of economic individualism. For example, the central place of economic individualism in tax policy differs from its role in health policy. Many of the current manifestations of economic individualism have a common historical root. In the United States, a foundational and deep-seated mistrust of government (*political* individualism), when taken with the nation's special native brand of capitalism, results in peculiar public philosophy that affects nearly every realm of public policy and most aspects of civic life. Despite differences among the Founding Fathers there was some consensus about the importance of the individual and the need to protect individuals from the state. The state was decidedly *not* viewed as the friend of the common citizen. Consider Thomas Jefferson's words: "That government is best which governs the least, because its people discipline themselves." Addressing the Virginia legislature in 1779, Jefferson proclaimed, "Experience hath shown, that even under the best forms [of government], those entrusted with power have, in time, and by slow operations, perverted it into tyranny."

Economic individualism is the forest in which a great many American public policy trees grow. Most Americans, understandably more occupied with growing trees than watching forests, know there is no widely accepted public interest theory and seem generally content to have economic individualism move into this vacuum. Everyone understands something about American capitalism and about the role of individual political rights in the nation's political culture, but it may not be so obvious just how the two have woven themselves together into a policy philosophy more powerful than any public interest theory.

While it seems ironic that economic individualism could work as an organizing principle for public law and public policy, the logic is not so different from that used by Gary Wills (1999) in explaining how and why American citizens use the nation's constitutional and statutory foundations to make antigovernment arguments. According to Wills (16), "Americans believe they have a government which is itself against government . . . [T]here is a positive determination to see even in the organs of government itself only anti-governmental values." He further points out that antigovernment mythmaking began very early in the life of the nation as "the arguments of Antifederalists *against* the Constitution were said, only a decade or so after the document's ratification, to be embodied in the Constitution" (17). More recently, we have the spectacle of individuals vying to become the most powerful *government* official in the United States, individuals (Ronald Reagan, Jimmy Carter, Bill Clinton, and George W. Bush) who had been chief *government* executives in large U.S. states, advancing as a major qualification their status as "outsiders" removed from and untainted by government. Such a history seems to suggest that "*individualism*" and "*public interest*," terms that seem logically to defy connection, can, at least in the unconventional logic of American politics, coexist and even run together.

THE DIFFUSION OF IDEAS: MODALITIES OF ECONOMIC INDIVIDUALISM IN PUBLIC LIFE

While much of economics provides support for the central premises of economic individualism, our concern here is with theories that are especially pertinent to public policymaking. The major focus of the remainder of this chapter is the intellectual embodiments of economic individualism. However, before delving into the theoretical bases by which economic individualism affects the reflective citizen and the public policymaker, we take a brief detour. Because so much of this book deals with competing ideas or even meta-ideas, it seems appropriate to at least briefly consider how ideas hold sway and ultimately affect policymaking and implementation.

To the casual observer of public affairs, and perhaps even to some more attentive observers, it may seem that the course of public affairs is a result of random events and the unpredictable human reactions to them. To be sure, randomness and uncertainty are always important elements of public affairs. President Clinton's affair with a White House intern becomes public, he is impeached, and all manner of political stakes are changed in a vast ripple effect. Hurricane Katrina devastates the southern United States, and policy attention is diverted to issues—relief and emergency preparedness—barely discussed the week before. Yet despite these sweep-all-away events, there remains a role for ideas, though the impact of ideas occurs in quite different ways and generally at a much slower pace. Whereas the big events shaping policy leap from newspaper headlines in 60-point type or appear for weeks at the top of the endless loop of 24-hour cable or Internet news, ideas generally exert their influence on policies and social choice in subtle, indirect ways.

Perhaps economist John Maynard Keynes's is the best-known insight about the power of ideas to shape public affairs':

> The ideas of economists and political philosophers, both when they are right and when they are wrong, are more powerful than is commonly understood. Indeed the world is ruled by little else. Practical men, who believe themselves to be quite exempt from any intellectual influences, are usually the slaves of some defunct economist. Madmen in authority, whom hear voices in the air, are distilling their frenzy from some academic scribbler of a few years back. I am sure that the power of vested interests is vastly exaggerated compared with the gradual encroachment of ideas. . . . [S]oon or late, it is ideas, not vested interests, which are dangerous for good or evil. (1964, 383)

FROM IDEAS TO POLICY: SOME OF THE SWITCHBACK PATHS

The veracity of Keynes's point notwithstanding, there is little so challenging as trying to understand the history of an idea, its development, evolution, and diffusion. However, there is little that is unique about the route to influence taken by the ideas of microeconomics and economic individualism; they take much the same course as nearly all "big ideas" that hold sway. The challenge in understanding the course of influence in economic discourse is that one finds so many big ideas under the single conceptual umbrella, economic individualism. The ideas under the heading of economic individualism have evolved for hundreds of years, producing thousands of significant tributaries and countless applications.

Rather than present an in-depth analysis of the many influences of economic thinking that shape public policy and management, let us consider here some of the *modalities* of influence and the accompanying social dynamics by which the ideas of economic individualism diffuse. Absent some basic understanding of the diffusion of knowledge, it is difficult to understand the indirect and oblique ways in which ideas shape policy and practice.

In semiotics, "modality," the study of signs and meaning, refers to the reality status associated with a sign or text (Chandler 2001). It is useful to think of economic individualism in terms of modalities because it reminds us that this root philosophy has many expressions, including but not limited to formal economic theory. When one speaks of the influence of economic individualism, theory is only one among many modalities of influence. A partial list of modalities includes the following:

Formal theory
Applied theory
Popular accounts of theory
Models and guidelines issuing from theory
Tools based on or issuing from theory
Rhetoric

The chief purpose of identifying the various modalities is simply to make the point that the influence of economic individualism in policy and management comes from many sources that intermingle and influence one another. Only rarely does formal theory have a direct and immediate impact on public policy and management. While there is no need to deal specifically with each of these modalities, some elaboration is required.

With respect to "tools based on or issuing from theory," the implication is that theories usher in tools that contain many of the assumptions or proofs from a theory. An example from the recent history of technology is the development of the physical infrastructure for what came to be called the Internet, a technological embodiment made possible by packet-switching theory (see Abbate 1999). But examples need not be confined to physical technologies. For example, cost–benefit analysis is an economics tool enabled by aspects of economic theory. Similarly, political polling is a social technology enabled by developments in statistics and especially sampling theory.

In considering modalities one must examine the sometimes convoluted paths by which ideas affect collective action. However, understanding the conversion of ideas to action does *not* require an in-depth discussion of the remarkably complex requirements and nature of theory in the sciences and social sciences (Hempel 1966). For present purposes, let us simply think of a theory as a broad explanation of phenomena. Thus Karl Marx's dialectical materialism is a theory, in this sense at least, as is Keynesian economics. Economic individualism is perhaps best viewed as a philosophy (because its broad assumptions and premises do not themselves lead directly to cause-and-effect statements or to predictions). However, economic individualism is a philosophy that has accompanying theories; indeed, most of contemporary neoclassical economics is either directly rooted in economic individualism or at least is quite consistent with the philosophy.

"Formal theory" in economics, as in the sciences, means that the explanations of a theory can be expressed in terms of mathematics or logic (Rosenberg 1976). Whereas most theories in the social sciences are not in this sense formal ones, a distinction of economics is that much of it is amenable to formalization. Most of contemporary microeconomics can be traced to formal theory foundations (Solow 1991). These formalizations do not have wide exposure and typically are published in academic journals and, less frequently, academic books. Typically, the readership of these academic books and journals is measured in hundreds. Most of the people who are influenced by formal theories have never read them. This is not an indictment. Most educated people have some understanding of the causal mechanics of physics but not because they have read physics journals.

In academic disciplines formal knowledge is diffused to nonspecialists through textbooks (Faulkner 1994). In the past, formal theories of any sort found their first mass audience in textbooks. For example, many students and adults are familiar with the notion of public goods, but few have read Samuelson's (1954) economic theory of public goods. Textbooks still serve as a major source for conveying theory to the masses, but increasingly, they are not the first source. For philosophies, new theories, and "big ideas," in both the social and natural sciences, the first source for the layperson is popular media, especially newspapers and magazines. More and more, popular media have served as the means by which people are introduced to new developments in knowledge (Friedman, Dunwoody, and Rogers 1999), with those that can be communicated in just a minute or two finding major exposure in television or Internet streaming (Treise et al. 2003).

These "knowledge broker" media are the means by which most who are not professional economists are introduced to both the traditional theory of the economics canon and new developments in economics research and theory, both formal and applied. Similarly, policymakers and those who influence them typically derive their ideas about economics (and other ideas used ultimately for shaping public policy) from these knowledge broker media, at least when they are not directly interacting person-to-person with the individuals who originated or applied the knowledge (Lindblom and Cohen 1979).

Knowledge based on the philosophy of economic individualism and its attendant theories is especially well adapted for mass distribution. In the first place, it is amenable to simple but powerful analogies, albeit ones that are sometimes misleading, such as equating a nation's expenditures with household expenditures. Most important, every member of society is a consumer and everyone understands, at least at a personal level, the nature of discrete consumer choice. Even social isolates have some experience with markets. The most fundamental bases of economics—scarcity, supply, and demand—are intuitive concepts easily communicated to those who know little or nothing of economic theory.

It is simple to see how the philosophy of economic individualism can be easily understood and can influence even minimally educated persons in any society. The core ideas are simple, familiar, easily communicated, salient by definition (self-interest), and pertain to behaviors that are part of daily life. The fact that economics has advanced to the point that it has generated highly sophisticated and formalized theories that no one can understand in depth unless trained in economics or mathematics has not proved a stumbling block to the diffusion of ideas. Similarly, we do not need to know astronomers' equations to have some knowledge of the periodicity of Halley's Comet. This is not only due to the various broker media available to all or nearly all citizens; in the case of economic individualism it is also due to the rhetoric and shorthand symbols generated by contemporary economics and those who apply their ideas. Persons who have never seen an economics textbook or even the business and economics page of the local newspaper can nonetheless understand and use the rhetoric of popular economics. Such rhetoric as "the bottom line" or "there is no free lunch" have nearly universal recognition, and years of experience have shown competing politicians that these symbols have power.

While economic individualism and its assumptions provide the intellectual taproot for much of public policy discourse, its influence is only rarely direct. Most of those who either make or contribute ideas to public policy (i.e., elected officials, representatives of interest groups, policy analysts, and public managers) do not draw directly from the philosophy of economic individualism or even the theories flowing from it, but rather from the applications, tools, guidelines, and rhetoric issuing from economic theories. Perhaps the most familiar tools having firm roots in neoclassical economic theory are cost–benefit analysis and expected values models (for an overview, see Weimer and Vining 1999). In many instances, cost–benefit analysis, when performed with the requisite technical expertise, proves quite useful. However, bastardized forms are often used in policy deliberations, typically giving limited attention to long-term effects. For example, in the movement to privatize Social Security, as discussed in chapter 2, some supporters of privatization used the *concepts* of cost–benefit analysis, without having themselves performed a technically proficient study. Certainly it is unfair to call economic policy analysis to task because the techniques are bastardized and concepts misused. But the persistent use of accompanying rhetoric does suggest the need for counterbalance.

More recently, economists and policy analysts have begun developing analytical tools akin to the traditional approaches but designed to take into account perceived limitations. One such tool, contingent value analysis (Portney 1994), was developed to examine the costs and benefits in cases (such as preservation of ecologies) where this is not a true market but where preferences can nonetheless be expressed and quantified.

While the techniques flowing from modern microeconomics are employed widely by policy analysts and by some public managers, these tools typically are used to support major policy decisions rather than serving as the impetus for them. Perhaps the means by which economic individualism has the strongest direct influence is through the conceptual models it generates. Models provide systematic ways of thinking about the world and do not necessarily require calculations or analysis. Recently there has been considerable attention to the role of "mental models" in public decision making (Morgan et al. 2001; Bostrom et al. 1994), the psychological frameworks people bring to decisions. In many cases these frameworks relate closely to individual experience and self-interest and are quite distinctive if not unique to the individual (Johnson-Laird 1983). But in other cases we can identify commonly held mental models, including those of economics scholars and persons appropriating economic knowledge, which have much in common (Arthur 1988; Denzau and North 1994).

The philosophy of economic individualism and contemporary microeconomics provide "ready made" conceptual models that are easy to understand, familiar to most persons working in public policy decision contexts, and widely used, often in bastardized form. One of the best known of these models is the "pure rationality decision model" (see Bozeman and Pandey 2004 for a summary discussion). The other is the market failure model to which we referred briefly earlier. We do not give much attention to the pure rationality decision model because it is typically more useful for individual and narrow-gauge decisions. But the market failure model (discussed later) seems to have been widely adapted for individuals' mental models and thus has become quite influential in guiding the course of public policy and management.

To summarize, the argument that economic individualism and its attendant economic theories have had enormous influence in public policy and management requires some understanding of the complex and myriad ways in which ideas evolve and diffuse. Economic individualism is part of the fabric of shared knowledge in most societies. Persons in public policy and management communities not only have the same broad familiarity as the general public but also are in many cases well versed in the details of the analytical tools and conceptual models flowing ultimately from economic individualism.

With this background, we examine three of the intellectual edifices that have had considerable influence in general thinking about public policy—market failure theory, property rights theory, and principal–agent theory. The ideas contained in these theories are part of the intellectual heritage and knowledge base shared by many people who influence public policy and management. Even if policymakers know only the bare bones of these theories, knowledge of the fundamental arguments often suffices, especially in the absence of other well-developed ways of thinking systematically about policy choices.

PROPERTY RIGHTS THEORY: A THEORETICAL ARGUMENT FOR GOVERNMENT INEFFICIENCY

While having developed along somewhat different intellectual lines than market failure theory, the economic theory of property rights provides a strong theoretical justification for the expectation that government will be less efficient than the private sector.

The property rights model traces its lineage back at least as far as the pioneering work of Berle and Means (1932), who were concerned about the rise of a managerial class and the separation of ownership and control of the organization. The property rights model (e.g., Alchian and Demsetz 1972, 1973; De Alessi 1969; Demsetz 1967, 1969) assumes that many bureaucratic dysfunctions arise from the absence of oversight from wealth-seeking entrepreneurs. In the private firm, the wealth-seeking entrepreneur works to combine the optimal production inputs to produce goods and services as efficiently as possible, the rationale being that the margin between input and price should be as large as possible because the entrepreneur's economic well-being hinges on that (profit) margin (Matouschek 2004). Not surprisingly, public-sector organizations are inevitably viewed as less efficient because there is such extreme separation of ownership (the public at large) from operation (by bureaucrats without a pecuniary interest in the organization). Consider the prison example in chapter 2, where private prisons were deemed more efficient than state-run prisons. The privatization of the prison expanded the distance between the citizens of Youngstown and prison management, thus complicating the ability of disgruntled residents to voice their concerns and affect public policy.

This ability to transfer property rights is viewed as a force for efficiency in the private sector even in those circumstances where there is a sharp distinction between ownership and control of operations. A related source of inefficiency is owed to the fact that there are no rights of property transfer in public agencies. Because public programs (most of them, at least) are financed indirectly through tax dollars and because the "investor" (i.e., taxpayer) is unable to make "portfolio adjustments" (i.e., choosing to invest in some public program and not others), there are natural tendencies toward inefficiency. Because public organizations are viewed as inherently flawed, at least from a technical efficiency standpoint, the property rights prescription is straightforward—put economic activity into the private sector if at all possible, through direct control, contract, or privatization of public operations.

The evidence for the property rights model is difficult to assess. Most of the work is in the positive economics tradition, and there have not been a great many efforts to verify empirically the claims of property rights theorists. Comparisons of public and private organizations and services have been made in a few organizational realms, including hospitals (Lindsay 1976; Clarkson 1980); utilities (Hausman and Neufeld 1991); and (Davies 1971, 1977) airlines. However, almost all these studies have exclusively focused on differences between public- and private-sector organizations' technical efficiency. While the findings are not perfectly consistent with the key assumptions of property rights theory, it would seem implausible that public-sector organizations, often operating *because* of market failure, would be as efficient as private-sector ones. The dice are loaded.

Despite its limitations, an advantage of the property rights model is that it provides a simple but plausible explanation for organization failure—the clouding of incentives due to the absence of a profit motive. Property rights theory tells us much about public organization failure, but it has little to say about private-sector failure or public successes. Despite the alleged advantages of owner-induced efficiency, most business enterprises fail. If property rights is the explanation for the private sector's superior performance, privatization is both prescription and, sometimes, empirical test. In this chapter my concern is with the fundamental ideas advanced as rationales for such market-oriented approaches as privatization. For the present, it is sufficient to define privatization as the shifting of responsibilities and performance from government to private-sector organizations. Useful introductions to the prescriptions flowing from privatization are provided by Savas (1987, 2000). Privatization is considered in more detail in chapter 4. As we shall see in that chapter, it is not easy to provide a definition of privatization.

PRINCIPAL–AGENT THEORY

In nearly all large, multifunction organizations, some significant portion of management activity entails overseeing work done for one's own organization by other organizations. This external work may take many different forms, including, for example, outsourced information technology, transportation services, new construction, or almost anything that helps the focal organization produce its goods and services. Since the 1970s a body of theory and research (e.g., Spence and Zeckhauser 1971; Jensen and Meckling 1976; Ross 1973) has developed to examine these relationships, termed principal–agent relationships, focusing particularly on the reasons why such transactions are so often inefficient and the approaches to making them more efficient. Questions arising from principal–agent theory (PAT) include "What type of incentives should a principal provide to an agent?" "How can the principal monitor the agent's task performance?" and "What is the role of risk to the principal–agent relationship, and how should risk be accommodated?" Given the nature of these questions, it is not entirely surprising that the discussion of PAT has evolved within the realm of insurance (e.g., Harris and Raviv 1978; Spence and Zeckhauser 1971).

The core of the principal–agent problem is how to ensure that the agent (a contractor or employee) will act in the best interest of the employing principal, given differences in motive, information, and preference. Generally, it is rational for the principal to seek the most effective performance of the activities for which the principal has contracted with the agent. At the same time, it is rational for the agent to perform at a level that is satisfactory (i.e., that will meet any stipulations in the contract) but, at the same time, to expend as few resources as possible and to not "overperform" (i.e., provide goods and services at a level in excess of the minimum agreed upon contractually). Moreover, in many instances, the principal will not have sufficient information to fully evaluate the performance of the agent, which can lead to subpar performance.

A key question in the principal–agent relationship is the optimal level of monitoring. On the one hand, if the principal invests no resources in monitoring, it is plausible (absent excellent outcome indicators) that the agent will not perform at a high level. On the other hand, monitoring has its cost in terms of the principal's resources and can be viewed as a transaction cost not contributing directly to the production of goods and services. For example, consider the substantial transaction costs associated with outsourcing national defense in Iraq.

Gary Miller (2005) provides an excellent summary of the features and assumptions of the principal–agent model. The following summary draws extensively from this.

ASSUMPTIONS OF THE PRINCIPAL–AGENT MODEL

1. *Agent impact.* The agent takes actions that may be presumed to affect the principal's ability to achieve a value or values, and there is a degree of potential risk with respect to the implications of the agent's actions for the principal's value. For example, if the head of a government agency (principal) contracts with a consultant (agent) to train the agency's personnel in the use of a new software, the subsequent ability of the staff to use the new software will depend in part on qualities of the contract (teaching ability, level of effort, knowledge, preparation), but will also depend on factors beyond the agent's control (e.g., staff attendance, quality of the computers used in the training, the availability of the software).

2. *Information asymmetry.* While the principal likely has some knowledge of the outcome, the principle has less knowledge of the agent's role in

the outcome. In part this is because of an inability (and often undesirability) of completely monitoring all the actions of the agent and the many factors that might constrain the agent's effectiveness. For example, the principal may be dissatisfied with the staff's ability, after the training, to use the software, but the principal may not know whether that inability is due to a shortcoming of the agent, the staff, learning conditions independent of either, flaws in the software, or some combination of these and other factors. Due to the costs and often the impossibility of complete monitoring, the principal will seek to substitute incentives for good performance for actual monitoring. But information asymmetry makes it difficult to know whether those incentives (or sanctions) are effective.

3. *Asymmetry in preferences.* No two individuals' preferences are ever completely identical, except in very circumscribed domains, and this is true also of the agent and the principal. In some cases, however, these preferences may not only differ but also be at cross-purposes. A crucial concern of PAT is the case of "shirking" (much as discussed earlier in property rights theory). That is, the agent may feel that the activities that would provide greatest benefit to the principal will not provide greatest benefit to the agent. A simple example: When the principal provides a contract to the agent, it is in the principal's interest to have the contracted activity performed at the highest possible level (or at least the level of performance contracted).

4. *Initiative that lies with a unified principal.* This includes a simple but important set of enabling assumptions including the following: (a) the principal has a set of preferences, (b) the principal acts rationally in pursuit of these preferences, and (c) the principal is authorized and capable of offering a contract in pursuit of activities believed to advance the principal's preferences.

5. *Backward induction based on common knowledge.* The principal and agent share some knowledge and assumptions. Both know the general structure of the rules pertaining to any joint activity, both have some knowledge of likely costs of tasks associated with a contract, both have some knowledge of the range of outcomes that could occur as a result of the contract and its attendant activities, and both know that the agent will respond to any incentives that sum to slightly more than the agent's perceived costs (including opportunity costs).[1] This, of course, implies that it is useful for the principal to know as much as possible about the agent's perceived benefit from the contract and the cost of doing business, and it is in the agent's interest to reveal as little as possible about this information and associated calculations. The idea of "backward induction" is that the principal, using such shared knowledge as is available, can make inferences about the agent's resources, preferences, and calculations and then use these inferences in the framing of contract incentives.

6. *Ultimatum bargaining.* According to this assumption, the principal is expected to use knowledge of the agent's resources and calculations to provide a take-it-or-leave-it contract offer to the agent (assuming, of course, that the goods and services to be provided by the agent are not unique to that agent).

As Miller (2005) notes, these six assumptions give rise to two predicted results. One is "outcome-based incentives," the expectation that the principal will base the contract on performance, thus shifting risk to the agent. The second prediction is "efficiency tradeoffs," implying that the efficiency of the transaction between the principal and agent will be diminished by the fact that the agent will require increased incentives due to the burden of assuming risk. Risk bearing increases costs, and generally, the greater the risk, the greater the cost. This implies a "bonus" for the agent, above and beyond the returns that would be required were there no uncertainty about outcomes.

According to principal–agent theory, the seeming inefficiency of bureaucracies, and especially government bureaucracies, can be accounted for by the difficulties principals face in monitoring agents' behaviors. At one level, the principal may be a legislature delegating authority to the bureaucracy. Whereas the bureaucracy has the required human resources and expertise to implement the policy ("contract"), the legislature has limited ability to monitor or to provide performance-based incentives. If we shift the analysis focusing on the government agency as principal, then when the government bureaucracy contracts for the delivery of goods and services with providers, the government organization likewise has an information deficit, especially in instances where contract management capacity is inadequate.

In the context of the public bureaucracy, privatization is often advanced as a partial remedy for various principal–agent problems. The presumption is that market competition, while it does not eradicate principal–agent problems, can reduce them by providing alternative providers (agents) who have incentives for continued good performance (and sustained contracts), thereby reducing, at least to some degree, the need for extensive monitoring and, thus, lowering transactions costs (Williamson 1979, 1981).

Empirical tests of PAT have yielded mixed results. Experimental research by Miller and Whitford (2002) call into question the idea that incentives are needed to ensure that risk-averse agents will perform effectively when not monitored. They underscore the role of trust in contracting and show how trust can often result in favorable outcomes for both principal and agent, even absent extensive incentives. More generally, DiIulio (1994) argues that PAT underemphasizes the social and moral underpinnings of bureaucratic behavior, with the result that the rational economic predictions of PAT cannot account for behaviors that are not, in the narrow sense, self-interested.

MARKET FAILURE THEORY AND ECONOMIC INDIVIDUALISM

Property rights theory and PAT are of interest chiefly because they provide theoretical rationales explaining why government organizations tend to be less efficient, at least with respect to market efficiency, than private organizations. However, market failure theory is of more direct and immediate interest because it provides specific criteria for making judgments about the allocation of duties between government and private organizations. Market failure, the most familiar and pervasive rationale applied to public policy decision making (Zerbe and McCurdy 1999), has the merits of providing a strong theoretical underpinning and, at the same time, a practical guide to policy choice and implementation.

Market failure theory presents an excellent case example, perhaps an unrivaled one, in the ubiquitous public policy impact of a broad set of ideas. It is perhaps the premier example of a relatively complex and multifaceted theory that, despite its complexity, a great many people carry as part of the mental models framing their values and decisions.[2] Market failure is rooted in the theory of private value and is driven by concern with pricing efficiency. Various cases and illustrations presented subsequently demonstrate market failure's limited utility for understanding public value and outcomes where the technical efficiency of prices is not a primary consideration. It is important to make this point because market failure has emerged as perhaps our most familiar theory for policy-level decision making, our premier set of guidelines for institutional performance and responsibility. The pervasiveness of market failure reasoning ensures a built-in conservatism in public policy and often results in neglect of public values, generally because the model marginalizes collective values by simply not dealing with them. The model deals with the efficiency of markets and how one knows that markets are not efficient. Beyond this there is little prescription and, despite widely held beliefs, no necessary endorsement of government action as a solution to market problems. The efficiency of markets is important, and market failure provides heuristics useful for public managers and public officials, but they are imperfect heuristics.

Pioneered by Bator (1958) and Samuelson (1954), the market failure model centers on questions of externalities (spillover effects) and the ability to set efficient prices for goods and services. Because ideas about market failure criteria and economics-based concepts for allocation decisions are quite familiar, a brief description may suffice.[3] Donahue (1991, 18) provides a succinct description: Market failure occurs when "prices lie—that is, when the prices of goods and services give false signals about their real value, confounding the communication between consumers and producers." Most economists agree on the broadest causes of market failure. One of these is externalities, though not all types of externalities (e.g., Bator 1958, 363–70). Externalities occur when goods are "nonrival"—when one person's consumption of the good does not mitigate its availability to others. Market failure also occurs owing to steep transaction costs, information deficits, monopolies, and other such competitive failures.

Charles Wolf provides one of the most cogent, concise descriptions of market failure criteria, but one that is a bit at odds with other definitions. According to Wolf (1993, 17), "The principal justification for public policy intervention lies in the frequent and numerous shortcomings of market outcomes. . . . But how is the success or failure of market outcomes to be judged? Two broad criteria are usually and properly, though sometimes ambiguously, employed: efficiency and distributional equity."

Wolf goes on to say that market outcomes are efficient if "the same level of total benefits that they generate cannot be obtained at lower cost, or, alternatively, if greater benefits cannot be generated at the same level of cost" (1993, 18). Not all economists recognize Wolf's second criterion, distributional equity. But public finance economists, interested in taxation and tax incidence, must grapple with distributional issues. Economists' focus on distributional issues usually centers on the economic efficiency of various approaches to distribution of income and goods, not on any inherent qualities of equity or social justice.

One of the more complete definitions of market failure is provided in the *Penguin Dictionary of Economics*. As market failure plays a key role in this book, the quote is extensive:

> [Market failure is an] outcome deriving from the self-interested behavior of individuals in the context of free trade, in which economic efficiency does not result. Market failures provide a ubiquitous argument for intervention of some form or other [not necessarily government intervention]. But they have two main sources. First, they derive from the fact that many transactions which would need to occur for the sake of economic efficiency simply do not occur. This may be on account of transaction costs. Or, there may be a deficiency of information to the parties involved, or there may be asymmetric information. . . . Or, the necessary transaction may be deterred by the fact that the efficient price is not set. . . . Or there may be strategic behavior by the individuals involved, who fail to engage in a trade, in the hope that they might extract a better deal from their adversary if they "play it tough." A large number of "missing trades" are those involving the many resources over which no properly defined property rights exist (such as clean air) and thus over which no trade can occur. . . . The second main category of market failures derive from the fact that there are sometimes collective interests that are unable to be served by self-interested, individual behavior. There are goods or services that have to be consumed collectively . . . ; there can be free-rider problems in which, for example, citizens hope to avoid paying for a service on the grounds that someone else will pay. (Bannock et al. 2004, 211)

The length and precision of this definition notwithstanding, one of the greatest appeals of the market failure model is that its fundamental idea is easily understood: the private sector is the best problem solver except in instances where market competition is flawed and prices are distorted. In the words of one introductory economics text (Marlow 1995, 61), "Under ideal conditions related to competition, information and the absence of externalities, private competitive markets allocate resources efficiently. For government to play a legitimate role, then, either ideal conditions must not be present or *efficiency must not be the most important criterion for directing resource allocation"* [emphasis mine].

It is important to note the putative legitimizing role of market failure on government action. The fact that government can play a "legitimate" role only in cases of market failure does not mean that government should *necessarily* play a role when there is market failure or that there is any expectation that government action will necessarily remedy problems in instances where markets have failed to do so (see Wolf 1993 for a discussion of "nonmarket failure" and criteria for choosing between the "imperfect alternatives" of government vs. private provision of goods and services).

The market failure model fits hand-in-glove with American traditions of economic individualism, but this is only one reason for its appeal. Perhaps its strongest point is that its basic premise is easily understood and rarely questioned: private market solutions are the most efficient. Often this strong claim is shifted to a weak and poorly defended one: that private market solutions are the most effective. Another reason for its appeal is that the market failure model offers a number of diagnostic criteria. Are there externalities? Are there monopolies? Are there excessive transactions costs? As policymakers and the general public seek easily understood, easily communicated but nonetheless plausible guidelines for decision making, the market failure model has allure.

Market failure can be a useful tool, but it does not follow that market hegemony in policy and public management is thusly warranted. Peter Brown (1992, 1994) has provided an especially useful analysis of the limits of market failure models. Among other problems, market failure is premised on a shallow utilitarianism and, as a result, holds little promise for dealing with equity questions. It is prisoner to its foundations in economic individualism. One might object that the basic premises of market failure theory assume collective outcomes, and thus market failure seems an unlikely means of activating economic individualism. Despite appearances to the contrary, market failure and economic individualism are mutually reinforcing.

Defining the government role in terms of the *failure* of markets (i.e., pricing inefficiencies) seems to imply that the public interest is something else, perhaps some condition pertaining to externalities or the "jointness" of goods and services. But the fact that goods are nonrival and can be consumed simultaneously by n persons contains no implication of joint consumption or any sort of collective action or even a manifest collective interest. The theory of public goods is just that—a theory about the properties of goods and services, not one about the people, institutions, or procedures of consumption. Rival goods, externalities, and market failure are entirely consistent with economic individualism and, indeed, premised on such notions. From a public interest standpoint, one of the chief accomplishments of market failure models is to define government and collective action as a *residual*, as a possible (not necessary) alternative to pursue after private solutions have, for one reason or another, failed.

PUBLIC VALUE AS MORE THAN AFTERTHOUGHT

In most instances, those interested in *public* values have at their disposal only their deeply held beliefs, sentiments, and perhaps the ambiguous generalities derived from political philosophy or the public interest, but no analytically powerful theories or attendant tools derived from those theories. It is only at the level of grand deliberation that public interest theory and public value concepts are nearly on an even footing with market-based theories and tools. Iraq was not invaded because of cost–benefit results. Generally, such history-framing decisions are made in accord with some combination of political calculation, personal idiosyncrasies, perceived economic interest, and estimates of public interest. However, most government decision making and policy analysis is not about invading Iraq, ending apartheid in South Africa, or piecing together Europe after the fall of the Soviet Union. In the mundane and highly practical day-to-day decisions about allocation of responsibilities among public and private institutions (i.e., the 99 percent of all public decisions), proponents of public value often find themselves poorly armed. This is one of the reasons perhaps (certainly not the most important one, though) that questions about allocation of goods and services so often receive market answers.

A crucial question is this: "Given the many advantages of economics-based management and decision approaches, does public interest or public value theory, either in previous forms or reformulated, offer a useful alternative in those cases where public value seems at least as important as economic efficiency?" The answer to this question is not at all straightforward. Only the most resolute ideologues believe that decision approaches and tools derived from microeconomics are sufficient to every decision. But it does not follow from the limitations of economics that public interest theory provides acceptable alternatives. Indeed, public interest theory has thus far presented so few *practical* or operational approaches, one might reasonably argue that it is best to leave sleeping theory dogs lie.

The many advantages of market failure criteria notwithstanding, there are several reasons why market failure and related economic efficiency approaches should not preempt other approaches to choosing sector roles. In some cases, there are practical, easily communicated reasons to search beyond market failure criteria. Later sections discuss some of these empirical justifications related to institutional advantage. But it is also worth noting that the reaction against the economic hegemony of analysis is sometimes as much visceral as intellectual. For example, most noneconomists (and not a few economists) squirm when economic analyses favor the saving of male lives over female lives for the sound economic rationale of males' greater "discounted future earnings" (Rhoads 1985). While there is no destructive intent in Becker's (1974, 300–301) characterization of children as commodities "presumed to have modest price elasticities because they do not have close substitutes," one hopes that such a view does not dominate decisions about, say, public schools or child health care. Similarly, many feel there is much more to government than just a body called upon to provide "a good possessing jointness . . . also characterized by nonexclusion" (Davis and Hulett 1977, 36). As Brown notes (1992), market failure models and other schemes rooted in economic individualism often produce vocabulary that seems to trivialize what is at stake in public issues.

Setting aside the emotional hot buttons, let us frame the question in this manner: If we assume that economics, despite its insensitivity to common linguistic usage and its occasional dehumanizing assumptions, provides a powerful, well-articulated, and generally useful approach to analyzing allocation of goods and service among sectors, are there respects in which, to paraphrase Bator (1958), market-based approaches simply "will not do"?

Contemporary discourse is too often dominated by technical efficiency of markets and the private value of things public, often at the expense of public values. The search for a satisfactory conception of the public values and public interest should continue unabated, even in the face of an abundant, often valid criticism. Some justifications include

1. *public value* is something more than collective private value,
2. much of importance is missing in market-based expressions of public value,
3. the fact that public value or public interest are ideals is not a sufficient justification for ignoring them or assuming that they cannot be systematically studied, and
4. (perhaps most controversially) government service sometimes offers something not easily attainable in operations and participation in efficient markets, namely individuals' commitment to the collective good.

These views are more harmonious with decades-old public administration theory than with either the New Public Management or most other contemporary theories of public management. However, these points are not entirely out of step with contemporary economics. The limitations of market theories of governance, public policy, and social choice have been compellingly demonstrated (as discussed later) by many economists, including some who propounded those theories. More than most, economists are aware of both the uses and limitations of market reasoning for issues in the public sphere. In most instances, the contributions of market theory have not been designed as competitors to public interest theories or as means of obscuring public values but, instead, as an available and obviously powerful analytical alternative to having no useful, applicable alternative.

Often economic values are literally irrelevant to public choices. In many instances markets are highly competitive, pricing is efficient, and enormous public problems remain. In other instances, markets are noncompetitive, pricing is inefficient, government has "intervened," and enormous public problems remain. When considering public value, market failure is often simply not the point. Nevertheless, market-based reasoning often dominates public policy deliberation.

Why is public value so often marginalized as nonmarket, market intervention, or market failure? As mentioned earlier, one reason is that decisions about public versus market allocation of goods and services are not made on an even playing field. Arguments about public values or public interest often find themselves at a considerable disadvantage, a disadvantage accruing not from the veracity of argument but from the difficulty in framing the argument (Kuttner 1997). Market failure, pricing efficiency, and economic individualism provide decision theories and criteria; these analytical approaches are powerful and plausible, and, most important, there is often little analytical "competition." Often, theories of the public interest provide useful insights and focus on crucial public value issues. But economic and public interest rationales do not operate at commensurate levels of theory and application. Whereas economic analysis is backed with the diagnostic tools of market failure theory, the arguments of public interest typically operate above the fray, rarely having sufficient presence in the bloody battleground of day-to-day policy deliberation. Thus public value often remains a residual category or ideal construct, and its attendant theories, theories of the public interest, provide little or no guidance as to the key issues of public policy and public management: "What should be done and by whom?"

Nevertheless, there is considerable concern about finding the means to discussion of public value in policy and public management deliberations. Many concerned with public value find economics approaches inappropriate to the most fundamental questions of governance (see especially Stone 1997). Philosopher Peter Brown (1992, 1994) is among those who have contributed to our understanding of the limitations of market failure as a guide to public value. More recently, Zerbe and McCurdy (1999) provided a trenchant critique, concluding that transactions-cost approaches hold much more promise for public policy analysis.

Anticipating contemporary social capital arguments (e.g., Putnam 2000; Skocpol and Fiorina 1999), Lane (1991) argued that efficient markets often have very little to do with development or human happiness, and thus market frameworks are inadequate to the task of social allocation of goods and services. Thus, Kirlin (1996, 170) complains, "Economists sometimes adopt a view of the functions of government to fit their tools of analysis. In support of their chosen approach, they distort the history of government, making it subordinate to economics when it clearly is not." He goes on to argue that government *creates* value, value not easily understood within a market framework. Interestingly, some economists agree with Kirlin. Wittman (1995) argues that democratic political institutions create value, often quite efficiently, as they reduce transactions costs and encourage efficient exchange of political rights. Some public management scholars argue that public managers themselves create public value (e.g., Moore 1995; Van Wart 1998).

Economists are among the most convincing critics of the role of microeconomic theory in public value. Professional economists are well acquainted with limitations raised by Arrow's Impossibility Theorem (alleging the impossibility of an adequate social choice framework).[4] Similarly, economists employing Pareto efficiency (the conventional utilitarian calculus) in social choice generally understand its irrelevance to the distributional issues so often at the heart of public value questions. Some time ago, economists began to agree on the validity of the "theorem of the second best" (Lipsey and Lancaster 1956–57), which suggests the hazards of applying competitive market reasoning when there are significant competition barriers. Richard Nelson (1987) presented compelling arguments that the pervasiveness of market failures inhibits the usefulness of the model as a set of practical criteria.

Economists have made major contributions to overcoming the strictures of traditional microeconomic theories of value. For example, social choice theory (Sen 1979, 1995; Suzumura 1997) aims to "provide a general approach to the evaluation of, and choice over, alternative social policies" (Sen 1999, 349). Bator (1958) recognizes that the provision of public goods or the legitimacy of public action cannot always be determined on the criterion of economic efficiency alone. In her constitutional theory of public goods, Marmolo (1999) argues that the rationale for the public provision of goods is not dependent on economic efficiencies and arguments of nonexcludability and joint consumption, but instead on the public values inherent in institutional design and the definition of public powers. The problem, then, is not unawareness of the limitations of market failure, but a lack of suitable alternatives for facilitating dialog about public values (White 1994).

Chapter 4 examines the public interest theories that have been advanced, classifies them, and considers their strengths and weaknesses. While we will see that none of these provides a set of crisp guidelines for policy and public management, public interest theory is nonetheless useful for framing arguments, especially those in which "is" and "ought" questions begin to intersect.

Before considering public interest theories as a possible alternative framework to theories based on economic individualism, we turn in chapter 4 to the role of economic theories in public management and the implementation of policy. The so-called New Public Management approach to government reform strongly affected the delivery of goods and services in many nations, especially during its zenith in the late 1990s. In the United States, the New

Public Management is not so familiar as a brand name for importing private-sector assumptions and approaches into government chiefly because market approaches have such a long and deep history in the United States that no "reform" was required (Kettl 2005).

NOTES

1. The term *opportunity costs* refers to the value of an alternative use of a resource, compared to the contemplated use of the resource. Thus, one who uses capital to pay, reduce, or pay off the principal on a home mortgage loan might well consider the "opportunity costs" relative to the return that would accrue from paying off one's credit card debt. In this case, the opportunity costs should include the foregone opportunity of a tax deduction from mortgage debt (whereas credit card debt is not deductible). A more general and perhaps more relevant illustration: a contractor who expends resources to earn a profit in connection with a given contract may not have those same resources fully available should another contract be tendered.
2. Let us consider a simple but significant indicator of the pervasiveness of market failure concepts. A May 5, 2005, Internet search on the exact terms *market failure* and *syllabus* yielded 17,400 "hits," the vast majority relevant to the purpose of identifying college courses dealing with the topic *market failure*. (For comparison, *public values* and *syllabus* yielded 379 hits, and *public interest theory* and *syllabus* yielded 20 hits.)
3. Readers who wish a more detailed account of the market failure model, its assumptions, and its relation to public policy and public finance issues may wish to consult several basic texts treating the topic. Especially recommended is the cogent and relatively detailed (but still introductory) account provided by Bruce (1998).
4. For years, economists have wrestled with the Impossibility Theorem that argues the inability of choice mechanisms to provide for common welfare under any but the most draconian of assumptions (e.g., dictatorship). More recently, several economists (e.g., Sen 1970; Gevers 1979; Suzumura 1997) have demonstrated results that are less pessimistic.

CHAPTER FOUR

ECONOMIC INDIVIDUALISM
IN PUBLIC MANAGEMENT

We forget at our peril that markets make a good servant, a bad master and a worse religion.

—AMORY LOVINS, CEO, Rocky Mountain Institute

The ideas of economic individualism affect not only the design and analysis of public policy but also its management and implementation. Indeed, it seems fair to say that the great preponderance of public management reforms and innovations of the past two decades have primarily been ones based on market or quasi-market theories and concepts. These market-based public management approaches take different names in different contexts. In the United States, both the literature and the practice of public management have for more than twenty-five years been strongly influenced by market-oriented public management. Sometimes it is in the name of privatization or contracting out and sometimes it is more general notions of "managing government like a business." Market-oriented public management owes a considerable debt to the Reagan Revolution, not so much for developing new approaches as providing a forum and a demand for them.

This chapter considers two closely related topics concerning the application of markets and values of economic individualism: privatization and New Public Management (NPM). As Starr (1988) observes, privatization is a "fuzzy concept." Among the many available definitions, a particularly useful one has been provided by the U.S. General Accounting Office (now the U.S. Government Accountability Office). According to this definition (1998, 3), privatization is "any process that is aimed at shifting functions and responsibilities, in whole or in part, from the government to the private sector through such activities as contracting out or asset sales." The definition seems useful because it is encompassing. A broad definition serves best simply because it covers the many activities that are generally referred to as "privatization."

If privatization is a fuzzy concept, NPM is a fluid one. Most agree that, whatever else NPM might be, it is a set of approaches to public management reform. So let us begin by defining public management reform. Pollitt and Bouckaert (2000, 8) provide a perfectly serviceable definition of public management reform as "deliberate changes to the structure and processes of public sector organizations with the objective of getting them (in some sense) to run better." There is nothing in that definition that necessitates a focus on markets or quasi-markets, but as Pollitt and Bouckaert note, the majority of recent reform efforts have tended be market oriented. Indeed, one observes a long history of market-oriented reforms predating the NPM concept.

In the United States many of these have been budget reforms such as performance budgeting, planning-programming-budgeting systems, and zero-based budgeting. But other reforms, such as management-by-objective and, more recently, the reforms associated with the Government Performance and Results Act (U.S. Congress 1993) have been more encompassing. The idea of "reinventing government" was a Clinton-era catchphrase but also a set of activities that changed some important aspects of public management in the U.S. federal government (see Frederickson 1996 for a critical overview). Each of these reforms, whether budget reforms or broader reforms, has included an element of market-oriented management, measurement, or evaluation.

Sorting out all the differences between NPM and "privatization" requires an observer more astute than the present one. However, the following distinctions seem safe. First, privatization is the older term. While it is not clear to whom the term *privatize* should be attributed or exactly when it entered the popular vernacular, we do know when the term entered the dictionary. It was relatively recently, 1968.[1] This makes the term about fifteen years' senior of NPM.[2] A second distinction is that the NPM seems to have more management strategy trappings than privatization. NPM is a loosely integrated managerial philosophy. While privatization efforts have broad influence, one thinks about policy and management as tools more than as a philosophy of management. Privatization is about moving public performance and functions to the private sector, but NPM includes many other trappings such as, for example, viewing the client as customer. It is perhaps accurate to say that privatization is a broad tool kit, whereas NPM is, as advertised, an approach to management reform. But it would be a mistake to make any hard-and-fast claims about specific boundaries between NPM and privatization.

To a large extent, the term *New Public Management* has become a brand, one signifying market-oriented governance. While the approach embodies a number of activities and orientations to government—discussed in more detail later—the basic thrust is use of markets and competition. The term emerged from the Whitehall reforms in the United Kingdom during Prime Minister Margaret Thatcher's era (1979–90) and was exported to many nations both in Europe and other parts of the world. Conservative governments in New Zealand and Australia emerged as two of the most enthusiastic exponents of NPM (Kettl 2005). While each of these nations, and especially New Zealand, has in recent years reversed many of the NPM elements, each retains important NPM vestiges.

Regardless of the ups and downs of NPM, the "marketization of the state" (Pierre 1995) has proven an influential and robust trend. This chapter considers more of these trends. Rather than documenting specific instances of market-oriented public management, our primary concern is the *underlying theoretical bases* of these reforms (Kickert 1996, 1997). The object is to consider these premises in comparison to those of public value.

I begin by examining privatization, the older concept, and then move to the issues of NPM. This is not only because NPM is of more recent vintage but also because NPM is more akin to a philosophy of management. Privatization seems less integrated and less tied to specific management nostrums, as opposed to the grab bag of management tools provided in specific market-based approaches to public management. But it is also worth noting that approaches such as privatization, contracting out, and institutions such as public enterprises and public authorities predate NPM and make up much of the NPM tool kit.

PRIVATIZATION

One interested in a detailed description and analysis of privatization can consult any of a great many sources, providing different flavors (see Brooks 2004). Donahue (1991) provides a straightforward and generally balanced introduction, one that includes information about the historical roots of privatization and examples of particular instances of privatization and that is also useful for helping one understand the rationales for privatization. Savas's work (2000) provides the perspective of the advocate. He has studied privatization for many years and for several years served as a practitioner implementing privatization policies, which convinced him of the value of privatization. Savas's book not only describes privatization but also provides numerous examples and practical guidelines for effective privatization.

Sociologist and professor in public affairs Paul Starr (1988) provides one of the earliest but still most useful efforts to sort through the thicket of privatization concepts. According to Starr, "Privatization has come primarily to mean two things: (1) any shift of activities or functions from the state to the private sector; and, more specifically, (2) any shift of the production of goods and services from public to private" (4). This seems a broad definition, but it does provide some limits. For example, Starr's concept excludes shifts of public organizations into hybrid organizations such as public authorities. Similarly, when private, nonprofit organizations become for-profit business organizations, that transformation does not qualify as privatization. The Starr conceptualization is in one respect too expansive (at least for present purposes). In his view, privatization occurs not only as a result of direct government action but also because persons outside of government have, of their own independent initiative, begun to provide legal alternatives to government goods and services. We shall not speak of this as privatization simply because it muddies the waters. With the exception of a very few government monopoly goods and services, there are always private alternatives. If one views all private schools, private security firms, and private trash haulers as *privatization*, then the term begins to lose its policy and strategic management implications.

While many of the best-known books about privatization are focused on the United States, many books are available about experiences in other regions, including countries in Eastern Europe (Engerer 2001), developing countries (Birdsall and Nellis 2005), Africa (Tanyi 1997), and most anywhere else. Likewise, one can find information about privatization of nearly any function including schools (Walford 1990), police (Benson 1998), garbage (Cointreau-Levine 1994), or just about any government function. One can even find books on privatization of national defense, the classic "public good" (Camm 1996).

While some of the best-known works on privatization are positive in orientation (e.g., Savas 2000), criticism is abundant. Sclar (2000) and Kuttner (1997) provide especially trenchant and more general criticisms of privatization. However, more specific criticisms are plentiful. Indeed, there are so many criticisms of privatization that subgenres have emerged for various policy fields. Thus an abundant critical literature is available for specific policy domains such as water privatization (e.g., Galiani, Gertler, and Schargrodsky 2005; Jurik 2004) or prison privatization (e.g., Useem and Goldstone 2002; Sheldon 2005).

In short, the literature on privatization is voluminous. For those interested in learning more about privatization, the works described earlier provide a beginning. But our concern is not about privatization per se, but about its relation to economic individualism and, particularly, public value. Because of this focus, the literature criticizing privatization is more relevant than the general introductions, the case studies, the "how-to" books, or the ideological treatises. From the scores of evaluations of particular instances of privatization, not only the ones cited earlier but also scores of others, one feels confident with the following summary statement: Privatization is neither a magic bullet nor a colossal dud; it is an approach that works sometimes. Of greater interest here are the *values* underpinning privatization.

VALUES AND PRIVATIZATION

In many instances the values implicit in privatization are manifest. This is particularly the case when the rationale for privatization is a less sophisticated one and seems more a mantra than an idea (Beckett 2000). But in other cases, values are implicit and often more subtle. In most instances privatization is undertaken for multiple reasons and reflects a set of values rather than a single, overarching value (Feigenbaum, Henig, and Hamnett 1998). In many cases privatization is something more than a practical approach to improving government; it is part and parcel of an ideological view about government and its role in society (Appel 2000; Miller 1997).

The following section shows that privatization and New Public Management, while not the same, are closely interwoven, so much so that the two share many values. Thus we revisit these values in the subsequent discussion of NPM.

Cost Savings and Cost-Effectiveness

Let us begin with the most common, the crudest, and in some respects the most insidious of rationales for privatization. Cost savings is the most popular rationale for privatization. Policymakers expect to achieve reduced costs with privatization because they anticipate greater efficiency among private providers because of, among other factors, market competition (Van Slyke 2003). Saving tax dollars is, of course, an entirely legitimate objective and one always popular with taxpayers. Demonstrably, privatization sometimes results in some reduced costs and, it often follows, reduced tax burden (Savas 2000). In at least some instances, privatization introduces competition, reduces transaction costs, and saves money, often with no decrement in the quality of service. Three-fourths of the U.S. city and county executives responding to a 1987 survey reported savings of 10 percent or more from a wide variety of privatization efforts (Vickers and Yarrow 1991). When the profit motive is clear, privatization more often provides efficiency motivations and management oversight (Vickers and Yarrow 1991; Savas 2000).

Despite clear and documented privatization successes, a by-now vast accumulation of studies of privatization and studies comparing government versus private provision of goods and services have provided quite mixed results, even if one uses relatively simple measures of cost (see Rainey 2003 for an overview). If one uses a more sophisticated assessment of costs, that is, not just immediate expenses but also long-run costs, cost measures incorporating cost avoidance, or costs of contract management and supervision, then the results from privatization are even more diverse. For example, Van Slyke (2003) finds that contracting out social services neither increases competition nor increases cost-effectiveness. If one moves to the even more complicated question of the contribution of privatization versus other factors in net cost savings, then calculations become more challenging (Joassart-Marcelli and Musso 2005).

Cost savings is rarely a sensible cardinal value for public managers (except perhaps those cases when the only alternative to cost savings is abandoning the provision of a particular good or service). Instead, most public managers pursue cost-effectiveness, and, indeed, many define their mission in part by the pursuit of cost-effectiveness in service delivery (Nutt and Backoff 1995). If it is difficult to ascertain cost savings from privatization, it is inordinately more complex to determine net cost-effectiveness. This is simply because it is almost always more difficult to measure effectiveness than cost, except in those rare cases where there is a generally agreed upon concept of effectiveness and when increasing its value does not impair other important values that an organization seeks to achieve.

Liberalization of Government

A more fundamental value underpinning privatization, one more closely aligned with economic individualism, is the liberalization of government. The fundamental value of classical liberal government is small government with sharp limits on its control. This value is sometimes conflated with government costs but, of course, is actually independent. It is possible to have a large efficient government just as it is possible to have a small inefficient one. The value of a reduced role for government may be more fundamental even than the value of efficiency. Indeed, classical liberal political theory such as that of Hobbes and Locke had little to say about the cost of government and a great deal to say about its potential for tyranny.

Privatization is neither necessary nor sufficient for the achievement of liberalization, but many view privatization as closely related to their goal of reducing the scope of government. There are many ways this can occur. For example, if a function previously reserved as a government monopoly now permits private competition, one can achieve liberalization.

The important point here is that it is possible for one to favor privatization not as an efficiency ends but expressly for the purpose of shrinking government, its funding, its employees, and, especially, its influence. One pursuing such values would not, then, be as readily satisfied with managerial reforms aiming to increase the efficiency of government while leaving its scope and influence intact. Thus, internal competition with government would not directly promote the value of liberalization. Likewise, the contracting out of government services would not necessarily serve the value of liberalization if government maintained responsibility for close supervisions and management of the contracts, including rigidly enforced policies and standards from the contracts.

Decentralization and Community Action

Related to the idea of liberalizing government is the value of decentralization. According to this value, one commonplace in policy discourse—the closeness of government—has inherent value to citizens. This is, of course, the hallmark of the Jeffersonian ethos. To the extent that privatization shifts the emphasis of governance from more distant to more proximate units, values of decentralization and community responsiveness may be enhanced. However, Alford (2002) and Frederickson (1997) argue that privatization and outsourcing devalue citizenship and ignore the responsibility agencies have to the public interest.

Indeed, the evidence is not so straightforward, and some studies debunk the idea of government liberalization leading to decentralization and proximity to citizens. For example, one study (Barnett and Newberry 2002) of privatization of mental health programs in New Zealand showed that decentralization achieved through privatization was relatively modest and was offset by difficulties in accountability. Specifically, the privatization led to considerable local and regional variations in the structure of contracts, granting more flexibility but sometimes at the cost of performance. As often seems the case, the privatization of services redistributes power but seems to provide few if any benefits for citizen control or empowerment. Studies in developing countries suggest that there often is an even larger gap in those countries between decentralization and accountability objectives of privatization and the actual results (e.g., Caulfield 2006; Parker and Kirkpatrick 2005).

TRANSFORMATIVE PRIVATIZATION

Elsewhere in this book, and particularly chapter 6, I discuss the familiar concept of "transformative democracy." At the risk of inventing new terminology, we can also speak of "transformative privatization" as a value. The basic idea is that public managers exposed to privatization will be changed such that they will develop new perspectives on the meaning and importance of market competition.

The transformative privatization value, as other values, takes various forms, some more sophisticated than others. Cruder versions seem to assume that most public managers are by nature profligate and disregarding of public funds. The reasoning, in many instances, is something like this: public managers do not suffer direct adverse consequences of spendthrift behavior, and thus they have neither the incentive nor the inclination to guard the public purse. More sophisticated variants (e.g., Acemoglou and Verdier 2000) posit "rent-seeking bureaucrats" who are concerned with their own advancement, a personal agenda, or corruption and squander funds in service of these. Richer conceptualizations (Duch and Palmer 2004) of public management behavior begin with the assumption that public managers have multiple motives, including perhaps public service, but that when competing motives clash, the lack of "market discipline" pushes the public managers to spend when they should conserve.

The causal paths by which public managers are to be transformed, with market exposure, to higher levels of performance are not generally well articulated. A notable limitation is that few pay much attention to the social psychological dynamics that affect such causation (Lee and Webley 2005). The basic idea is that incentives will change and managerial behavior will respond to these incentives. But this chain of reasoning is weak. In the first place, the market imposes no particular discipline in the absence of competition, and many studies (e.g., Van Slyke 2003; Bozeman and Wilson 2004; Caiden and Sundaram 2004) have suggested that the competition introduced by privatization is, variously, absent, disappointing, spurious, or mismanaged. Moreover, what we know from decades of studying managers is that their motives and behaviors are complex and deeply embedded. The likelihood that fundamental changes will occur because of transitory exposure to market forces seems modest. When organizations move toward market reforms and contracting, managers' long-term values, coworker and peer influences, authority patterns, formal education, and political constraints provide powerful alternatives and sometimes rival influences. Moreover, the "market experience" usually (excepting recent experiences in former socialist or communist nations) is not a new one. Most managers whose organizations have begun privatization programs have themselves been active participants in markets. In the United States, for example, more than half of all middle class families have stock and mutual fund portfolios. If the market is transformative, it likely transformed long ago.

This questioning of the limits of transformative privatization should not be taken as a repudiation of the idea that public managers can be changed by work involvement with contracts and market mechanisms. The only point is that the effects are likely to be more incremental ones rather than wholesale transformations.

Coercion

In some instances privatization is a response to, essentially, external coercion. Perhaps the best example is the history of the World Bank or the International Monetary Fund (IMF) requiring management reforms, including privatization, as a prerequisite to its loans and other services (Henisz et al. 2005). As noted in the water case presented in chapter 2, the majority of efforts to privatize water systems in the developing world have been in response to overwhelming pressure from the World Bank and the IMF. When countries introduce privatization to curry favor with the World Bank, the IMF, or various international organizations, the values become as complex as all the reasons why assistance is sought in the first place—economic development, political stability, prestige, national identity, and international political and economic integration, to name just a few of the more prominent values.

Latent Values

Several decades ago sociologists began to distinguish between manifest and latent functions. Robert Merton generally is credited with this conceptual distinction. Perhaps most famously Merton used the distinction between manifest and latent functions in his analysis of urban political machines. But one early example was based on Hopi rain rituals. According to Merton (1957, 64), rain ceremonies served not only manifest meteorological functions but also "the latent function of reinforcing the group identity by providing a periodic occasion on which the scattered members of a group assemble to engage in a common activity."

In many cases privatization seems to serve both manifest and latent functions. However, the rain-maker function, unlike the Hopi case, is more often a latent function. That is, politicians and other public officials sometimes embrace privatization not so much as a solution or a reform as evidence that *something* is changing even if conditions seem to be getting no better. Similarly, public officials and public managers sometimes use privatization as a symbol. Market reforms send a cue about the persons who design or implement them. These cues differ in context but they may, for example, signal a hard-nosed interest in efficiency (whether or not reflected in real behaviors or outcomes), commitment to innovation, or receptivity to business influence. Aside from any direct outcomes, these symbolic outcomes and the latent values attendant to them may have value to public officials and public managers.

NEW PUBLIC MANAGEMENT

Michael Barzelay (2001, 2–3) notes that the term *New Public Management* "expresses the idea that the cumulative flow of policy decisions over that past twenty years has amounted to a substantial shift in governance and management of the 'state sector.'" It seems noteworthy that a book titled *The New Public Management* comes no closer than that to a definition of the term. Instead, Barzelay examines NPM as manifested in its activities in various nations and follows Aucoin's (1995) lead in conceptualizing NPM as a set of arguments or a "network of claims." In some respects NPM is more a catchphrase for market-based reform than a unified approach to governance. But NPM is more than market advocacy because there are many aspects to NPM that do not impinge on market-based reform. As Hood and Peters (2004) note in their recent retrospective, "Like most divinities, NPM turned out to be somewhat mystical in essence, as no two authors . . . listed exactly the same features in enumerating its traits." It is perhaps fair to say that the only common point among various conceptions of NPM is a deep respect for the use of market discipline in governance.

One of the reasons why NPM is difficult to pin down is that the focus of scholars and practitioners has shifted somewhat since its inception. According to Hood and Peters (2004), NPM is now in "middle age" and has experienced three periods of development. The earliest writing about NPM began in the late 1980s, but the common use of the term seems to have appeared in the 1990s, in part due to a series of papers aiming to articulate or codify NPM precepts (e.g., Flynn 1990; Pollitt 1990). By now NPM is perhaps beyond middle age and in its declining years. While interest in market-based governance remains strong—as indeed was the case *before* NPM—some of the nations that have been most closely associated with NPM reforms, conspicuously New Zealand (Boston, Dalziel, and St. John 1999) and the United Kingdom, have begun to move away from NPM reforms and especially NPM rhetoric. Many of the European nations that flirted with NPM (e.g., the Netherlands,

Denmark, and Germany) never fully embraced the experiment. In the United States only a few of the NPM-like reforms of the Clinton administration's National Performance Review (Gore 1993) survived intact the two elections of George W. Bush. But if NPM is no longer on the tongues of scholars and policymakers around the globe, neither is it yet relegated to the dustbin of managerial reform fads. NPM remains influential, especially in the British Commonwealth nations from which it originated, and, even if the term *NPM* and its many "arguments" are not so often advanced, market-oriented governance remains strong in most parts of the globe.

During its emergent years NPM was influential, as a concept and in practice, in the "New Right" agenda of member nations in the Organization for Economic Cooperation and Development, and especially in Anglo-heritage countries including the United Kingdom, Australia, and New Zealand. In the early 1990s the term had barely made a dent in U.S. public management circles, in part because U.S. scholars and practitioners had already begun to develop different terms for many of the same approaches (e.g., "reinventing government") and in part because market-based approaches had taken root in the United States long before the term and ideology of NPM originated. Many of the European governments then infatuated with NPM were transitioning from a democratic socialist tradition and from a welfare state that was much more extensive than ever experienced in the United States. Thus, the ideas of NPM had more power to startle, whereas in the United States, with many existing commitments to market-based government, there was perhaps more a sense of (no pun intended) business as usual. In the late 1980s and early 1990s in Europe and other nations captivated by the idea of NPM and the Whitehall reforms, there was a period of multiparty reflection and criticism about fundamental values of governance and the relationship of markets. This same period of reflection seems not to have occurred in the United States, though something much like it developed in the early 1980s with the Reagan Revolution.

The second NPM period, according to Hood and Peters (2004), focused on analysis of the different variants of public management reform and the diverse expression of NPM in various nations. Predictably, as the NPM concept came to be more influential and a powerful symbol, its meaning was shaped by local political issues and controversies. Various papers documented, lauded, and sometimes criticized the development of NPM, and others (e.g., Savoie 1995; Zifcak 1994) provided contrasts of nations' applications of NPM reforms.

The third (and contemporary) NPM period, according to Hood and Peters (2004) dates from the late 1990s and seeks to institutionalize NPM and to provide its intellectual underpinnings. Part of this effort is providing textbooks devoted specifically to NPM and formalization of the field, including understanding NPM within the historical context of government reform (Barzelay 2001).

Despite some progress in institutionalizing NPM, it still, even at this late period of development, means many different things. One of the most useful recent "enumerations of traits" is provided by Christopher Pollitt (2003, 27–31). Perhaps the best early "enumeration of traits" is Christopher Hood's (1991). Recognizing that NPM has evolved, stabilized somewhat, and begun to be institutionalized, it is useful to compare these two summaries, one from the earliest days of NPM and the other from its latest period of development. Table 4.1 provides a comparison.

The book's concluding chapter considers NPM in much more detail. However, it is worth dwelling here on the core issues highlighted by this comparison of emergent and developed NPM. Despite a span of more than ten years between their respective publication dates, the core values between the two are not much different, and these two lists of traits have much in common. NPM has not evolved into something quite different than it was at its origins.

These summaries show that the leitmotif of NPM, in either the earlier or later version, is competition. Almost casually, the two treatments disparage

Table 4.1   New Public Management Traits, Emergent and Developed

Emergent Characteristics of NPM	Developed Characteristics of NPM
Preference for "hands-on" professional management; active, visible control from top managers	A shift in management focus from input and processes to output
Preference for quantitative indicators and explicit standards and measures of performance	A shift toward more measurement and quantification, especially in the form of systems of performance indicators
Emphasis on output controls; resources linked to performance and decentralized forms; personnel management	A preference for more specialized, "lean," "flat," and autonomous organization "arm's lengths" relations among agencies
Disaggregation of bureaucratic units; unbundling of management systems into corporatized units centered on products and service and with decentralized budgets, dealing with one another "at arm's length"	Use of contracts or contract-like relationships in lieu of formal and hierarchical relationships
Shift to greater competition, term contracts, and competitive bidding	Much wider than hitherto deployment of markets or marketlike mechanisms for the delivery of public services
Emphasis on private-sector style management practices; greater flexibility in hiring and rewards	Broadening and blurring of the frontiers between the public sector, the market sector, and the voluntary sector
Stress on greater discipline and parsimony in resource use; cutting direct costs, resisting union demands, limiting businesses' compliance costs	Shift in value priorities away from universalism, equity, security, and resilience toward efficiency and individualism

Source: Adapted from Hood (1991, 4–5); Pollitt (2003, 27–28).

interdependence and interagency cooperation, instead urging "hands-off" relations, formal contractual relations, and a shift in values from universalism to individualism. The retreat from government interdependence is a more radical departure than the encouragement of market mechanisms and competition (though the two are obviously interrelated). Historically, most scholars have argued that there are some ineradicable differences between business and government management (for reviews, see Rainey 1989; Rainey, Backoff, and Levine 1976). However, that difference is not related (as has often been alleged) to the "bottom line," profit retention, user charges, or performance incentives. Each of these approaches has been used for years in government, though none is dominant in government management. But the idea that government entities should be independent of one another, that they should be "hands off," is not at all common. In government agencies, their common foundation in legitimate political authority (see Bozeman 1987) ties them to one another, to political superiors, and, by proxy, to the citizens. If there is a key to understanding the difference between a "customer orientation" and a "citizen orientation," this is the role of political authority in mitigating the relationship between the individual and the government-as-corporate actor. I will return to this theme, one pivotal to understanding differences between market values and economic individualism, on the one hand, and public values and citizenship, on the other.

VALUES EMBODIED IN NPM

Just as it is possible to identify a set of values pursued in privatization, so is it possible to enumerate broad values and motivations underlying NPM. In *Bureaucracy and Red Tape*, Bozeman (2000) provides a "Balance Model" for assessing administrative reform. The basic idea is a simple one. The Balance Model begins with core values of public management: efficiency, accountability, performance, and fairness. These terms are used many different ways but in the present context, *efficiency* is using the minimum level of resources to achieve a desired level of results. *Accountability* is achieved if policies and procedures are implemented in conformance with the purposes prescribed by higher governmental authorities (with citizens being the highest authority in a legitimate democratic state). *Performance* refers to the extent to which the values represented in policy objectives are achieved. Perhaps most complicated among the core values, *fairness,* means that people are dealt with in the legitimately prescribed manner. Fairness may imply impartial treatment and "neutral competence" in the bureaucracy, or it may imply differential treatment, such as special preference for the underprivileged, veterans, or minorities. That is to say, fairness must be considered in the context of policy statements and assumptions.

Inasmuch as the values of the Balance Model were developed for assessing administrative change and reform, the model seems relevant for understanding

NPM. It seems clear that, according to almost all descriptions of NPM, the driving values are performance and efficiency, while fairness, by any definition, rarely receives much emphasis in NPM. Perhaps the most interesting core value of the Balance Model, at least from the standpoint of NPM, is that of accountability. Whereas most descriptions of NPM at least pay lip service (and sometimes much more) to the value of accountability, there seems little recognition that accountability and, respectively, performance and efficiency often are inimical to one another.

Perhaps the best and most thoroughgoing analysis of the trade-offs of values involved in managerial reform is that provided by Pollitt and Bouckaert (2000). This approach is quite compatible with the Balance Model, but more detailed. Table 4.2 is adapted from the "contradictions" identified by Pollitt and Bouckaert.

SUMMING UP

Privatization and NPM certainly are not the only managerial reforms rife with contradictions, inconsistencies, and paradoxes. As we will see in a subsequent chapter focused specifically on value analysis, it is rarely easy to cut through the thicket of ends, means, and empirical realities to achieve multiple goals.

It is easy to surmise why management reform more often than not includes multiple, conflicting values. No management scheme can sensibly promote just one type of values. Managers know instinctively that their art and

Table 4.2 Contradictions and Trade-offs in Public Management Reform

Core Management Reform Value	Contradictory or Trade-Off Value	Comments
Increase political control of the bureaucracy	Free managers to manage; empower service consumers	The history of public management reform suggests that this trade-off will always be toward political control. Managerial freedom occurs by subversion and chance.
Provide flexibility and innovation	Increase citizen trust and government legitimacy	Citizens are rarely excited by innovation, absent obvious performance or costs benefits. For many public managers and political officials, innovation=quality. The citizens are right about this one!
Give priority to making savings	Give priority to improving performance	The managerial shibboleths abound: "do more with less," "lean and mean," and such. But there is always a nexus after which decrements in

Core Management Reform Value	Contradictory or Trade-Off Value	Comments
		resources necessarily leads to declining performance. The key is identifying the point where the curves intersect.
Make government more responsible	Reduce range of government's tasks	This is the privatization trade-off, or perhaps better described as the privatization myth. Making government more responsible by taking away its functions is addition by subtraction. This works in management as well as in arithmetic.
Motivate staff	Weaken tenure and downsize	No contradiction involved if we take this to mean "shore up the hopes of troops as they see their comrades falling around them." But expecting highly motivated employees even as the organization withers remains an unreasonable aspiration.
Reduce control and paperwork	Sharpen managerial accountability	See Bozeman (2000) on this particular misguided pair of conflicting goals. While there are multiple causes of red tape, many flow from increases in accountability.
Create more single-purpose agencies	Improve horizontal coordination	The evidence suggests that single-purpose agencies create fragmentation, not coordination (Gregory 2002).
Decentralize management authority	Improve program coordination	While not necessarily a contradiction, this works only with strong, active, and effective networks.
Increase effectiveness	Sharpen managerial accountability	Pollitt and Bouckaert (2000) see this as a tension, not a contradiction. The tension is between a focus on outputs and a focus on outcomes. While these seem reasonably connected, the managerial world usually spins about on outputs, not outcomes.
Improve quality	Cut costs	Not a contradiction when the organization is afloat in excess funds.

Source: Adapted from Pollitt and Bouckaert (2000, 154–71).

craft necessitates trade-offs. While managers need not embrace the exact specifications of the Balance Model or the Pollitt and Bouckaert (2000) contradictions, even the most modest work experience quickly brings the practicing public manager into touch with the juggling of values necessitated by a managerial environment characterized by multiple constraints, multiple authoritative actors, and limited resources.

While recognizing the multiple conflicting values of NPM and privatization, it is nonetheless possible to understand the economic individualism roots of these approaches. Each of these approaches includes values based on use of market mechanisms, contracts, and, ultimately, choice. There is little in each approach pertaining to communal values, trust, collective choice, or even that fourth leg of the Balance Model table, fairness. This is not to say that NPM and privatization are inured to public value and public interest. It is certainly possible to specify many different circumstances under which privatization or the various doctrines of NPM could be closely aligned with public interest and public value. But neither begins with core public values or with a clear-cut notion of public interest. The values embodied in privatization and NPM, while not identical to one another, are efficiency and effectiveness values, not equity, fairness, or communal values. While there is certainly more to NPM and privatization than either the market or economic individualism, one would not stray off the mark in asserting that, on balance, these approaches have been forces for moving the world closer to neoliberalism and organization by markets. When public values follow, so much the better. But there is no insistence on them.

Recent discussion and debates about public management have been dominated by neoliberal, economic individualism, and reforms have focused on market mechanisms. Indeed, these trends have so long been in ascendance that it is easy to forget that, between the 1920's zenith of Progressive Era intellectuals such as Charles Beard, Frederick Jackson Turner, Lincoln Steffens, and Walter Lippman and the 1960s, philosophers and political scientists viewed questions pertaining to public values and the public interest as the centrepiece of normative discourse. Perhaps contemplating public interest seems far removed from contemporary public management and policy challenges? Chapter 5, focusing on the public interest traditions in philosophy and political science, seeks to show why public interest theory fell out of fashion, and, at the same time, why it is worth resurrecting.

NOTES

1. See http://www.etymonline.com/index.php?search=privatize&searchmode=none, downloaded June 13, 2006.
2. One cannot yet find "New Public Management" in any standard dictionary, but it is an entry in Wikipedia, albeit a much smaller one than "privatization." (To be more precise, NPM was a Wikipedia entry on June 13, 2006: http://en.wikipedia.org/wiki/New_Public_Management.)

CHAPTER FIVE

PUBLIC INTEREST THEORY
AND ITS PROBLEMS

Living adults share, we must believe, the same public interest. For them, however, the public interest is mixed with, and is often put at odds with, their private and special interests. Put this way, we can say that the public interest may be presumed to be what men would choose if they saw clearly, thought rationally, acted disinterestedly and benevolently.

—WALTER LIPPMANN, *The Public Philosophy*

One commonly held distinction between government and market organizations is that government should work in the "public interest" (Appleby 1952; Flathman 1966). It is not only citizens who expect public interested government (Goodsell 2003), so do public managers (Perry 1996; Crewson 1997; Wittmer 1991). Yet, despite the convergence of citizens' and public managers' views about the importance of the public interest in government service, there is little agreement about the meaning of the public interest, either in general or as applied to particular issues and controversies. Essayist and journalist Walter Lippman's definition of the public interest, perhaps the best known, gives some insight into the problems of using the concept, but, as do so many other definitions of the public interest, provides little practical guidance. Were one to take Lippman's definition as a starting point for public policy, one would be stymied.

This chapter has two major objectives. First, to examine some of the dominant ideas of public interest theory and to consider how they relate to one another, and second, to examine the recent intellectual history of public interest theory, paying particular attention to two questions: "Why did public interest theory begin to buckle under its critics' assaults?" and, perhaps even more interesting, "Why does public interest theory, despite the ebb and flow of intellectual fashions and despite powerful criticisms against it, nevertheless have continuing appeal?"

As noted in chapter 1, nearly fifty years have passed since the relentless criticisms of behaviorally oriented political scientists derailed the formal study of the public interest. Schubert's (1961, 348) scathing dismissal of the public interest as "childish myth" and Sorauf's (1957, 638) comparison of the public interest to "fables" were not the worst of it. In addition to over-the-top rhetoric, these two critics, and others (e.g., Downs 1962), provided sound, convincing criticisms of concepts of the public interest. Among the various criticisms advanced, several seem incontestable: (a) the term is vague and ambiguous, (b) individual authors are not consistent in their usage of the term, (c) many concepts of the public interest are virtually indistinguishable from more general concerns of morality, and (d) there have been few efforts to measure the public interest, none entirely successful. With respect to this latter point, political philosopher Brian Barry's (1965, 196) idea that "the only really satisfactory way of approaching 'the public interest' would be to take a great number of examples of actual uses—from court cases, newspapers, books, speeches, and conversations—and see what could be made of them" has not been taken up by researchers.

Most of the many criticisms of the public interest can be traced back to a taproot problem: ambiguity. So long as public interest concepts are hopelessly ambiguous, usage will necessarily be inconsistent, measurement efforts have little likelihood of success, and it will be difficult systematically to consider "a great number of examples." This ambiguity is one reason (there are more important ones) why the concepts of economics, market failure, and economic individualism have so easily held sway in public deliberations. Compared with Lippman's definition of the public interest as what men (and women) "would choose if they saw clearly, thought rationally, acted disinterestedly and benevolently," the assumptions economists make to advance their theories, assumptions such as perfect information and perfectly competitive markets, seem almost down to earth. This, then, is the conundrum that has faced us since ancient times: that nearly everyone is convinced that the public interest is vital in public policy and governance, but there is little agreement as to exactly what it is.

According to Richard Flathman, the ambiguity of the public interest is not adequate justification for its abandonment:

> Public interest is a normative standard, and it raises the whole panoply of problems associated with standards in general. The history of moral philosophy testifies that problems of standards are not easily solved. There is no reason to think that they will be easily solved in the case of the public interest. But difficulty of analysis is not ordinarily considered a valid reason for abandoning a problem. The problems associated with "public interest" are among the crucial problems of politics. (1966, 13)

PUBLIC INTEREST THEORY: REPUDIATION AND RESURRECTION

Cochran (1974) argues that the waning of political scientists' enthusiasm for public interest theory is a result of the discipline's focus on the politics of group interest. This argument goes hand-in-hand with political scientists' rejection (at least in the 1970s) of topics deemed "unscientific" or not amenable to scientific study. Whereas this is a disciplinary trend that crested in the 1970s and early 1980s, the substitution of a scientifically more tractable group interest focus for the public interest can be traced back to one of the founders of the scientific study of politics. Arthur Bentley (1908, 167) rejected such "idea ghosts" as community, public good, society, and even values because "they stand for certain regularities and tendencies in activity stated as individual conduct."

Political scientists took their time following Bentley's lead, but by the 1950s the scientific study of politics, with the study of pluralism and group interest, had emerged as a dominant trend in the discipline (Lowi 1964) as one of its principal axes. This focus on group interest resulted in a view of the public interest less as a concept of collective good and more as an outcome of group process. The result of this view, according to Sorauf (1957, 630), "is a surprising, and unbecoming, political Darwinism that naively presumes that the public interest will automatically be served if all men pursue their own interests," a sort of political and procedural "invisible hand."

Even though behavioral political science has ebbed somewhat since the 1970s, with the rise of postbehavioral, naturalistic, and postmodern schools of thought, the public interest has not enjoyed a restoration. If Cochran (1974, 327) is correct that attention to theories of the public interest is "an accurate weathercock for determining which way the wind is blowing in contemporary American political science," then one must conclude that wind is barely blowing. Between 1995 and 2006, only one paper (Goodin 1996) published in any of the five major political science journals (the *American Political Science Review* and the four journals sponsored by regional political science associations) has used the term *public interest* in the title, and only a handful have in any way dealt with public interest theory.

Despite political scientists' retreat from public interest theory, it has not disappeared; rather it seems to have become the province of fields and disciplines other than political science. During the past decade or so public administration journals have published many articles dealing directly with the public interest or public values. Among U.S. public administration scholars, papers dealing with the public interest are plentiful (e.g., Brewer 1996; Box 1992; Rogers and Kingsley 2004). The topic seems even more popular in the United Kingdom and Canada (e.g., Mintz 2001; James 2000; Grant 2000; Campbell and Marshall 2000; Elcock 2006) and Western Europe (Kooiman 1999; Jørgensen 1999; De Bruijn and Dicke 2006). Nor is public interest research the exclusive preserve of political scientists and public administrationists. Scholars in disciplines such as sociology (Burstein 2000), economics (Barber 1999; Champlin and Knoedler 2002), and history (Kirkendall 1997; Selgin 1999) focus on the public interest. Although mainstream American political scientists seem to have essentially given up on the public interest, it is alive and well among other nations' scholars and in many fields and disciplines.

WHY THE "PUBLIC INTEREST" SURVIVES

Policymakers' and scholars' attention to public interest theory has fluctuated a great deal over the decades. While the idea of elucidating public interest seems a bit out of place in theory environments dominated by postmodernism, relativism, or positivism, it is an approach completely consistent with liberal political philosophy and the philosophical cornerstones of the U.S. federal government's framing documents. Michael Sandel (1996) notes that the frequency of the term *public interest* is unrivaled in the early documents of the United States. He marks the post–World War II era as the period during which the "civic strand of economic argument faded from American political discourse" (Sandel 1996, 274). Gawthrop (1998, 8) argues that, since the 1930s, the U.S. democratic political system has been dominated by a "pluralist-bargaining-incremental process," one in which the future is best predicted as a marginal change in the past and whereby political change has been characterized by relatively modest, politically negotiated adjustments.

Public interest theory never goes away. It changes disciplinary foci, it receives more or less attention from scholars, but it remains and, during the past decade, seems again on the upswing. Certainly it is easy to explain the endurance of concern with public value, but why with public interest theory? Concern with public value is sustained by the obvious need to account for public preferences and common good (by some concept and by some accounting) in politics and policy. But, as mentioned in chapter 1, public value and theories of the public interest are certainly not the same thing. Public value is a palpable force in all governance, not only democratic government but also authoritarian government (even when public value is ignored, the ignoring of public value exerts a toll). Public interest theory is a means of conceptualizing, explaining, and, sometimes, prescribing collective good. Thus it may seem surprising that a concept as ill-defined as the public interest, a concept that rarely yields instrumental measures, indices, or precise analytical tools, has so long held sway.

While attacks on the ambiguity of public interest theory have had important impacts, it is unlikely that any area of political inquiry will be abandoned solely because key concepts seem ambiguous. The definitional precision and the ability to quantify have never been the determinants of political concepts' popularity. Many of the concepts that capture the popular imagination are just as ill-defined and just as subject to disagreement as public interest concepts. If we consider the ideals that societies, governments, and individual citizens hold dear, ideals such as liberty, freedom, equality, benevolence, social justice, and democracy, we know that these terms have many definitions and that there is little agreement as to how to measure them or whether to measure them at all. If we extended criticisms of the public interest to all the political concepts we use—that is, if we insisted on using only those that are unambiguously defined and conveniently measured, then public discourse and perhaps even governance itself would be sharply diminished.

Let us consider some of the reasons public interest theory remains of interest, conceptual difficulties notwithstanding.

The Power and Appeal of the Ideal

As Fesler argues, the fact that the public interest is an ideal provides both its power and its ambiguity.

> The simple fact is that public interest is an ideal. It is for administrators what objectivity is for scholars—something to be strived for, even if imperfectly achieved, something not to be spurned because performance falls short of the goal. If there is not a public interest then we must denounce the idea of ideals. . . . If it is illusory, so are justice, liberty, and integrity. . . . [T]hese and other ideal values cannot be absolutes but must be reconciled when in conflict in concrete cases. (1990, 91)

This is not much different than the view that the public interest is, and should be, a normative concept, exempt from the requirements of scientific study. (The normative conception of the public interest is explored in some detail later in this chapter.) In a argument similar, but not identical, to Fesler's, Cassinelli (1958, 48) suggests that the reason to study the public interest is more or less self-evident: it is the benchmark against which we consider public policies, and it is "the ultimate ethical goal of political relationships, and institutions and practices are to be judged desirable or undesirable to the extent they contribute to or detract from the realization of the public interest."

Flathman (1966, 82) suggests that consideration of the public interest is essential, even if it remains an ambiguous or undefined ideal. He acknowledges that the public interest has no general, invariant meaning and argues that "a non-arbitrary descriptive meaning can be determined for it in particular cases." Flathman suggests that a retreat from the public interest would signal abandonment of efforts to achieve morally justifiable public policy.

Promote Community and Shared Values

Cochran (1973) sees the public interest as, essentially, an antidote to fractional and divisive politics of interest. His concern is that a focus on individual and group interests undercuts the experience and nature of political community. According to Cochran human experiences, sorrows, and joys are not well represented in terms of self-interest: "It obscures the nature of these human relationships to designate them only as self-interested behavior, and it obscures the wide variety of types of order, which take their characters from the types of relationships which constitute them, to speak in political theory only of the order of partnership in mutual self-interest" (1973, 764). In Cochran's view the politics of interest is amoral. If one is concerned with morality in politics, the public interest provides a path to deliberating political morality and the morality of specific public issues.

Reaction to Market-based Governance

Chapter 1 has already alluded to the rationale of market-based governance. But it is worth noting that it is an increasingly popular rationale. A number of public administration scholars have been seeking to resurrect public interest theory in part because of their belief that the widespread use of market-based reforms for the delivery of public goods and services has begun to alter relationships between the citizen and the state and to negate legal and motivational commitments to the collective good (Pierre 1995; Kettl 1993; Kobrak 1996). Blancard, Hinnant, and Wong (1998) compare roles of citizens as beneficiaries, participants, and owners with the NPM's thinking about citizens as "customers." They conclude that a customer concept of the citizen changes the sets of obligations and the political authority relations of the states' social contract. This tendency is exacerbated with increasing privatization and contracting out such that there is a very different "social subcontract," one that trades political empowerment for economic empowerment.

Despite obvious concern about perceived trends of market-based public management driving out or reshaping the public interest, the critics of this trend have, by and large, failed to provide notions of the public interest, collective good, or civic responsibility that are sufficiently coherent to serve as a sharp counterpoint to "marketization" (Pierre 1995). The analytical challenges remain.

This chapter does not and cannot resolve the many analytical difficulties posed by various concepts and theories of the public interest. (However, chapter 4 argues that some of these difficulties are overblown and others can be reconciled.) Nevertheless, it is important to understand the extant meanings, issues, and problems posed by the public interest. The public interest approach and the public value mapping model presented later in this book are positioned in reference to the controversies.

The specific questions requiring attention include the following:

1. How has "the public interest" been defined? What are its alternative concepts?
2. How do public interest concepts and concerns relate to core issues in public management and public policy?
3. What is the relation of the public interest to political authority and to the market?

CONCEPTS AND CATEGORIES OF THE "PUBLIC INTEREST"

There are so many and such diverse treatments of the public interest that an entire subgenre of literature includes articles and books categorizing the public interest (e.g., Held 1970; Leys and Perry 1959; Sorauf 1957; Schneider 1956). Among the many ways of organizing concepts of the public interest, Cochran's (1974) fourfold typology is one of the most familiar. Cochran distinguishes among "normative," "abolitionist," "process," and "consensualist" approaches to the public interest. Following Cochran, little attention is given here to the "abolitionist" approach, those scholars whose chief point is that the public interest is a concept not worth studying.

Normative Public Interest

Normative theories advance the public interest as an ethical standard for evaluating public policies and as a goal public officials should pursue (Cochran 1974, 330). While normative political theory is, in general, alive and well among scholars, normative theories of the public interest are not as common as they once were.

A normative concept of the public interest assumes that there is a common good that is different than the aggregate of private benefit and, as usually expressed, that common good is something that is in the interest of the community as a whole, even if against the interest of some of the individuals in the community. Philosopher and pragmatist John Dewey (1927, 35), who will be discussed in depth in the next chapter, distinguishes public interest as applying when there are important consequences of individual and group transactions that extend to individuals not party to the action: "Those indirectly and seriously affected for good or for evil form a group distinctive enough to require recognition and a name. The name selected is 'The Public.'"

Anthropologist Gail Kennedy (1959) provides a useful rationale for the existence of a public interest apart from aggregated private interests. She notes, first, that individuals are inevitably members of multiple groups and that the multiple memberships may provide joint public interests. Second, many problems have both an outcome that maximizes individual (private) benefit and one that maximizes the group benefit (with any attendant benefit the individual receives as being part of the group). She notes that it is reasonable to expect that many will in their deliberations seek the shared benefit of the group because "to be human is to be a member of some social organization and to be within a social organization is *ipso facto* to have commitments which engender both privileges and obligations" (Kennedy 1959, 261).

One issue upon which normative theories of the public interest diverge is whether the public interest requires that the interest of all members be served (i.e., holistic interest) or whether it is necessary only to serve the interests of most individuals, even if the interests of some others are negated. Brian Barry (1967) views the public interest as necessitating benefits to all parties—that each has preference for the same policy. He gives as an example preference for medical insurance policies where it is in everyone's simultaneous interest to pool medical expense risk. While this seems an unusually stringent public interest concept, it is important to note that Barry, unlike many theorists, distinguishes between the public interest and the net common interest. Thus a policy that benefits most citizens but is against the interest of some would, in Barry's terms, be in the net common interest. Presumably very few policies would be truly in the public interest, by this distinction, and a great many would be in the net common interest. Examples of public interest policies might include those protecting against nuclear destruction and policies to eradicate or ameliorate potentially pandemic diseases.

One reason for preferring a more stringent definition of public interest as that which is in the interest of all is that it avoids the possibility of a Bentham-like utilitarian calculus and, instead, treats the public interest as an ideal (Fesler 1990). It is useful to maintain the ideal concept of the public interest, for much the same reason as it is useful to maintain the ideal of a perfectly competitive market—each provides a benchmark, one approached but almost never attained. When considering the ideal of perfect competition in economic models it seems acceptable to proceed even while recognizing that such precursors of the ideal (including perfect information and purely rational decision makers) have little correspondence to reality. Having the target in mind keeps one on course, even if it is not possible precisely to hit the target. Why should this be less true of a public interest ideal than an ideal such as the perfectly competitive market?

Barry's (1967) public interest concept is similar to Braybrooke's (1972), except that Braybrooke defines the public interest in terms of the character of its opposition. If an individual, group, or organization has set its special interest against that of the society or community as a whole, then that interest of the whole is the public interest. He suggests that the opposition to the public interest will vary from time to time such that nearly everyone will be part of a group or coalition that strives for a private interest counter to the interest of the whole.

Cassinelli (1958) makes a particularly strong case for a normative public interest as a theory to be applied in public dialogue. According to Cassinelli, the public interest "is taken to comprise the ultimate ethical goal of political relationships, and institutions and practices are to be judged desirable or undesirable to the extent that they contribute to or detract from the realization of the public interest" (48). Cassinelli gives little attention to expanding upon the concept or approaches to divining the public interest. Instead, he considers a number of problems with alternative conceptions of the public interest, including the public interest as the interests possessed by the public and the public interest as the counterpoint to private interests. His chief argument, one very much at odds with procedural and with pluralistic views of the public interest, is that the public interest cannot be coincident with the majority values and interests and that elections and majority rule have no direct correspondence to public interest, even in democratic polities. Further, in Cassinelli's view there can be no balancing of public and private interest because the public interest is in the interest of all citizens and, thus, a "balancing" defies logic. The role of government, then, is to adjust competing individual interest, using the public interest as a guidepost for doing so.

Consensualist Public Interest

The consensualist view of the public interest, according to Cochran (1974, 347) emphasizes interests broader than individual or special interests but not requiring an invariant or universal public interest. Some view the public interest as a reflection of the majority interest. Cox (1973), for example, views the public interest as, essentially, nothing more than majority interest and argues that in a democratic polity the majority interest provides a useful measuring stick—voting in elections. One common feature of consensualist views is an emphasis on the role of democracy and elections in framing the public interest. Thus, Anthony Downs (1962, 4) contends that the public interest is "closely related to the minimal consensus necessary for the operation of a 'democratic society.'"

In one of the best-known scholarly treatments of the public interest, Richard Flathman (1966) argues that the public interest is a normative standard, one used to express commendation and to provide justifications. But Cochran categorizes Flathman as a consensualist because Flathman, unlike most normative public interest theorists, underscores that the public interest is neither invariant nor self-evident. Flathman draws from moral philosopher R. M. Hare (1952), who explains that the virtue that makes a public policy (or any other action or commodity) "good" requires us to know specifically what "good" means for the set of policies in question. Each set may have a unique group of criteria defining the value of "good." These criteria change not only according to set but also according to time. The example Hare uses is the telephone. The requirements for a "good" telephone in the 1920s are not the same as for today. With respect to the public interest, this is a crucial issue. Throughout time, some political and moral philosophers have sought invariant moral principles and notions of "the good." Plato, in particular, emphasized the limited role of context in determining "the good."

If one takes Flathman's (and Hare's) position on the public interest, determining specifically what is "in the public interest" is a nearly impossible challenge. However sensible the idea that the public interest is changeable, the implication of their view is that each set of policies may have unique or distinctive public interest criteria *and* these may change over time. Moreover, even before undertaking the extraordinarily difficult task of identifying for any set of policies their distinctive criteria for "the good," one must first determine the rationales for considering policies as part of a comparable set. Are all crime policies a set? Or is the set all policies for reducing violent crime? Or is it all policies for reducing violent crime in New York? Or is it all policies for reducing violent crime in New York by affecting drug-related activities? Or is the focus much more general, such as all social policies, or even all those policies affecting all citizens?

The remarkable analytical challenges one faces with a Flathman-Hare notion of the public interest fail to diminish the most important lesson of the consensualist view of the public interest—that the public interest, even if not precisely defined, can aid public deliberation. While insisting that there is no invariant meaning of the public interest, Flathman (1966, 82) contends that the public interest has a nonarbitrary meaning and that this meaning "is properly found through reasoned discourse which attempts to relate the anticipated effects of a policy to community values and to these that relation by formal principles."

If there is a latter-day counterpart to the consensualist view of the public interest, it is communitarianism. While developed from a somewhat different philosophical base, the two schools of thought have many common features.

Consensual Public Interest and Communitarianism

Whereas consensual public interest has a decidedly liberal moral tone, communitarian theory has encompassed a broad spectrum of political values. In various images communitarian views have been embraced by market efficiency disciples and governance theorists, by garden variety liberals and neoconservatives. Contemporary political philosopher Michael Sandel (1996) sees privatization as, potentially, a substitution of efficiency criteria for a community. In his view liberal distributional politics, focused on redress of economic inequality, have in some respect contributed to the partitioning of society. He does not favor preserving economic inequality, but recognizes that "separate but equal" works no better in crime, housing, health, or other policy realms than it has in education. Redress of economic inequality, as market and nonmarket failure is insufficient:

> "Civic conservatives have not, for the most part, that market forces, under conditions of inequality, erode those aspects of community life that bring rich and poor together in public places and pursuits. Many liberals, largely concerned with distributive justice, have also missed the civic consequences of growing inequality(.) . . . A more civic-minded liberalism would seek communal provision less for the sake of distributive justice than for the sake of affirming the membership and forming the civic identify of rich and poor people alike." (332–33)

Sandel is one among many who pits communitarianism against traditional liberalism, a close philosophical relative of economic individualism. Whereas traditional liberalism "focuses mainly on individual rights and equal treatment . . . with citizen capacity consisting mainly in the power to retrieve these rights" (Taylor 1989, 178–79), communitarianism postulates "a shared consciousness that arises from the identification with the . . . traditions of one's own political and cultural community" (Habermas 1996, 499). In the communitarian view market criteria, as the pluralistic criteria of traditional liberalism, undermine the single most important value in society, the sense of being part of a whole and, through self-determination, the acceptance of one's rightful place in the political culture. According to this view neither political-faction-based governance nor market-based politics can preserve the requisite sense of shared identity and stake in other political actors' well-being. Weatherford (1992) provides some empirical support for this notion and, more generally, for the assumptions of consensualist public interest theorists. In his study using public opinion measures as indicators of political legitimacy, Weatherford concludes that "the more effectively the [political] system's representational institutions work to connect citizens meaningfully to the world of politics, the more optimistic they are likely to be about the prospects for collective social efforts" (160–61). This seems to suggest not only that political deliberation and public discourse point the way to the public interest but also that they contribute directly to it.

Process Public Interest

According to Cochran (1974), "process" theories of the public interest come in three varieties: (a) an "aggregative" conception, in which the public interest is the sum of individual interests; (b) a view of the public interest as the competition among interests (the "pluralist" conception); and (c) a view of the public interest as interest reconciliation and fair procedure (I use the term *procedural* conception). To some extent the process view of the public interest embraces those who cannot accept a normative view of the public interest but are not ready to altogether abandon the concept. Scholars professing this view "find many 'publics' rather than one community or public and many interests rather than one held by the community" (Cochran 1974, 339).

The aggregative conception of the public interest has roots in Bentham and the Utilitarians (Bentham 1977) and the notion that the public interest is equivalent to the greatest good for the greatest number. Bentham utilitarianism is particularly compatible with economic individualism.

Bentham viewed individual interest as the motivating force underpinning all political acts. While reflection and ideology often play a role in the individual's enacting a political role, these occur as a result of a motivating self-interest. Attention to issues, motivation to political action, curiosity, and intellectual interpretations of politics—all these, to Bentham, flow from individual interest. Taking this beginning assumption, what could the public interest mean other than the aggregation of individual interests?

Even if one accepts Bentham's central assumption about the primacy of individual interest, the means of aggregating interests is not self-evident. Whether one ponders the "greatest good for the greatest number" or "the aggregation of all interests," the possibility of a canonical scheme for calculation does not (indeed, cannot) emerge. No voting scheme ensures the greatest good for the greatest number nor does any decision process. Among other problems with the aggregative view, there is no intersubjective meaning of "the good." Even if a satisfactory aggregation scheme could be identified, there is no evidence for assuming that individuals' interests and the valuation schemes for those interests are in any important sense commensurate. This does not, of course, imply that the Bentham conception or other aggregative views of the public interest are without value. Contemplating "the greatest good for the greatest number" may prove a worthwhile intellectual exercise. But the approach is no more operational than other ideal conceptualizations. To be sure, there are analytical approaches akin to an aggregative view of the public interest—Pareto optimality comes to mind—but such approaches suffer from a common limitation, the inability to provide a valid aggregation.

The pluralistic conception of the public interest requires only minimal truck with the concept. Schubert (1961, 202) observes that for this group of scholars the public interest is really no more than a slogan symbolizing the "compromise resulting from a particular accommodation or adjustment of group interaction." Smith (1960) provides a pluralist conception of the public interest and argues explicitly against a normative concept of the public interest on the grounds that it is likely to lead to authoritarianism, presumably because of the possibilities for trampling minority interests.

The procedural conception of the public interest makes virtually no distinction between political processes and the substance of the public interest; indeed, some adherents deny the possibility of a substantive public interest. Benn and Peters's *Social Principles and the Democratic State* (1959) presents one of the best-known cases for a proceduralist view of the public interest. They argue that the public interest is a procedural principle, not a substantive concern. Unlike most political theorists, they argue that the public interest should not be a substantive goal of public policy but an element of political process. A policy is in the public interest because it was passed in a spirit of impartiality, that is, the policy has not been captured by a special interest. In criticizing this approach, Flathman (1966) notes that the Benn and Peters conception does not correspond to the meaning of public interest in common discourse. More telling, he notes that if one were to poison everyone in United States, one passes the test of impartiality and disinterestedness, and thus something more is required for an act or policy to be "in the public interest."

More moderate views of procedural public interest have been popular among political scientists. Many political scientists who are "realists" emphasizing the role of group conflict and interest group accommodation easily embrace the procedural concept of the public interest. Theodore Lowi's classic *The End of Liberalism* (1969) includes ideas of procedure-based public interest. Lowi argues that factional politics is not, as James Madison famously argued, a blot on the body politick; rather it is a means of reducing the role of government, especially government regulation. As private interests compete to win resources, hearts, and minds, a sort of political invisible hand guides outcomes. While these outcomes are not themselves the public interest, a sound process for shaping outcomes is something much like the public interest.

EXTENDING THE LEYS AND PERRY MODEL: MARKET CONCEPTS AND PUBLIC INTEREST THEORY

Leys and Perry (1959) provide one of the more useful attempts to grapple with various concepts of the public interest. In many respects their scheme is like Cochran's (1977). Leys and Perry divide the uses of the term into "formal meanings" and "substantive meanings." Formal meanings are easily identified; the formal meaning is the express objective of "duly authorized governmental action." The substantive meaning of the public interest is the "object that *should* be sought in governmental action" and that is subdivided into several categories of use. The "aggregational conception" views the public interest as "the maximization of particular interests, whereas the "procedural conception" holds that the public interest is served when the proper procedures have been employed to arrive at public decisions. A third type of substantive meaning of the public interest is the "normative conception," in which some substantive value, such as social equality or economic opportunity, must be maximized for the public interest to be served.

As one of the chief objectives of this book is to consider the public interest and public values in connection with market failure and market valuation, it is useful to modify the classic Leys and Perry framework and contrast it with a market application. Interestingly, if we take the Leys and Perry framework and apply market-based criteria, we find that it is relatively easy to translate most public interest categories into market terms. Table 5.1 shows how this might be accomplished.

As the table suggests, market failure and economic criteria, when one takes them at the broadest level, have many of the same characteristics of public interest criteria, including a lack of precision and multiple interpretation. If we consider formal public interest, there is no obvious market equivalent. While both market authority and public authority are institutionalized in a variety of ways, there is no market equivalent of legitimate polities that require compliance by virtue of their legitimacy. However, when we consider substantive notions of the public interest, there are many parallels to market theory. In one important respect a substantive theory of the market is "easier": the ideal

Table 5.1 The Public Interest as Market Value

Leys and Perry Category	Public Interest Description	Market Application	Government Application
I. Formal	The object of government action	[No equivalent]	Implementation of legitimated policy
II. Substantive	The object that *should* be sought	Efficient market	Unarticulated public interest ideal
A. Aggregational	The maximization of particular interest	Pareto optimality	Bentham utilitarianism
B. Procedural	The proper decision procedures are employed	Pure rationality	E.g., integrity of democratic elections
C. Normative	A substantive value is maximized	Profit	E.g., public health

Source: Adapted from Leys and Perry (1959).

construct of an efficient market is more easily conceived than "the (public interest) object that should be sought" and has the virtue of universality. From the standpoint of market theory, efficient markets are always good.

Within the substantive public interest category, each of the three subtypes has an equivalent in market theory. In aggregational public interest, the traditional criterion is maximization of particular interest—this implies a Bentham-like calculation of the greatest good for the greatest number. This seems to have close market equivalence in Pareto optimality. An allocation of goods and services is Pareto optimal if no one can be made better off without making another worse off. While this is certainly not the same thing as Bentham utility maximization, it is certainly an alternative form of utility maximization, one that avoids some of the logical flaws of the Bentham approach (Flathman 1966, 17–22). With respect to procedural public interest, the most obvious economic parallel is with pure rationality models. If a procedure is purely rational it is to be prized, independent of substantive outcome. Indeed, rationality is often privileged in economic theory in many of the same ways and to the same extent democracy is privileged in public interest theory. Finally, normative public interest theory's notion of maximizing a substantive value, such as public health or Rawlsian justice-as-fairness, has a more widely agreed upon market counterpart, the maximization of profit.

This comparison of public interest concepts and applications with economic concepts and applications is superficial. Were one interested in a more in-depth comparison of these ideas, one would need much development, and the implicit arguments would require stronger defense. But this simple comparison and this modest level of articulation is perhaps adequate to make the point that public interest theory and its attendant values are not so far removed from market theory and its values. Whether, in fact, one wishes to take the next step—considering economic individualism as a sort of "public interest theory"—depends on the degrees of freedom one is willing to extend to analogies and, of course, to one's interpretation of the power and meaning of market theories in the political arena.

MARKET THEORY VERSUS PUBLIC INTEREST THEORY: AN ANALYTICAL MISMATCH

Only the most extreme market glorifiers suggest that public *interests* (as opposed to theories of the public interest) are irrelevant or inferior to market interests. Most observers respect the market and its uses and, at the same time, understand that the market cannot contain, allocate, or arbitrate all values important to a society. In other words, nearly everyone recognizes that markets have limits. In the words of Francis Bator (1958, 378–79), the person most often credited with inventing market failure theory, "If markets be ends as well as means, their nonefficiency is hardly sufficient ground for rejection. On the other hand, efficient markets may not do; efficiency of the 'invisible hand' does not preclude preference for other efficient modes of organization, if there be any."

While individuals differ tremendously in their predilection for market approaches to public policy, almost all concede the need for both a government role and public values that are not fully contained in market values. However, public interest theory does not provide a practical means for deliberating and facilitating collective decisions. Judging solely from their respective analytical properties and measurement possibilities, economic theory is much superior to public interest theory as a tool for guiding decision making. Flathman (1966, 13) observes correctly that "we are free to abandon the [public interest] *concept,* but if we do so we will simply have to wrestle with the *problems* under some other heading." But accepting the validity of Flathman's argument does not require us to shrink from the many practical and analytical problems of public interest theory.

As compared to market theory, the most important limitations of public interest theory seem to be the following:

1. In public interest theory there is no generally agreed upon measure or surrogate for value, no equivalent to money and price in market theory. As a consequence:

    a. Public interest theory, unlike market theory, cannot provide value substitutions (measured by a commensurate index: price).

    b. Public interest theory often cannot measure the extent to which a value has been obtained; with the partial exception of electoral votes, there is no obvious or general equivalent to monotonic indices of profit or wealth and no equivalent to price equilibrium or to perfectly competitive markets.

c. There is no widely agreed upon means of intersubjective understanding of public values.

2. Because the ideal of the public interest is a more ambiguous ideal, at least as compared to the more understandable and easily expressed ideal of perfect market competition, it is not possible to posit a single theory and proceed to deduce propositions or to connect inductively obtained propositions. There is no one path from the analytical thickets of public interest theory. In moving from the public interest ideal to action, the particular path from ideal to calculation, analysis, and action depends on unique starting points.

As a result of these seemingly irresolvable analytical shortcomings of public interest theory, it is difficult for it to "compete" with market-based theories of value and collective decision. A vast army of public values arguments proceeds, valiant, but armed with only the crudest, ineffective weapons. A better organized army of economic arguments proceeds, mercenaries (of course), armed with an ever expanding assortment of analytical weapons. Until the last hundred years or so, there was no intellectual mismatch when public interest theory was pitted against market theory. In the wake of positive economics and microeconomic theory, that has changed. Public interest theory versus market theory is certainly not a moral mismatch but an analytical mismatch. An advocate armed only with public interest theory is at a serious disadvantage.

THE USES OF PUBLIC INTEREST THEORY

Granting the convincing argument that public interest theory holds little if any promise as a rival to microeconomics and economic individualism in practical decision making, what role can it play, if any, in enhancing public values? One possibility is to follow in the path of the critics of public interest theories, those Cochran so aptly terms the "abolitionists," and give up on public interest theory. Obviously, that is not the path I have chosen. Several other possibilities come to mind. In the first place, one can follow Fesler and bask in the ideal. There is some value in having a poorly articulated ideal that many can embrace and bring to diverse uses. Second, one can seek to develop public interest theory, recognizing that there is no immediate prospect (and perhaps no long-term prospect) that it will rival market theory with respect to its analytical properties. This is a useful approach if one believes that theoretical schemas are helpful even when they are not precisely articulated and cannot provide precise measures. Third, one can seek to develop more limited, middle range theories that, if not true public interest theories, at least have much in common with them. This is the approach taken in chapter 8, in which the public value mapping model is presented. Fourth, one can seek applicable public interest theory by eschewing normative public interest or the search for Cassinelli's (1958) notion that public interest can refer only to those values that serve all citizens and to roughly the same degree. Proceduralist and consensualist approaches to the public interest shift the focus away from identification of a substantive "good" to identification of institutions and procedures that will help formulate an acceptable idea of "good." This is the approach taken in chapter 6.

In chapter 1 the following definition of *public interest* was provided: *An ideal, public interest refers to those outcomes best serving the long-run survival and well-being of a social collective construed as a "public."* The overview presented in the present chapter shows that this general definition of public interest in only one of many possibilities. Chapter 6 not only expands on the definition introduced here but also provides arguments as to why this concept, one combining a proceduralist and an ideal approach, can, despite its lack of specificity, prove to be of some practical utility to public policy and public management.

CHAPTER SIX

TOWARD A PRAGMATIC PUBLIC INTEREST THEORY

All the evolution we know of proceeds from the vague to the definite.

—C. S. PEIRCE, *Collected Papers,* Vol. 6

A MISSPECIFICATION OF THE PROBLEM: THE PUBLIC INTEREST

Encapsulating the substance of the previous two chapters and the major concerns of this book, we can say that the de facto public interest theory of economic individualism has become dominant in public policy and public management while more conventional public interest theories have not been able to compete, in part because of the apparent fecklessness of rival public interest theories. This chapter argues that the major alleged weakness of the public interest concept is not, in fact, a limitation but a misapplication of inappropriate utilitarian standards to public interest theory. The crux of the argument: the public interest is often thought of as a choice between, on the one hand, a murky ideal that has little or no intersubjective meaning and, on the other, a Bentham-like utilitarianism that is really little more than an expression of economic individualism (except that utilitarianism is even less useful because there is no accompanying calculus such as Pareto optimality, expressed as cost–benefit analysis). This is a false choice.

The apparent murkiness of the ideal in conventional public interest theory is not such a problem as it seems; market failure and the public interest require very different intellectual and practical policy starting points. With market failure one *starts with the ideal* (i.e., the perfectly competitive market) and frames policies that should move toward either remedying market failure or providing optimal allocation of resources in the face of market failure. But the benchmark is axiomatic. It is an *ideal*.

According to many conventional theories of the public interest, especially procedural approaches, there is no claim to identify an invariant and monolithic public interest but, instead, there is a search for a public value or set of public values that serve the collective good. The public value quest *starts with the social problem* and then works toward a limited ideal—a practical solution to a recognized public failure. In market failure theory the markets are unstable but the theory is not. In public interest theory the problems are concrete (e.g., poor quality public health, failing schools) but the ideals (e.g., adequate public health, quality education) are unstable. Public interest theory has been faulted for being ambiguous (i.e., having multiple meanings), but in fact the public interest, viewed as public values, *should* have multiple meanings.

If we follow the lead set decades ago by pragmatist John Dewey (1927), we can conceive of a pragmatic approach to public value in which the pursuit of the public interest is a matter of using open minds and sound, fair procedures to move ever closer to an ideal that is revealed during the process and, in part, by the process. A lively debate has been provided in the journal *Administration & Society* concerning the merits of Dewey's pragmatism (e.g., Evans 2000; Garrison 2000), as well as alternative approaches to pragmatism (e.g., Snider 2005; Shields 2005). However, much of the recent works applying Dewey's philosophy are somewhat diffuse. In this chapter we revisit Dewey's writing on public interest and discuss particular ways in which it can be applied in the development of a more pragmatic public interest, one serving multiple public values.

LIBERAL UTILITARIANISM AND PRAGMATISM IN PUBLIC INTEREST THEORY

It is common for observers of the public interest to note its association with two broad traditions in political thought (Benditt 1973). The first and clearly the dominant notion of the public interest in contemporary public life is the "Benthamite" or liberal utilitarian tradition, a tradition quite consonant with economic individualism and market failure theory. As we saw in the preceding chapter, utilitarian public interest, commensurate with the premises of economic individualism, is thought to be derived directly from the mechanical or mathematical aggregation of individual interests. According to utilitarian notions of the public interest, the community or "public" is not real in any meaningful sense and thus cannot properly be said to have any interest or good apart from the sum of the interests or preferences of its distinct individuals (see James 1981). As mentioned earlier, the advantage of such an approach is that it can, ultimately, be measured according to economic standard.

The second and historically less pervasive view is a more socialized and communal accounting of the public interest as the shared, common good of citizens comprising a recognizable political community. This notion (Flathman 1966; Benditt 1973; Diggs 1973), typically associated with thinkers such as Rousseau and Edmund Burke—and earlier, with Aristotle and Aquinas—focuses more on the moral and even metaphysical notion of common good (often in an objective sense) and thus stands in stark relief from the individualist and subjective account of interests and preferences in the liberal model.

This communal reading of the public interest as common good has, however, largely been clouded over by the utilitarian-individualistic understanding in modern life, although recent revivals of this tradition among political theorists and policy scientists (such as the civic republicanism advanced by Michael Sandel) suggest that change is perhaps in the air.

Douglass (1980) traces the historical ascendance of the liberal utilitarian public interest over communal notions to the crumbling of medieval feudalism and the capture and transformation of the idea of the common good by "Royalist" monarchs as an instrument for political power. According to Douglass (1980, 106), the claim to a "public interest" arose in this environment as a liberal democratic argument of the people agitating for freedom from the exploitation and abuses of the Crown. The public interest thus became thoroughly entangled in the moral language of individualism; in the process, it was effectively purged of its earlier communal aspects and the notion of a shared good among citizens.

As suggested earlier, contemporary treatments of the public interest that have attempted to shine analytic light on the concept have generally met with mixed results, chiefly because of ambiguity in usage. Are we, for example, to take the notion of "interest" referred to in the "public interest" to be an objective good independent of the will of individuals? Or does it refer to the subjective desires and preferences of individuals qua citizens (or perhaps qua consumers)? Or is it something else altogether? Can a policy (action, decision, or proposal) be said to be in "the public interest" and yet nevertheless be rejected by the majority of the citizenry? Related to these questions are a host of epistemic issues: How is the public interest (however it is defined) to be known? Is it indeed something that may be discovered by identifying and then aggregating hundreds, thousands—perhaps millions—of individual expressed preferences? If so, how meaningful (and feasible) can it really be as a substantive normative standard? Can the public ever be mistaken about its interests? These are just a few of the thorny questions that work to make the public interest a vexed concept in political and moral discourse. This conceptual fuzziness and, in particular, the "nonscientific" character of the public interest led Arthur F. Bentley (1908, 167), writing in the early part of the twentieth century, to memorably declare it an "idea ghost," one that right-thinking political scientists would do well to avoid.

Chapter 5 summarized the scholarly literature on the public interest that formed in the 1950s and 1960s as political scientists grappled with many of the previously listed questions (e.g., Cassinelli 1958; Barry 1965; Flathman 1966; Held 1970). Some observers, especially Souraf (1957) and Schubert (1961), following in the skeptical footsteps of Bentley, criticized the public interest for its perceived conceptual incoherence and meaninglessness as a rational standard for public policy. Despite his generally negative views of the public interest, especially as a topic of research, Souraf did acknowledge its value in symbolizing the interests of the underrepresented and voiceless in power politics (Souraf 1957, 639). Souraf even proposed an acceptable "minimalist" association of the public interest as the democratic method for orderly settlement of citizen conflict.

Other scholars were less critical of public interest theory and more receptive to its potential for enhancing democracy. The political philosopher Brian Barry (1965) concluded that the public interest was directly attached to the social role of the citizen, describing it as "those interests which people have in common *qua* members of the public." More recently, and following Barry's lead, the political theorist Robert Goodin (1996, 339) has suggested that a policy or action is in the public interest "if and only if: (1) It is an interest that people necessarily share (2) by virtue of their role as a member of the public (3) which can best or only be promoted by concerted public action." The public interest, in Goodin's view, is therefore not contingently public, but rather necessarily so; it arises out of shared public roles and requires deliberate and coordinated collective action to secure and promote.

One of the most nuanced, extensive, and best studies of the public interest is Richard Flathman's (1966). While Flathman agreed with many of the concept's critics, that there probably was no all-inclusive and universally valid descriptive meaning of the public interest, he argued that descriptive meaning could nevertheless be determined in specific contextual situations as reasoned discourse worked to "relate the anticipated effects of a policy to community values and to test that relation by formal principles" (1966, 82). These formal principles included a utilitarian principle that directed inquirers to look for the full consequences of proposed policies, and a "universalizability" principle by which individual interests were to be generalized and subsumed under rules or maxims that flowed from shared community values. As Clark Cochran (1974) observes, Flathman's approach, while largely procedural in nature due to its reliance on the method of vetting community values through formal principles, is not aggregative à la the Benthamite model. Yet it is also more than a procedural account of the public interest since, as Cochran notes (1974, 351), Flathman's definition serves as "a reminder to decision-makers to remember moral considerations, to abide by formal principles, to employ community values as well as individual interests, and to give reasons in terms of these values for their decisions."

PRAGMATIC PUBLIC INTEREST: DEWEY RECONCILIATION

Public interest theory seems, on the one hand, too idealistic and impractical (e.g., moral theories) and, on the other, insufficiently attentive to community and public values (e.g., utilitarianism, economic individualism). One rarely evoked name in the historical development of public interest theory is the American pragmatist philosopher and democratic theorist John Dewey. Dewey held an intriguing notion of the public interest that was an alternative to both the liberal aggregationist rendering and the classical conceptualization of the "common good." What is more, Dewey's understanding of the public interest may be seen as sharing several features with Flathman's approach, including the emphasis on the role of community values and the contextual nature of the public interest. Dewey also anticipated Souraf's (and others') later association of the public interest with the democratic method of dispute resolution. Yet Dewey's work adds at least two additional critical elements to public interest theory: a method of democratic social inquiry modeled after the ideal workings of the scientific community, and a focus on the key role of deliberation, social learning, and interest transformation in this process. His philosophy offers an approach to reconciling the need to preserve public value ideals and to enable practical application. The Dewey approach focuses on public value but not a monolithic concept of public interest; rather it focuses on a public interest in action.

Dewey's best-known treatment of the public interest takes place in his landmark work in political philosophy, *The Public and Its Problems* (1927). In that book he describes the pressing political and intellectual challenge of the public in the age of industrial capitalism: to organize itself so that it might intelligently control and attain its shared interests. According to Dewey, this proved to be a difficult task, mostly because of the fragmenting economic, technological, and social forces of modern life:

> Indirect, extensive, enduring and serious consequences of conjoint and interacting behavior call a public into existence having a common interest in controlling these consequences. But the machine age has so enormously expanded, multiplied, intensified and complicated the scope of the indirect consequences, has formed such immense and consolidated unions in action, on an impersonal rather than a community basis, that the resultant public cannot identify and distinguish itself. And this discovery is obviously an antecedent condition of any effective organization on its part. Such is my thesis regarding the eclipse which the public idea and interest have undergone. (Dewey [1927] 1988, 314)

On the surface Dewey's understanding of the public interest here sounds analogous to what one might refer to today as "market failure"; that is, the situation in which private transactions produce externalities that spill over onto nontransacting individuals—a state of affairs commonly thought to require some sort of government intervention in the private realm. Yet there is more at work in Dewey's notion of the public interest than this, and his conceptualization is not reducible to a purely economic reading. Dewey demonstrates a commitment to a strong normative notion of the public interest in his discussion of the interest of citizens in securing desirable social consequences, suggesting that where many share a particular good there is an especially compelling reason to realize and sustain it (Dewey [1927] 1988, 328). For

Dewey the common awareness of this shared interest ultimately defines the social and moral aspects of the democratic ideal, and it is through public talk and participation in the affairs of the local, face-to-face community that this consciousness is formed and solidified (Dewey [1927] 1988, 368).

But how does a community go about identifying its shared good or public interest? For Dewey this involved experimental social inquiry into actual public problems and conflicts, a process modeled after the method of the natural and technical sciences. As he wrote in his 1935 book, *Liberalism and Social Action*:

> Of course, there *are* conflicting interests; otherwise there would be no social problems. The problem under discussion is precisely *how* conflicting claims are to be settled in the interest of the widest possible contribution to the interests of all—or at least of the great majority. The method of democracy—inasfar as it is that of organized intelligence—is to bring these conflicts out into the open where their special claims can be seen and appraised, where they can be discussed and judged in the light of more inclusive interests than are represented by either of them separately. (Dewey [1935] 2000, 81)

By holding narrower special interests up to the scrutiny of the wider community, Dewey believed, their merits could be assessed from the perspective of the emergent "more inclusive interests" of the public, identified through open discussion and free debate. This in turn would reveal the true public interest partially embedded within a particular problem solution or policy proposal. The glare of publicity would expose private interests masquerading as public ones, and through this process of debate and deliberation the community could test alternatives, ascertain social consequences, and identify the most widely shared good among citizens. Indeed, Dewey thought it is one of the virtues of democracy that it "forces a recognition that there are common interests, even though the recognition of what they are is confused; and the need it enforces of discussion and publicity brings out some clarification of what they are" (Dewey [1927] 1988, 364).

Dewey sets a criterion often difficult to meet in today's media-structured politics of dichotomy, where "hardball" political issues are presented as debate fodder for a representative "from the left" and another "from the right," as though there were no possibility of either a correct view, a synthesis view, or even a nuanced view. For Dewey effective democratic participation in the affairs of the community requires that individuals come to public deliberations with an open mind. They must be willing to listen to others and accept the possibility that their own views and, ultimately, their preferences, may be misinformed or short-sighted and that they may change (perhaps dramatically) in the process of engaging in reasoned and respectful argument with their fellow citizens. As Matthew Festenstein writes, these Deweyan norms of inquiry, read off of the practices of the scientific community, also condition participants to look for ways in which to establish common interests as they make meaningful personal and psychological connections with others:

> In Dewey's presentation, the epistemic virtues of tolerance and open-mindedness shade into imaginative sympathy with the travails of others. . . . The commitment to participate, to offer arguments and to hear the views of others, has the psychological corollary of leading participants to think in terms of possible criticisms and alternative views, and to conceive of their own interest is in a way which takes account of the interests and views of other participants. Traditions of shared communication tend to establish bonds of trust and sympathy and to lead individuals to identify their interests with those of the broader community. Moreover, in the process of communication, the interests of separate persons and groups are harmonized with one another. (Festenstein 1997, 89)

While Dewey's notion of the public interest is partly procedural in nature, it is clear that his conceptualization was not grounded in simple utilitarian methods of preference aggregation or the mechanical balancing of individual interests. Dewey's approach also avoids the pluralist conflation of the public interest with the outcome of interest group struggles. In some situations, he concluded, conjoint activity may produce such a significant and large public interest that it requires organized intervention in and "reconstruction" of the affairs of a group (Dewey [1927] 1988, 281). This is a far cry from the traditional pluralist view of the state as little more than an "umpire" among competing interest groups.

Yet neither was Dewey's understanding of the public interest premised on prepolitical or metaphysical notions of the "common good" in a classical sense. Instead, in Dewey's model, the public interest was to be discerned through the workings of social inquiry and democratic discussion and deliberation; it was thus a political, rather than an economic, construction. As indicated earlier, consumer sovereignty was rejected: individually held preferences and private interests bearing on the public good were not taken as given but were to be submitted to the test of free and open debate among citizens, a process in which they could be challenged, enlarged, and transformed as citizens engaged and learned from each other in deliberative settings. Dewey defended this process in 1939:

> Democracy is the belief that even when needs and ends or consequences are different for each individual, the habit of amicable cooperation—which may include, as in sport, rivalry and competition—is itself a priceless addition to life. To take as far as possible every conflict which arises—

and they are bound to arise—out of the atmosphere and medium of force, of violence as a means of settlement into that of discussion and of intelligence is to treat those who disagree—even profoundly—with us as those from whom we may learn, and in so far, as friends. A genuinely democratic faith in peace is faith in the possibility of conducting disputes, controversies and conflicts as cooperative undertakings in which both parties learn by giving the other a chance to express itself. (Dewey [1939] 1991, 228)

For Dewey this educative potential of democracy and democratic deliberation in particular suggested that citizens could not only broaden their interests and moral outlooks to take in the larger public good but also sharpen and improve the intellectual and communicative skills necessary to participate in this process over time (Dewey [1927] 1988, 366).

This faith in the intellectual capacities of the common citizen and the potentially enlightening and ennobling power of education distinguished Dewey from democratic realists such as his colleague and frequent critic Walter Lippmann, who took a much less sanguine view of the political and administrative capacities of the public. Whereas Lippmann memorably defined the public interest as "what men would choose if they saw clearly, thought rationally, [and] acted disinterestedly and benevolently" (Lippmann 1955, 40)—and came to the elitist conclusion that citizens were intellectually incapable of effectively governing themselves in such a manner—Dewey retained an unyielding faith in the educability of citizens and their ability to develop the necessary ability and motivation to identify and secure their shared interests through democratic deliberation. Noting that such social and political knowledge was not an innate possession but rather a "function of association and communication" (Dewey [1927] 1988, 334), Dewey believed that the institutionalization of the scientific spirit in education and public life would foster the kind of democratic diffusion of knowledge of social consequences that would allow citizens to chart their own political and policy course. This knowledge would also promote the intelligent control and direction of economic and other social forces for the greater public benefit: "Economic agencies produce one result when they are left to work themselves out on the merely physical level, or on that level modified only as the knowledge, skill and technique which the community has accumulated are transmitted to its members unequally and by chance. They have a different outcome in the degree in which knowledge of consequences is equitably distributed, and action is animated by an informed and lively sense of shared interest" (Dewey [1927] 1988, 333).

We must remember, however, that Dewey understands that the public is fallible; it can be mistaken about what is in its interest at any point in time and in any given situation. Incomplete information about the causes and consequences of particular social problems, and widespread commitment to beliefs that subsequent inquiry determines to be false, can lead communities astray, as can more insidious forces such as ideological bias, political secrecy, and the ubiquitous corrupting influence of economic power. Yet, like the ideal of scientific inquiry (even if it often falls short of the scientific ideal), for Dewey this democratic social intelligence is potentially self-correcting, progressively rooting out error by casting its epistemological net out to the widest possible range of alternative beliefs and experiences and vigilantly maintaining its open and transparent character:

> It is of the nature of science not so much to tolerate as to welcome diversity of opinion, while it insists that inquiry brings the evidence of observed facts to bear to effect a consensus of conclusions—and even then to hold the conclusion subject to what is ascertained and made public in further new inquiries. I would not claim that any existing democracy has ever made complete or adequate use of scientific method in deciding upon its policies. But freedom of inquiry, toleration of diverse views, freedom of communication, the distribution of what is found out to every individual as the ultimate intellectual consumer, are involved in the democratic as in the scientific method. (Dewey [1939] 1989, 81)

The public interest, in Dewey's view, is thus not an absolute, universal, or ahistorical good. It is constructed in each policy and problem context as conjoint activity produces indirect social consequences that the democratic public wishes to direct into collectively identified and validated channels. It follows, then, that there will be many "publics" just as there will be many public interests in various times and places. That is to say, the designated public interest on any given policy question cannot be stated in advance of the democratic appraisal of causes and consequences and the contextual, cooperative search for a wider shared interest in a specific problematic situation. For Dewey it is therefore always a good to be discovered by a public motivated to secure its shared interests as a democratic community, a commitment that ensures not only the identification and maintenance of such interests but also the development of individuals as fully self-realized and enriched citizens (Dewey [1927] 1988, 328). Conflict is not ignored; rather, deliberation within the method of democratic social inquiry can promote the discovery of new courses of action and reveal underlying shared interests. In Dewey's understanding this process could in fact result in the transformation of the underlying conditions that produced such conflict among individuals and groups, making it possible for a common political culture to be established and maintained (Caspary 2000, 17).

DEWEY'S PUBLIC INTEREST AND TRANSFORMATIONAL DEMOCRACY

Dewey's pragmatic but hopeful approach to public interest theory in many ways resembles a contemporary strain of political science theory, transformational democracy or, in Warren's (1992, 1995) term, *expansive democracy*. Process public interest scholars place great faith on procedure, usually democratic procedures. In some respects the faith of procedural public interest scholars resembles the views of democratic theorists who emphasize the transformational aspects of democracy.

According to advocates of transformational democracy, participation in democratic governance has a redeeming, transforming effect. By this view (e.g., Habermas 1996), participation in democratic institutions, whether the workplace, school, or government, often results in a more public-spirited, tolerant, and attentive citizenry, results not accruing from market transactions and, generally, results not valued by market criteria. The transformational aspects are realized even when decisions cannot possibly provide widely acceptable representations of preferences (Radcliff and Wingenbach 2000).

The transformation aspects of democracy are widely disputed, even among proponents of liberal democracy. The fabric of U.S. government, with its limited democracy, representative assumptions, and checks and balances, runs counter to transformational democracy tenets. The cornerstone assumptions of pluralism—that interests groups aggregate the raw self-interests of individuals and that interests must be held in balance—come closer to the mainstream. But, as Warren points out (1992, 12), one need not accept uncritically the claims of transformation theorists to find validity in the notion of inherent value of participation in governance: "Democracy has an intrinsic, as well as an instrumental, value. Although some values of democracy are means to nonpolitical values, others grow out of democratic processes themselves. Participation completes individuals, in part by enabling them to discover and develop their *public dimensions* [emphasis mine], in part by providing the kinds of interactions that develop capacities for autonomous judgments."

Warren argues that the self-transformation thesis is not equally valid for all configurations of goods and interests and introduces a typology based on the character of goods—excludable or non-excludable, symbolic or material, scarce or abundant. "Public material goods" (Warren 1992), ones involving conflict and requiring common action, are especially strong candidates for the inclusion of transformational criteria.

While it would be extremely difficult to develop a large-scale, societal level test of Warren's transformative democracy theory, research (Halvorsen 2003) focused on public meetings indicates that participants involved in quality participation do feel that the organization is responsive to public concerns and indicate an increased tolerance for differences of opinion. This finding may be mitigated somewhat by other empirical research (Brewer 2003) showing that public employees are much more likely in general to be civically engaged and may thus respond differently to participation opportunities. Other studies (Bowler, Donovan, and Hanneman 2003; Anderson and Guillory 1997) indicate that the effects of democratic participation differ across nations and may be culturally dependent as well as dependent on general characteristics of political systems in which the participants are embedded.

Even if some of the tenets of transformational democracy are in dispute, we can consider a Dewey-style approach to public interest theory on its own merits. Whether or not well-structured democratic participation warms the citizen soul, it may nonetheless be a useful vehicle both in connection with particular decisions and for the strengthening of decision institutions.

PRAGMATIC PUBLIC INTEREST AND DELIBERATIVE DEMOCRACY

The public interest in the pragmatic view is a contextual and pluralistic good, one constructed in each policy and problem context by a democratic public committed to the cooperative and deliberative process of experimental social inquiry. It follows, then, that there will be many "publics," just as there will be many public interests in various times and places. In the Deweyan account the designated "public interest" on any given policy question cannot be known prior to social inquiry and public discussion and debate. The public interest is therefore always created by a public motivated to secure its common interests as a political community, a commitment that ensures not only the identification and maintenance of such interests but also the development of individuals as fully self-realized and enriched citizens (Dewey [1927] 1988, 328). Conflict is by no means ignored in Dewey's project; rather, deliberation within the method of democratic social inquiry can promote the discovery of new courses of action and reveal underlying shared interests that may not be immediately obvious in light of the previously stated proposals and positions. In Dewey's understanding this process could even transform the conditions that produced the conflict in the first place, making it possible for a common political culture to be established and maintained (Caspary 2000, 17). Democracy was for Dewey many things: a moral ideal, an aesthetic good, an institutional framework, a way of life. But it was also, in his hands, a powerful method of problem solving, one that possessed an informal logic of inquiry that must sound quite familiar to contemporary observers and advocates of public dispute resolution methods and techniques (e.g., Fisher, Ury, and Patton 1992; Susskind and Cruikshank 1990).

The student of contemporary political theory will recognize the many sympathies between Dewey's emphasis on cooperative inquiry and the recovery of face-to-face political experience and the articulation of the tenets of deliberative democracy by scholars in the early 1980s. Indeed, Dewey is frequently claimed by contemporary deliberative democrats as a significant historical voice in the development of a more active, reflective, and discursive understanding of democratic politics (see Bohman 2000). For deliberative democrats, political legitimacy rests primarily on the exercise of public reason or, more prosaically, open public debate and discussion by free and equal citizens (Cohen 1997).

Many varieties of deliberative democratic theory have taken hold in the past two decades, including models couched within the traditions of liberal constitutionalism (e.g., Ackerman and Fishkin 2004), civic republicanism (Sandel 1996), civic liberalism (Barber 1984), and critical theory (Habermas 1996; Dryzek 2002). Despite their differences, all of these projects share a significant family resemblance: each offers an alternative to merely aggregative approaches to the public interest. Deliberative democratic approaches also promise a more thoughtful style of democratic politics, one premised on a dynamic or transformative view of citizen preferences and recognizing the opportunities for social learning in deliberative settings. Deliberative democrats therefore advance a much more activist (and to some critics, overly idealistic) view of democratic citizenship than that countenanced by conventional representative democratic models, which generally regard the mechanical (and solitary) act of voting as the ultimate expression of citizens' political judgment.

The deliberative turn in democratic theory has been criticized on a variety of counts, including its proponents' faith in the willingness and ability of large numbers of citizens to engage in meaningful political deliberation. Even its most sympathetic critics and its more candid boosters admit that the requirements of deliberative democratic institutions raise compelling issues of logistics and practicality (e.g., Posner 2003; Goodin 1996; but see Ackerman and Fishkin 2004). Other objections have focused on deliberative democrats' apparent neglect or slighting of considerations of political and economic power and domination, distorting forces that can erode the legitimacy of deliberative democratic models as true expressions of the unforced will of the public (e.g., Shapiro 2003). There have also been worries voiced about the inclusiveness of deliberative democratic proposals and the accommodation of social and cultural difference (Young 1996).

There are, of course, no pat answers or easy solutions to these kinds of questions and problems: they can be met only by the methodical and painstaking process of reconstructing institutional design to allow a more active democratic citizenry the space to deliberate (freely and fairly) and to afford sufficient access to the necessary mechanisms for registering their values and interests. As Dewey observed in 1927, the real challenge lies in the careful and steady reform of the techniques and environment of democratic deliberation: "The essential need . . . is the improvement of the methods and conditions of debate, discussion, and persuasion. That is *the* problem of the public" ([1927] 1988, 365). Dewey's emphasis on this process—in particular his more implicit though ultimately very powerful argument that deliberative democracy could draw attention to widely held public values and promote more intelligent and effective public problem solving—marks him as an important theorist of the public interest in the American political tradition, one who worked in the space lying between the aggregative/utilitarian and meta-physical expressions of the concept. Moreover, the pragmatic approach to public value (i.e., considering questions of normative political import only within the context of specific, experienced public problems requiring coordinated action), begins to remove some of the philosophical muddiness that has clouded the concept historically.

While a Deweyan approach to public values and the public interest does not suggest any particular procedural model, other than deliberative democracy, it does hold promise for developing alternatives to market failure and economic individualism, alternatives with fertile implications for public policymaking and implementation. One advantage of the approach is that it recognizes that there is no single public interest ideal, but, at the same time, it acknowledges the pragmatic importance of pursuing a changing ideal as opposed to positing an economic ideal and neglecting its public value consequences. A pragmatic approach to public interest theory seems most suitable for developing a vital, activist orientation to public values and thus scaffolding for the sort of public values criteria presented in chapter 8. However, before identifying specific public value criteria, we consider in the next chapter the rudiments of value theory.

NOTE

This chapter was coauthored with Ben Minteer.

CHAPTER SEVEN

VALUES, VALUE THEORY, AND COLLECTIVE ACTION

The cause is hidden; the effect is visible to all.

—OVID, *Publius Ovidius Naso*

Much of the remainder of this book deals with public values—divining sources of public values, identifying problems in the aggregation of public values, comparing public values with economic values, and exploring the correspondence of public values to public interest. However, before we turn to the discussion of public values and public value criteria in chapter 8, this chapter deals with a prior concern—values and value theory.

Without some consideration of value theory, the particular niche of *public* values remains cloudy. Sometimes the scholarly work dealing with public interest and public values loses its way by passing over value theory. Scholars in many disciplines, especially philosophy, have devoted prodigious time and resources to fundamental values issues, and much of their work is directly relevant to public values and public interest. By considering some of this basic work, we can reduce the likelihood of a perpetual rediscovery of these fundamental issues of value theory.

This is not to say, however, that scholars concerned with values and values theory have reached much agreement or provided resolutions to significant analytical problems in value analysis. In fact, despite enormous attention to values and value theory, fundamental disagreements remain about such critical issues as the most useful concept of value, the differences between "value" and "valuing," the possibility for a hierarchy of values, the transitivity of individuals' values, and the justification for values-based collective actions—all issues pertinent to public values and public interest.

VALUES: MULTIPLE CONCEPTS

The concept "values" draws the attention of political theorists, psychologists, sociologists, and especially philosophers. An advantage of this attention is that the wisdom of many academic disciplines is brought to bear on the critically important concept. The disadvantage is that the disciplines, in bringing their particular insights into the study of values, bring with them the respective disciplines' peculiarities of language, divergent interests in values concepts, and different analytical traditions. This is one reason so many disagree about the meaning of values and about how values concepts should be used. For example, what is the relationship of attitudes to values? Many social psychologists (e.g., Maio and Olson 1995; Stern et al. 1995) view attitudes as the fundamental organizing principles from which values flow. Rokeach's (1973, 18) definition is typical; values are "a single belief of a very specific kind."

Economists tend to equate value to resource exchange (e.g., money, prices, barter), often recognizing that price is a substitute for inherent value but nonetheless preferring to focus on measuring the proxy rather than dealing with the conceptual muddle arising from any effort to deal more directly with value. It should be noted that many environmental economists are motivated by a concern that the attention to the proxies such as price results in value distortions. In response, they have devised several nonmonetary approaches to measuring value of ecological elements, species, and a variety of natural resources (see, e.g., Farber and Costanza's [1987] analysis of the value of wetlands).

What "market" is to economists, "value" is to moral philosophers, and it is philosophers who have given the most intense and systematic attention to values. Given the bedrock position of values in philosophy, it is not at all surprising that there is great variety in philosophers' treatment of values. Some utilitarian theorists, such as political philosopher Robert Goodin (1995), view values much as economists do—as the expression of transitory preferences and desires. But most philosophers tend not to agree with economists and social psychologists that values are subordinate expressions of discrete preference. In one of the best-known treatments of moral philosophy, Rawls (1971) views values as ideally flowing from a "plan of life" and giving shape to it. Most philosophers seem to view values as motivating behavior, as permitting judgments about others' behavior, and as at the center of deliberations about moral questions, but beyond these very general areas of agreement there is remarkably little consensus.

VALUES AND VALUING

Discussions of values often become confused as one common meaning of value becomes conflated with another. One sense of value is an individual's broad-based, emotio-cognitive assessment (I explore this view later). In this sense of the noun *value*, one possesses values that may influence action. But there is another important sense of value. When we ask, "What is the value of *x*?" we are not talking about a complex emotio-cognitive aspect of one's guiding life principles but, instead, a much more narrow question of the specific value of a specific object. Thus we might ask the value of a mint condition 1957 Ford Thunderbird. This question may induce any of several answers, including a price ("The car is worth $35,000"), an explanation of personal meaning ("I treasure the Thunderbird because it was given to me by my father as a graduation present"), a technical appreciation ("It is a great car because I have modified the V-6 so that it will now go from 0 to 60 in 7.5 seconds"), or an aesthetic statement ("It has graceful lines and a classic design"). Moreover, much of value discussion in applied social science, especially economics, examines "value" in the second sense of the noun (a value judgment) rather than the first, broader sense of the noun.

DEFINING VALUE

In his excellent and comprehensive overview of value theory, political and social philosopher Gaus (1990, 2) begins by identifying the points upon which philosophers' deliberations about values have centered. Table 7.1 is adapted from Gaus's list.

Given the purposes of this book, there is no need to devote extensive attention to individual values and the ways in which individuals develop and change their values. This book is concerned most with public values and with the ways in which individual values can be combined or aggregated. Yet despite this focus, it is good to begin at the beginning and define *value*. As suggested earlier, scholars have not developed an accepted approach to studying values nor have they agreed upon a conceptualization of values. There is no need to inventory the range of uses of the concept of "value"; the chief point is to be as clear as possible about the perspective taken here.

With respect to the concept of value used in this book, a first assumption is that a value expresses an evaluative judgment. However, many concepts imply evaluative judgment, including (but not limited to) value, preference, desire, opinion, and attitude. A second assumption is that there is *both* a cognitive and an emotional aspect to values. That is, one thinks consciously about the object (i.e., person, concept, commodity, work of art) being evaluated, has at least some information about the object, and has an emotional or affective reaction to it. Thus a purely emotional response (e.g., rage, lust, or elation) does not qualify as a value. Similarly, a dispassionate assessment of information (e.g., Samuel is a tall) does not qualify as a value. Even when there is a judgment based on information, it is not a value if there is no emotive aspect. Thus, if one judges that Roberta is an excellent rope jumper, according to self-identified or other-identified criteria (e.g., ability to jump high, jump with multiple ropes, jump for a long time), but one has neither a positive nor a negative feeling about rope jumping or any of its attendant attributes, then one does not have a value for rope jumping.

Table 7.1   Characteristics of Values Discourse and Practice

Characteristic	Relevant Studies
Values language is grammatically complex, distinguishing among the verb (*valuing*), the adjective (*valuable*), and the noun (*value*), each of which has multiple uses.	Gaus (1990), Harmon (2000)
Values provide reasons for action and choice.	Raz (1986), Herman (1985), Cooper (1981)
Values are not incommensurable; evidence of this is that we argue about values and what are "good" or "right" values.	Taylor (1989), Gaus (1990)
Values are impersonal; they do not require agreement for their identification.	Rescher (1969), Prall, (1921)
We can recognize differences of values while, at the same time, acknowledging that one person's values are no better than another's.	Bond (1981), Becker (1973), Lewis (1971)
Values and value judgments are grounded in the properties of the thing valued.	Cohen (1978), Hart (1949)
Values are chosen by the individual, and every individual has values that are in conflict with one another.	Cadwallader (1980), Nozick (1974)
Values can be divided into categories related to their primacy (instrumental and intrinsic) and their type (e.g., hedonic, aesthetic, economic, moral).	Wright (1971), Laird (1929)
Values are both positive and negative (disvalue), concerning good and bad.	Bond (1981), Gert (1973)
Values are related to emotion as well as cognition.	Becker (1973), Rescher (1969)

Source: Adapted from Gaus (1990).

Even with the previous stipulations we have succeeded only in separating the concept of "value" from those related concepts that exclude either a cognitive component (e.g., desire) or an emotive component (e.g., neutral assessment). However, let us further assume that a value (a) is relatively stable, (b) has strong potential to affect behavior, (c) changes (if at all) only after deliberation, and (d) helps define one's sense of oneself. With these provisions we see that "value" is conceived as much broader and potent than related concepts such as preference or even opinion. Thus, by the elements provided earlier, we can say that one might have response to the beauty of hummingbirds but probably not a value. One might have an opinion that labor unions reinforce greed, but this is not likely a value. One might prefer mountain vacations to beach vacations or prefer one political candidate to

Table 7.2   Values: A Summary of Assumptions

Summary definition: *A value is a complex and broad-based assessment of an object or set of objects (where the objects may be concrete, psychological, socially constructed, or a combination of all three).*

Assumptions

1. Values express evaluative judgments.

2. Values have *both* cognitive and emotional aspects.

3. Values are relatively stable.

4. Values have the strong potential to affect behavior.

5. Values change (if at all) only after deliberation.

6. Values help define one's sense of oneself.

another, but these are not values. However, one might have a value for the preservation of wildlife, including hummingbirds, and one might act on this value by supporting the setting aside of wildlife habitat in the face of urban development.

Note that while there is a requirement that one have some knowledge of the value object in order to have a value, there is no requirement that one have direct experience with it. Thus one might have strong values about war without having directly experienced war.

As a definition of value let us use the following: *A value is a complex and broad-based assessment of an object or set of objects (where the objects may be concrete, psychological, socially constructed, or a combination of all three) characterized by both cognitive and emotive elements, arrived at after some deliberation, and, because a value is part of the individual's definition of self, it is not easily changed and it has the potential to elicit action.*

While this is perhaps a more cumbersome definition than we might wish, it is a definition that separates value from closely related concepts, and it is consistent with much of the literature on values, particularly the literature in philosophy (see, e.g., Anderson 1993; Mackie 1977; and, especially, Gaus's [1990] Affective-Cognitive theory).

Table 7.2 summarizes the chief points about values, as the concept is used in this book.

VALUE THEORY: THREE PHILOSOPHICAL QUESTIONS

Many of the analytical issues in value theory are quite relevant for analysis of public values. This section considers three of the most important philosophical questions concerning values. These questions include the following:

1. Should values be judged in terms of intentions or outcomes?
2. What is the relationship between intrinsic values and instrumental values?
3. What are the justifications for public values and collective action?

Value Neutrality and Value Judgments

An enduring controversy (see Parfit 1984) is whether values-based actions should be assessed in terms of the actor's motivation (agent-relative) or in terms of the outcomes resulting from actions (agent-neutral). According to some scholars (Vallentyne 1988), assessments of actions depend entirely upon outcomes, not intentions, a moral code, or a set of a priori values. The idea that values-based action should be judged on results is known as "consequentialism" (Gaus 1990).

The agent-neutral, consequentialist perspective has some appeal. In particular, it avoids consideration of mental states and de-emphasizes the importance of motives. This is attractive, because one can think of historical and perhaps even personal actions in which calamitous outcomes occurred from actions taken with the best of motives. Thus the ability to judge outcomes independent of motives obviously has some appeal.

From the standpoint of assessing public values, it is especially tempting to look only at outcomes. However, many of the criticisms of agent-neutral conceptions of value are especially relevant to issues pertaining to public value. A purely consequentialist approach to assessing public values (and public policy and management incarnations of public values) provides little instruction about strategy or about the relation of actions to outcomes. Without some consideration of the motives and, sometimes, the moral reasoning of actors, it is not easy to develop a full understanding of actions and their outcomes and thus is more difficult to replicate good behavior (and outcomes) and avoid bad behavior (and outcomes). Perhaps most important for policy and public management, consequentialism and agent-neutral perspectives provide few clues about good behavior and bad outcomes, a common if unfortunate combination in public management (Pressman and Wildavsky 1973).

Philosopher Elizabeth Anderson (1993) sets three criteria for consequentialist value theory. First, it assumes that there are "intrinsic values" (ultimate ends) and that human behavior ultimately pursues these values. Second, values and moral judgments are to be assessed only in connection with "states of affairs" (i.e., actual, not conjectural or ideal, real-world conditions). Third, actions, motives, morals, values, and individual character are important only in the ways in which they affect real states of affairs. Consequentialist philosophy is sometimes referred to as "moral realism," emphasizing that only real outcomes are important in judging values (Schueler 1988).

Anderson (1993) rejects the idea that values and morality should be assessed only in terms of real outcomes because, among other reasons, it can lead to absurd or catastrophic outcomes (see Williams 1972), such as compelling a despicable action (e.g., assassination) because the long-run outcome would appear to be a superior state of affairs for a larger number of people. She uses the term *expressive theory* to contrast her approach and consequentialism. According to expressive theory, moral action based on individual values should also be based on interaction with individuals, not just aggregations or groups of individuals. Rather, authentic values compel us to judge effects of our actions on specific individuals. Expressive theory views moral behavior not in terms of ultimate outcomes, which may be unknowable, but in terms of the rational values they express. Thus motivations do make a difference under expressive theory. Expressive values are intentional; they imply that moral behavior can be based on goal-oriented principles and not just results.

While expressive theory seems to have much closer connection than consequentialism to the ways in which people actually behave, the approach has its critics (Sturgeon 1996; Card 2004). One objection is to Anderson's idea that real states of affairs are not intrinsically important because their meaning is socially constructed (i.e., they can be judged only with respect to posited or individual values).

The best-known consequentialist-oriented approach to values is utilitarianism. Sen and Williams (1982) note that the philosophy of utilitarianism is closely aligned with consequentialism, and many of their criticisms of contemporary economics and economic policy flow from their objections to utilitarianism. The philosophy of utilitarianism was discussed briefly in chapters 5 and 6. Utilitarianism judges values in terms of implications for aggregate welfare, the greatest good for the greatest number, judging actions in terms of welfare maximization. An advantage of utilitarianism, compared with most approaches to value theory, is that it can provide clear-cut prescription and has given rise to methods of calculation. A disadvantage, one widely discussed by both philosophers and economists, is that if taken strictly it can lead to absurd conclusions (e.g., advocating population increases so as to enhance the accrual of welfare in aggregate or the death of unhappy or unfortunate persons thus raising median levels of net benefit).

Utilitarianism argues that the approach can provide important guideposts, and problems can be avoided so long as one is not entirely dogmatic. A more important criticism is less easily countered: that utilitarianism influences one to think of humans in aggregate, sometimes clouding the morality of relations among individuals and undervaluing the distinctiveness of individuals (Rawls 1971; Stein 2003).

Values: Intrinsic and Instrumental

One interested in public values must pay special attention to the distinction between "intrinsic" and "instrumental" values. Intrinsic values are those that are ends in themselves; once they are achieved, they represent an end state of preference (see Lemos 1994 for a fundamental philosophical discussion). For example, some would view personal health (or public health) as an intrinsic value. By contrast, instrumental values have no value in themselves but are valued in relation to an intrinsic value. Thus public health vaccination has value because we expect that it will lead to improved health for the community (an intrinsic value), not because it has value in and of itself. If vaccination could be demonstrated to have no value to public health or to be harmful to public heath, we would likely retain no value for vaccination.

Both extrinsic and instrumental values are agent centered, meaning that the concepts have no independent existence outside individuals' expressions of value. Thus a paper monetary currency can be said to have instrumental value because individuals have agreed that this particular form of paper can serve as an instrument of exchange. In most cases, a roll of one hundred dollar bills has no intrinsic value. A hundred dollar bill may have intrinsic value for a numismatic hobbyist, one who collects coins, paper money, or tokens, but for most of us, the bill is only interesting because of the ways in which we can spend it. The money may be exchanged for something that does have intrinsic value (such as food) or it may be exchanged for something that has a different instrumental value (such as a bus ticket).

The fact that both extrinsic and instrumental values are agent-relative means that valuation (the act of valuing) is incommensurate among a group of individuals. Even if we know that two people agree that a given valuation object has positive value, we cannot assume that these two have commensurate value for the object. This is true even of the most fundamental goods such as food and continued existence. One who is well fed may have a very different value for a pound of rice than one who is malnourished. Similarly, a person who has taken religious vows of poverty may have a different extrinsic value for money than one who is an eager or even profligate consumer. One who believes in a heavenly afterlife may have a different valuation of corporeal existence than one who believes that corporeal existence is followed by nothing.

In the social sciences, the distinction between intrinsic and instrumental values is widely recognized, but many different terms have been used for the distinction, some with slight differences of meaning. Dahl and Lindblom (1953) refer to *prime* and *instrumental* values, but others (see Van Dyke 1982 for an overview) use the terms *proximate* and *remote*, *immediate* and *ultimate*, and *means* and *ends* (Kalleberg 1969).

Van Dyke (1982) speaks of instrumental values as conditions and intrinsic values as consequences. This helps clarify only so long as one remembers that instrumental values are not the only consequences affecting the realization of intrinsic values and that the assumptions we make about the conditions required for the achievement of instrumental values often prove wrong (Oddie and Menzies 1992).

Sorting out intrinsic and extrinsic values almost always proves difficult.

Many of the complexities come from the fact that values are agent-relative, but complications are also introduced by changes in valuation and by multiple valuations of the same object. Let us consider a valuation (not an encompassing value) to make this point. I may value my beer mug because it is very large and permits me to pour massive quantities of beer into it (instrumental). At the same time, I may value it because it was given to me by my friend who is a brewmaster and the mug reminds me of her (intrinsic). If the mug develops a crack and can no longer hold beer, it loses its instrumental value but not necessarily its intrinsic value. In this example, changes in valuation may occur for any of several reasons, including not only a crack in the beer mug but also a crack in the friendship or a foreswearing of alcoholic beverages.

Perhaps even more complicated, a valuation may be an instrumental value at one point in time and an intrinsic value at another point in time. Thus one may begin a commitment to jogging as a means of staying in shape or losing weight, and over time, one may begin to enjoy jogging for its own sake, either for relaxation, routine, or increased serotonin. When does this transition in valuing occur? In most cases, it occurs gradually and imperceptibly.

Two problems of values and valuation pose special difficulties for public policymakers and public managers—the possibility of conflict among values and the difficulty of connecting instrumental values to intrinsic ones (or, related, to real outcomes). It is easy to see that important values can contradict one another. For example, the value for "a healthy population" can conflict with the value for "reproductive freedom." Of course, values often conflict. The rub is when *intrinsic* values conflict.

For all the practical difficulties posed by conflicts in intrinsic values (and sometimes by conflicts in instrumental values), it is generally not so difficult to at least identify conflicts. Thus, when a government seeks to curb smoking and, at the same time, to preserve the economic viability of farmers producing tobacco, the conflict may be tricky to address but easy to identify. A much greater problem for policymakers is distinguishing intrinsic from instrumental values and in matching potentially efficacious instrumentally based actions to likely outcomes. The implicit forecasts from actions grounded in instrumental values and directed toward intrinsic values are notoriously complex and often catastrophically wrong (see Helmer and Rescher 1959).

Let us consider an example of the hazardous course between instrumental-value-based action and intrinsic-value-based outcomes. Examining a policy pursuing the arguably intrinsic value "clean air," Bozeman and DeHart-Davis (1999) analyzed the ends, the means, and the underlying reasoning behind Title V of the U.S. Clean Air Act amendments. Title V required state government environmental agencies to collect detailed information from almost all the regulated firms producing even relatively small amounts of air pollutants in their states. According to National Association of Manufacturers' estimates, the costs to industry of the information gathering and reporting was about $3,000 for the smallest firms, about $50,000 for larger ones, with a total national cost of several billion dollars (Bozeman 2000). Even if this figure is overstated, it is clear from the public record that companies often hired consultants for the permitting tasks, and the consultant companies' fees often exceeded $100,000. In other words, Title V included quite significant compliance costs.

The reasoning underlying Title V was that citizens armed with more information would file lawsuits against polluting firms, and this would in turn reduce air pollution directly as well as indirectly through the threat of future suits (see Bozeman 2000 for the full case analysis). The intrinsic value (cleaner air) would be served well, *provided* the following conditional probabilities occurred in the ways expected by the policymakers:

1. the massive information gathered by the states would be readily available to citizens;
2. citizens would be aware that the information was available;
3. information would be in a form the citizens could conveniently use;
4. citizens could mobilize;
5. citizens would have financial resources for lawsuits;
6. citizens would have suitable legal expertise available and interested in the work;
7. the courts would be receptive to the citizens' suits (favorable rulings on standing);
8. polluting firms would be aware of the fact that the information provided to the states is available to the citizens;
9. polluting firms would believe that the threat of the lawsuit is palpable; and
10. polluting firms would have the motivation and resources to change their processes and technology so as to be less polluting.

The evidence (Bozeman and De-Hart Davis 1999) gathered in connection with the Title V case shows that some of the assumptions were entirely incorrect and others realized objectives at a much diminished level. The point of the previous illustration is simple: connecting instrumental values and action to outcomes or principles representing intrinsic values is often fraught with difficulty.

Let us consider one final example of the difficulty of sorting out instrumental and intrinsic values, an illustration of how agent-relative values can vex planners and policymakers. If *any* policy domain can be said to address intrinsic values, then public health policy seems a strong candidate. While there is currently much debate about the ultimate value of some medical technology and even the previously sacrosanct goal of extending life, surely there is no question about the value of public health measures that increase the likelihood that persons in economically disadvantaged societies can have a biologically normal life span.

Consider the case of one of the world's greatest public health inventions:

indoor plumbing. As reported in the *New York Times* (2002, section 1, p. 1), a United Nations initiative to provide indoor plumbing to impoverished villages in Bangladesh met with little success. Even with full knowledge of the public health benefits, the villagers had no wish to diminish the community bonding processes that occurred with the daily defecation and water-gathering regime at a nearby river. The "obvious" advantage of water not infested with deadly microbes was simply insufficient to trade for a lower quality of communal life. Public health has its place in the hierarchy of values, and, as all other values, its place shifts according to time, place, persons, and, in this case, cultural preferences.

So long as one recognizes that there are no values that are invariantly intrinsic values, then cases such as the previously described ones need not always wreak havoc. Clearly, the only way there could be an invariantly intrinsic value would be if there were only *one* intrinsic value. There is always the possibility that what was formally an intrinsic value (e.g., avoiding hunger) will be called into service or even reversed in an attempt to achieve what is at any particular point in time viewed as a more important intrinsic value (e.g., making a statement of political protest).

From the standpoint of empirical social science, the fact that intrinsic values are not agent-neutral is vexing and limits the ability of social scientists to inform. But the role of social science is virtually unbound with respect to instrumental values. *All instrumental values can be viewed as causal hypotheses that are, in principle, subject to empirical tests.* Philosophers clarify values through logical analysis and argumentation. Through its research, empirical social science can often play a role in clarifying value–action relationships. To illustrate, consider the following mission statement for a fictional state government labor employment agency:

> The agency's mission is to contribute to the quality of life and economic security of individuals who are unemployed or underemployed due to their having few skills valued in the marketplace. After identifying persons eligible for the program and recruiting them to the program, the program objective is to provide one hundred hours of formal training in heating, ventilation, and air conditioning mechanics and repair and to place the program participants in internships that will prepare them for full-time employment heating, ventilation, and air conditioning (HVAC) repair and maintenance jobs.

In this case it is reasonable to assume that the agency mission is the (formal) equivalent of a intrinsic value—providing economic security—and quality of life seems a good "end point" or consumption point value, a value worth achieving for the benefits it confers. The program objectives—identifying and recruiting personnel and providing training and apprenticeships—seem to be instrumental values. True, there are some people who will likely derive aesthetic satisfaction from mastery of HVAC, even if it does not lead to an improvement in their employment status. Similarly, the recruiting of persons for the program may have some consumption point value for both the agency and the program recipients. If the recruits enjoy the social interactions and acquaintances provided by the program, participation may be easier, and, in turn, if the agency has more and better participants, it is likely to increase its ability to thrive and sustain itself. But, of course, it seems reasonable, even in light of these possibilities, to consider that program objectives are close equivalents to instrumental values.

Empirical social science and, in this case, program evaluation researchers (Mohr 1995), can play a vital role in determining if the linkage between the implied intrinsic value (economic security) is well served by the various instrumental values (program treatments such as job training). Taken by itself, philosophical analysis may be useful for helping us identify logical flaws in the relation between intrinsic and instrumental values and, of course, in shedding light on the moral implications of these values. But philosophy cannot perform the practical task of assessing the empirical connections of means to ends.

Justifications for Public Values and Collective Action

Little in philosophy aims directly at justifying collective action on public values, but there is much attention to the related issue of justifying a public morality, and many of the dilemmas are quite similar. Philosophers have two very different approaches to justifying public morality: deontological and teleological. Each of these relates ultimately to public value.

Deontological justifications are based on notions of one's duty, especially in connection with the rights of others (in Greek, *deon* means duty). According to such justifications, actions should be based on a moral code or set of principles (public values qualifying as one such set). Deontological approaches eschew any notion that ends justify the means, and thus they are antithetical to consequentialism. Likewise, those embracing deontological approaches are critical of situational ethics, insisting instead that principles, if not invariant, should dictate moral decisions unless or until the principles are carefully revised.

Teleological justifications, by contrast, are somewhat more sympathetic to consequentialism but are not identical to it. Teleological justifications are ends oriented, but the ends may be based more on estimates of common good and procedures from common good than any particular set of outcomes. Gaus (1990, 17) uses the term *constrained teleological justification*, arguing that "one way to show that a rational moral person is committed to accepting a moral rule is to show that it is . . . part of a public morality that advances the values of all in a reasonable way: a morality that promotes a common good." For present purposes, then, we may assume that either route, teleological or deontological, can lead to the rationalization of collective action on the basis of public values.

Regardless of whether one proceeds on the basis of a teleological or a deontological rationale for action, we are left with the problem of how to move from individual-level justifications (e.g., acting on the basis of the individual's public values) to consensus-based collective action. True, Gaus's "constrained teleological justification" provides a clue, but this approach only suggests the possibility of recognizing the positive consequences of collective action; it does not in any way show that individuals will agree on either the procedures or the content of collective action.

Many contemporary philosophers, including Habermas (1996) and Rawls (1971, 1982), have occupied themselves with the preconditions for collective action in a polity (Benn and Peters 1959) or a moral community (Warren 1995). One justification is based on a "community of valuing" (Gaus 1990). By this account, collective action is based on shared values. There is no competition among values or weighing of competitive values; instead people act in concert simply because they agree on values. While there is much to recommend this approach, it obviously has limited application for larger and more heterogeneous communities (Oakeshott 1975).

One of the oldest but still prominent approaches to rationalizing collective action is referred to as "contractualism." The idea of a social contract is a venerable one, preceding the works of Hobbes and Locke, but the nature of social contract still generates discussion among philosophers. The key question of contractualism is "Why should individuals band together and agree to submit to a moral code to which all are subject but in which any individual may in part disagree?" Thus, contractualism can be viewed as agent-relative. If values are construed as entirely neutral, then they are manifest (or at least can be learned), and there is little need for a coordinated or agreed upon social contract. But if values are agent relative, then some justification is required for particular individuals to set aside their values in favor of the values of the larger community.

One answer to the question about subjugating one's values to those of the community is that one rationally calculates that it is in her self-interest to subscribe to a community moral code rather than go her own way. The reasoning is straightforward: If one can achieve some desired ends only by collective action, but the price of those ends is cooperation in ways that prohibit action toward other desired ends, then the rational calculation is the valuation of what is achieved by collective action versus what is lost by submitting to collective moral governance. This is potentially a basis for a community moral code but also for a legal system or a broader social contract. In such a case, we can expect collective action to emerge when there is sufficient agreement about the returns to individuals in recompense for their allegiance. Thus such factors as values consensus, education, and social cohesiveness might well be expected to facilitate collective action or broaden the range of collective action (Dewey [1935] 2000). By this contractualist view of collective action, one begins not with an a priori set of values but instead considers the actual values held by individuals within the purported community and seeks to understand the relationships, especially the commonality, among individuals' values. The contract is then built on this meshing of values.

Let us note at this point that this approach, which we may refer to as "inductive contractualism" (implying that collective action is based on existing shared values and social contractual recognition of them), is the approach embraced in this book. Despite the fact that specific public values criteria are suggested in the next chapter, we assume no canonical set of public values and instead argue that all societies have public values that can be identified, in some cases aggregated, and employed in the design and especially the assessment of public policy and governance.

Inductive contractualism shares some common ground with utilitarianism and consequentialism. However, in contrast to utilitarian conceptualizations (excepting Goodin's variant utilitarianism), (a) there is no presumption of a "greatest good for the greatest number" calculus; (b) the approach is voluntary and adaptive, relying on the actions of individual citizens; and (c) the "consequential basis" of collective action is not rooted in any particular outcome set but in a shared belief in the values framing collective action.

ECONOMIC VALUE: A MODEST PROBLEM

Chapter 8 explores in some detail the moral and practical significance of public values. However, it is perhaps useful to precede the discussion of public values with some additional consideration of the limitations of economic value. It is these limitations that underscore the need for progress in public values.

Despite the many difficulties of determining precisely economic value (Jaffe 1972), economists manage to proceed quite nicely, buttressed by precise indices of economic value, usually money and prices. Moreover, once one is satisfied that money or prices capture most of what is important about economic value, building analytical devices to explain exchange processes and rules proves relatively straightforward and, with the introduction of enabling assumptions, permits the formalization that (for good or ill) revolutionized economics during the twentieth century.

However, one of the major reasons why economic analysis has made such impressive analytical progress is that it for the most part eschews any attempt to grapple with intrinsic values. Indeed, this is a major distinction between public value and economic value—public values are often (certainly not always) intrinsic values, whereas economic values are at best pale reflections of intrinsic values, generally converted into monetary indices. To say that a commodity, process, or an idea has "economic value" is to say nothing about its intrinsic value but only about its exchange value. Exchange value is, of course, an important index, but it is not a suitable grounding for a value theory, either public or private.

Economists provide useful, elaborate definitions and explanations of markets, money, and flows of capital. But when pressed about the absolute most fundamental issues, economist often struggle. For example, even definitions of economics itself sometimes have a curious ambiguity. One text defines economics as "the study of the allocation of scarce resources among alternative uses" (Link 1986, 16). Are all mechanisms for allocating scarce resources "economics"? One could define politics as "the study of the allocation of scarce resources among alternative uses." Indeed, one of the best-known definitions of politics is "the authoritative allocation of values" (Easton 1957). What about abundant or nonconsumable resources? Certainly, economics has much to say about this.

Discussions of economic value generally occur with *economic value* treated as an undefined term. But let us for the moment consider an issue so basic that it is usually ignored in such discussions. What does it mean to say that something has *economic value*? What constitutes economic value? In the economics literature, one of the oldest formal definitions of economic value is provided by Austrian economist Carl Menger (Mitchell 1917, 97 [see also Menger 1892]): "[Economic value] is 'the importance which concrete goods, or quantities of goods, receive for us from the fact that we are conscious of being dependent on our disposal over them for the satisfaction of our wants.'"

Chapter 1 defined economic value as "the exchange value of goods and services, usually based on socially sanctioned indices, especially monetary units." (In barter economies, economic value is best viewed in terms of direct exchange of goods and services, e.g., the economic value of one goat is equal to three chickens.) Economic value, one may say, is an index of the extent to which an instrument (e.g., currency, bond, equity) is convertible into something having fundamental utility (e.g., food, shelter, recreation). Generally, a good that has intrinsic value, such as food, also has economic value. But the economic value has little to do with the direct use of the good but instead with its convertibility (see Gaus 1990). If the good is consumed and not exchanged, its economic value is largely beside the point. The intrinsic value of food is in its ability to nourish or to provide hedonic pleasure. Its economic value reflects its utility for exchange.

This is not a new insight. In his *Wealth of Nations*, first published in 1776, Adam Smith (2006, chapter 4, paragraph I.4.13) distinguished "value in exchange" (i.e., economic value as instrumental) from "value in use" (i.e., intrinsic value):

> The word value, it is to be observed, has two different meanings, and sometimes expresses the utility of some particular object, and sometimes the power of purchasing other goods which the possession of that object conveys. The one may be called "value in use"; the other, "value in

exchange." The things which have the greatest value in use have frequently little or no value in exchange; and, on the contrary, those which have the greatest value in exchange have frequently little or no value in use. Nothing is more useful than water: but it will purchase scarce anything; scarce anything can be had in exchange for it. A diamond, on the contrary, has scarce any value in use; but a very great quantity of other goods may frequently be had in exchange for it.

One can only speculate as to what Smith would have made of today's prices for bottled "designer" water, but the point is an enduring one if perhaps the example is not. Economics deals with instrumental values and, as such, is an inadequate tool for elucidating the public interest ideal or particular public values.

A particularly compelling example of the difference between exchange value and value in use is presented by Mark Sagoff (1997, 14). Sagoff considers the economic value and the use value of cigarettes, demonstrating that the cost of a commodity and its value, especially its public value, often have little bearing on one another.

> The price of cigarettes reflects the costs of production, competition among suppliers, and levels of demand. The price has no relation to human well-being as society judges it. As a society, we have reached a judgment that cigarettes have a negative welfare value—a deleterious effect on actual human well-being. The more consumers are willing to pay to smoke, the worse off they are, according to doctors and other respected social authorities. Cigarettes, therefore, have a positive exchange value but a negative value in use.

One can quibble with the Sagoff interpretation. For example, the idea that cigarettes have only a negative welfare value due to harmful health effects neglects other values that cigarettes may have, including peer acceptance and personal image (which the tobacco industry understands all too well), relaxation, and even weight loss. But the basic point is a good one: prices often have no relation at all to intrinsic value or value in use.

Anderson (1993) presents an especially interesting analysis of economic value and value theory as it pertains to economics. Anderson's position, one that would perhaps seem radical to many social scientists, is that economic values are inherently monistic. Because of the fundamental structure of assumptions built into economic values, they cannot accommodate more pluralistic approaches to values. More troublesome, according to Anderson, is the fact that economic analysis of values, by insisting upon monistic interpretations of value, actively undermines richer and generally more useful pluralistic analyses. To put it another way, an analysis valuing exchanges, commodities, and services on the basis of market standards preempts simultaneous, comparable reference to other standards (see Marmolo 1999; Anderson 1993).

To illustrate some of the limitations of economics for understanding and indexing values we consider in the following section cases which seem at first flush quite disparate but which in fact have much in common: (a) knowledge from basic scientific research and (b) barter objects in peasant communities.

VALUE IN USE: THE CASE OF SCIENTIFIC KNOWLEDGE

In connection with Anderson's argument, let us consider a prominent example of a value in use that has long troubled economists seeking a useful index. As economists have never made much headway valuing scientific knowledge (see Machlup 1962), it provides an excellent case in point for understanding the relationships among intrinsic value, economic value, and public value.

Many scientists (e.g., Ziman 1968) have waxed eloquent about the communal and cultural value of scientific knowledge. However, possible cultural aesthetics notwithstanding, scientific knowledge not put to use has no value outside of the individual; once put to use, its value inheres entirely in its use or application (which may not be transitive and may not be amenable to economic indexing). Bozeman and Rogers (2002) argue that economic currency is a poor surrogate for valuing *scientific knowledge*. This is chiefly because scientific knowledge simultaneously presents many types of values. The history of fundamental scientific research shows (Jewkes, Sawers, and Stillerman 1958) that creating and deploying knowledge relates only obliquely to the creation of commodities and, from the standpoint of valuation, is not much akin to technology creation and use (Nelson 1959; Stephan 1996). True, basic research (much like music and sculpture) can be priced, but price is a less exacting measure than repeated, broad-domain use. Economists refer to this application robustness as the "public goods characteristics of knowledge" and cast it as a market failure. However, the problem is more fundamental and has less to do with failures of markets than with failures of market-based theories. Attempts adequately to value basic research fail not because of the economic properties of information but because of its *pre-economic* properties. Knowledge is put to use and uses confer value, and economics hurries to catch up with fundamental evaluation as use.

Perhaps the reason we sometimes make the mistake of confusing value with its economic index is that we have difficulty thinking outside the box. This is because most of the world lives in a highly functional and generally beneficial box: an institutionalized, government-backed economy. It is difficult for us to think of value independent of that economic box. One of the chief functions of economies is to promote standard instruments of exchange, and when we say that an article published in *Nature* costs $2.50 for the reader to reproduce, then we have, indeed, said something about value—but not anything *important* or discriminating about value.

One way to understand the meaning of economic value is to consider the implications of value in a context where there is no formally structured economy. In doing so, we can see that there is, in principle, little difference between scientific communities' valuation of knowledge about thermodynamics and Bangladeshi communities' valuation of community interactions at the river. In neither case are the transactions amenable to satisfactory economic measure. Economic anthropologists make a useful distinction between embedded and disembedded economies, and this distinction has much to say about the reasons why economic values and indices often prove unsatisfying when applied in connection with goods and services that have intrinsic value.

VALUE IN "DISEMBEDDED ECONOMIES"

Historically public value is prior to and takes precedence over economic value. The point is brought into relief when we consider the social basis of economies. James Scott's (1976) analysis of social transactions in modern peasant villages analyzes "embedded economies," ones in which there is no separation or boundary between economic and social life, indeed, no concept of economy apart from need. Exchange is based on collective interests where the transcendent interest is the need to maintain subsistence and to insure against calamity. Indeed, anthropologist Sahlins (1972, 76) maintains that "to speak of 'the economy' of a primitive society is an exercise in unreality. Structurally, 'the economy' does not exist."

In his essay on the "moral economy," political scientist Booth (1994, 654) argues that the appearance of a disembedded economy, an economy that is separable from communal life and joint interest, "challenges the governing right-to-subsistence ethos, together with its norms of reciprocity and charity, and in doing so brings on a revolutionary response." Premarket peasant village exchange is based on reciprocity norms and, generally, common agreement of the right to subsistence. The emergence of a disembedded, semiautonomous economy, premised on valuation of privately held goods, shatters the normative compass of the village. In its place is a set of norms, beliefs, and (ultimately) laws centering on alternative means of producing and allocating transitively valued commodities.

Especially relevant among those working on aspects of moral economy is the work of Farmer and Bates (1996), who focus on one particular public value in some agrarian societies, the equalization of endowments. They demonstrate mathematically the radically different market efficiency outcomes that occur once the equalization value is taken as a constraint on analysis. Using econometric analysis (Cobb-Douglas production functions), they show the possibilities for coupling rigorous analysis of market outcomes with some modeling assumptions quite different from traditional neoclassical microeconomics. The chief point is simple: scholars of every stripe assume economic value and focus on technical efficiency of exchange, and in so doing tell us very little about any particular value other than efficiency.

In their classic treatment of the convergence of politics and economics, Dahl and Lindblom contemplate reasons why economics centered on allocation efficiency is a central problem for the discipline. They observe: "How different this situation might have been had economists felt the same enthusiasm for defining an optimum distribution of income as for an optimum allocation of resources, if they had pushed with vigor the equalitarian notions that some of them believed their cursory explorations in ideal or preferred distribution forced upon them" (1953, 161–68).

It is this relative lack of attention to "optimum distribution" that, among other reasons, necessitates extended consideration of public values. While allocation efficiency is often crucial, so much so that it may in some instances serve as a public value, it is only one of many allocation issues that should go into the crucible of policymaking. Chapter 8 explores public values—their meaning, derivation, and content implications—in detail.

CHAPTER EIGHT

PUBLIC VALUES

The very existence of society depends on the fact that every member of it tacitly admits he is not the exclusive possessor of himself.

—T. H. HUXLEY, *Collected Essays I: Method and Results*

While public interest as ideal provides a good starting point for public affairs deliberation, any move from deliberation to action requires a tangible concept. "Public value" serves well in this capacity. Since its introduction in chapter 1 public value has not received much attention. As used here, "public values" are those providing normative consensus about (a) the rights, benefits, and prerogatives to which citizens should (and should not) be entitled; (b) the obligations of citizens to society, the state, and one another; and (c) the principles on which governments and policies should be based.

As noted in chapter 1, the chief concern in this book is with a society's or a nation's public values. However, it is certainly the case that individuals hold public values. Public value can operate at the level of the individual for much the same reason that altruism can operate at the individual level. Citizens can hold a public value that is not the same as their own self-interested private value. Thus an individual may hold a preference for high-quality public education even if he or she is unlikely to benefit personally and even if it will require him or her to pay more taxes. When octogenarians who do not have grandchildren vote higher millage, it is not because they expect personally to benefit from improved education. Similarly, one may have a self-interested value in privately saving for one's retirement to ensure a high standard of living during retirement, while at the same time supporting public policies that ensure some sort of minimal social security provision for others. When the wealthy vote for Social Security, they do not expect personal benefit upon retirement, but do expect public value of such policies.

When older people vote to spend their resources on children's education or when the rich support Social Security, is this a matter of altruism or enlightened self-interest? Generally, are public values "more altruistic" than private values? One could argue, for example, that people who choose to pay higher millage rates or vote for Social Security benefits when they will not receive direct benefits may have a rational preference for a better educated society, and this is in their indirect self-interest. Or it is possible that there is a direct benefit, a feeling of self-satisfaction. Ultimately, the answers to these self-interest versus altruism questions are not particularly relevant to policy or management or even to public values. Discussions about the possibilities of altruism easily descend into an infinite regress, but that does not affect charitable giving or other behaviors that show regard for others' well-being (Sawyer 1966).

More important than the motivational basis of public value is the relation (or lack of relation) of public values to social institutions. A theory of public value is *not* a theory of government or politics. There is no necessary correspondence between public value and either public policy, politics, governance, or markets. Individuals, groups, and institutions can ignore, serve, thwart, or achieve public policies. In some cases and for some individuals there may be a very close correspondence or even an identity between their own values and society's public values, but for other individuals there may be no correspondence at all. Moreover, there is no necessity that the aggregate individual values or individual public values in a given society coalesce into a normative consensus (however, if there is no discernable social agreement about important public values that is the very definition of anarchy). Finally, we observe that taking private value into careful account may itself be an important public value. Thus libertarians might be viewed as having a strong public value for enhancing private value and minimizing the public sphere. In economic individualism, enhancing private economic values is essentially the only public value.

LOOKING FOR PUBLIC VALUES

A beginning question for anyone interested in public values is "How do we know them when we see them?" In the case of *individual* values, including individual public values, identification poses no substantial problem: we can simply ask people. Assuming knowledge, self-awareness, and a willingness to reveal information (common assumptions in opinion polling and survey research), we can determine these values. But when one speaks of a society's public values, identification becomes a more troublesome issue. This section considers some possible ways to identify public values. It is helpful to note at the outset, however, that the search for public values has merit even if that effort fails to identify public values about which there is general consensus.

Looking for Public Values in Our Intuition

Some philosophers are quite critical of the role of intuition in reasoned judgment and evaluation (Brandt 1983; Hare 1952), arguing that intuition reinforces prejudices and undermines serious critical evaluation. However, others (see DePaul and Ramsey 1998) insist on the importance of intuition and on the near impossibility of eliminating intuition from value judgments. Sen

(1970) suggests that intuition is especially powerful in determining what we find repugnant, even when it does not clarify exactly *why* we are repelled.

If one agrees with the widely accepted view that value assessment includes an emotive element (see Gaus 1990), then one of the best places to start a search for public value is our intuition about what is repugnant and what such a response implies for public value. Naturally, both individuals and collectives of individuals will vary with respect to this intuition, but it is almost always worth examining. The following case focuses on a practice that some find repugnant, but one in which others see much merit.

The Market for Human Organs

Let us consider the case of human organ sales.[1] It is theoretically possible to develop an efficient market but one that, nonetheless, has the potential to violate some individuals' and some societies' public values. This seems an excellent case for a particular sort of trade-off analysis: market efficiency versus repugnance.

In the United States and many other countries, including but not limited to India, the United Kingdom, Canada, and more recently, China (*People's Daily* 2006), it is currently illegal to purchase a healthy human organ from a willing donor. Strict prohibitions were set forth in the National Organ Transplant Act of 1984 making the sale or purchase of human organs punishable by up to five years in prison or a $50,000 fine. Nevertheless, a few years ago a posting at the Internet auction site eBay provides evidence that if organ auctions were permitted they would prove highly remunerative. According to an account published in the *New York Times* (Harmon 1999), a September 2, 1999, posting from a Sunrise, Florida, Internet user offered a healthy, as yet still in place human kidney. The ad read: "You can choose either kidney. Buyer pays all transplant and medical costs. Of course only one for sale, as I need the other to live. Serious bids only."

The bidding, which started at $25,000, climbed to $5,750,100 before the eBay monitors pulled the plug on the illegal auction. While it is difficult to know whether the posting was serious (most media accounts treated the episode whimsically) and which, if any, of the bids were true to the "serious bids only" injunction, the posting raises a number of questions relevant to public values and markets.

In the United States issues pertaining to the market for human organs are, at large, played out in theoretical deliberations. However, in 2006, two U.S. doctors writing in *Kidney International* proposed the sale of kidneys because individuals are in control of their own body parts and because donating a kidney is comparable to the donation of blood and platelets, a common practice in the United States (*BBC News* 2006). But in other nations organ sales controversies have greater immediacy. In India as many as 5 percent of organ "donations" are from sales in the open market. The fact that the average worker is poorly paid, earning the equivalent of about $11.00 per month suppresses the market value of organs, with kidneys bringing only about $1,500 to the seller and corneas averaging less than $5,000 (Chandra 1991; Kumar 1994). Studies suggest that the Philippines is, likewise, an active market in private sales of human organs (*Medical Industry Today* 1998). Perhaps most disturbing is evidence gathered by Amnesty International and Save the Children that Brazilian children are being kidnapped for the purposes of forcibly extracting organs for sale to human organ syndicates (Pike 1998).

The previous example is an extreme and emotional one. There is no reason to believe that persons who, in general, embrace the philosophy of economic individualism would necessarily support a private human organ market. But the case brings into sharp relief the differences in perspective of the intersections of markets and public values.

Steven Shavell (1999, 22), a Harvard professor of law and economics writing in the *New York Times,* in response to an editorial (Groopman 1999) decrying the trade in human organs, argued, "If a desperately ill individual who would die without a kidney is able to buy one from a healthy individual, both are made better off. Why . . . stand in the way of market transactions that will not only make those who engage in them happier but also save lives?" (For an elaborate rejection of fairness and other deontological justifications in favor of utilitarian welfare, see Kaplow and Shavell 2002.)

Human organ sales provide an excellent illustration of emotive bases of public values *because* many find such prospects repugnant despite the fact that such sales are easily rationalized from utilitarian and economic efficiency bases: the purchaser would be better off, and if the donor is willing to take the risk of selling an organ and receiving the "going price," the donor is better off. To be sure, the individual selling a kidney is taking a significant personal risk, but this only suggests that the price will need to be high, compensating the individual for the risk of living with a single kidney.

One might bring the same objection to living human organ transactions that one brings to the controversy about forced wearing of motorcycle helmets. If one fails to wear a motorcycle helmet and, as a result, sustains major head trauma, the most lethal result from most motorcycle accidents, there is a major externality. In many societies the cost of medical treatment is not borne solely by the individual, and thus one's failure to wear a motorcycle helmet puts the rest of society at risk of having to pay for the individual's indiscretion. Not only does society take the burden of avoidable health costs, but it also provides payments to survivors and loses the productive value of an individual whose life is shortened (usually, in motorcycle accidents, young males, a demographic group who generally have high work-productivity value).

Much the same argument can be made against the trade in human organs. If the person who takes the risk of living with just one kidney turns out to have made a bad bet, then society, not just the individual, suffers the cost. This is especially likely because the sellers will come disproportionately from the poorer segments of society, selling their "natural resource" to the wealthy.

Proceeding on a market failure basis, one might suggest market palliatives for the efficiency problems in organ sales. For example, organ transactions should require indemnification. An escrow could be built in to the organ's purchase price such that those who take a risk and lose can draw from this privately provided insurance fund, thereby reducing the burden on parties external to the transaction. In this way, organ transactions remain economically efficient, and externalities are reduced.

The problem with a market failure analysis of organ transactions is that it avoids the factors that many would find reprehensible, the degrading of human beings and, in all likelihood, the victimization of the poor. From the perspective of economic individualism, human organ purchase is a purely private matter. From a public interest and public values perspective, the social collective has a stake, and the transaction is a public concern, at least if this issue is under the umbrella of the society's public values.

It is almost certainly the case that the issue of human organ sales would in most nations entail another important set of considerations in addition to secular public values and economic individualism. Many would decide about the acceptability of human organ sales not on the basis of market efficiency or public values but on the basis of religious conviction. Often religious conviction interacts dynamically with the forces of economic individualism and a society's public values.

One must consider that circumstances and consequences vary from one culture or nation to another. For example, might not the public values pertaining to human organ sales be different in the United States or Europe from, say, the Philippines (to use the case of one of the most active markets for human organs)? In the United States the 2005 average annual wage for an individual was $36,953 (Social Security Administration, 2005b). In the Philippines it was $2,400. This returns us to a point made earlier. Often public values yield to necessity and the ability to survive. There is perhaps no direr trade-off than between dignity or "humanness" and survival. At this nexus core economic and core public values generally converge.

While intuition and common sense can play an important role in judgments about public values, especially individual public values, it is nonetheless useful, even in cases we find emotionally repellant, to see if it is possible to articulate either an explanation or a generalization. Elizabeth Anderson (1993) provides some buttressing. She argues that if markets pose a constant threat to market participants' autonomy, or if they consistently degrade the quality of particular commodities (or commodity holders) within the market, then market incentives and their technical efficiency are not useful decision criteria or resource allocation criteria. (We should note that this is a position entirely consistent with Bator [1958] and Adam Smith [1976].) In making this point Anderson considers a case very much like human organ exchange—prostitution. Many of the arguments in the two cases are quite similar, and while individuals might well differ in their views about the relative repugnance of the two cases, the basic exchange of one's body for remuneration characterizes both cases. Anderson (1993, 154) argues: "The case against prostitution on the grounds of autonomy is (clear). The prostitute, in selling her sexuality to a man, alienates a good necessarily embodied in her person to him and thereby subjects herself to his commands. Her actions under contract express not her own valuations but [the] will of her customer."

An obvious objection to Anderson's reasoning is that her autonomy criterion seems to cut both ways. If prostitution (or selling one's kidney on the open market) diminishes autonomy by subjecting the seller to a dire, last-resort contract, does it not also diminish autonomy to abridge the individual's ability to dispose of this most personal property as he or she pleases? According to Anderson, society necessarily has a stake in this sort of choice. She poses the question in terms of weighing short-term narrow autonomy rights of the individual to the long-term autonomy implications for society:

> In democratically prohibiting the market alienation of certain goods embodied in the person, people exercise collective autonomy over the background conditions of their interaction. They determine that the judgments that should control their actions are the judgments they make as fraternal citizens rather than as isolated laborers unable to protect themselves from competitively underbidding one another. Their collective self-protection, while limiting certain choices at any given time, makes available to all a broader range of significant choices over time than complete commodification would. (Anderson 1993, 165)

Whether or not one agrees with Anderson either in principle or in a particular case, one should note that the public value views brought to such controversies do not equate with institutional arrangements. Public values and institutional arrangements are not logically connected. Public values may be viewed as a criterion by which to judge institutional arrangements for goods and services but should not be confused with them. Thus public values neither support government action nor abjure markets; they are orthogonal to each. Prostitution makes this case. If one agrees with Anderson that prostitution has the effect of violating individual autonomy and that autonomy is a public value (among the "rights, benefits, and prerogatives to which citizens should (and should not) be entitled"), then one might well deplore both free markets for prostitution *and* government regulated prostitution.

Chapter 1 introduced the term *normative publicness*—an approach to values analysis assuming that a knowledge of the mix of political and economic authority of institutions and policies is a prerequisite of understanding the potential of institutions and policies to achieve public values and to work toward public interest ideals. One of the premises of normative publicness is that achieving public values is not necessarily the province of government (or of the market). The "best" policy or institutional arrangement for goods and services is the mix of political authority best serving public values. Arguably, prostitution is in many instances an example of simultaneous market failure and government failure to achieve public values.

Looking for Public Values in Pluralistic Societies

One reason that it is easy to skirt public values questions in favor of questions more easily formalized is that highly differentiated, pluralistic societies inevitably have fundamental cleavages on public values. Madison tells us, "Different interests necessarily exist in different classes of citizens" (*Publius* 1996, 345). Whether the differences are between recent immigrants and citizens of longer standing (Garza 1996), whites and African Americans (Joint Center for Political and Economic Studies 1999), or a manifestation of religious and class-based "culture wars," there are many fundamental issues about which Americans disagree fundamentally (Hunter 1991). In the United States, unlike many European nations, there is not even much value or ideological consensus among elites (Lerner 1996). Consistent with economic individualism, one of the few points of consensus among most Americans is a strong value for individual rights and a limited value (at least compared with other Western nations) for collective goods (Lipset and Pool 1996).

A strength of the U.S. political system, compared with most other systems, is that it is structured to accommodate conflict; public discourse proceeds even when conflict is greatest. Neither the fragmented U.S. political system nor the lack of political consensus need prohibit discussion or analysis of competing values. Charles Goodsell (1989) has outlined several competing public values especially relevant to public administrators.

Competing preferences in pluralistic societies can be captured in elections, though there are well-known problems to using elections as an indicator of public value (Saari 2003). Furthermore, citizens' views about public values and preferences for government and other agents' action can be determined by polling, among other devices. The measurement of public opinion, even opinions about core issues of governance and commitment to the state, has a long and largely credible history. One answer to the question "What rationale should we use to make decisions about public values?" is the measured preferences of citizens. This does not imply, of course, either a plebiscite or a referendum on specific policy issues; only that the general governance preferences of citizens should be taken into account.

The most obvious and time-tested approach to tapping citizens' values is by public opinion survey. Already, there is abundant information about such issues as trust in government, division of responsibility between federal and state governments, political ideology, and responsiveness of government (see Nye 1997). It may be useful in some respects to ask straightforwardly, "Do you prefer government or a private company to manage prisons?" But the chances for abuse in such specific decision contexts likely outweigh any hope of gain. Nevertheless, the simple idea of using unframed citizen preferences as at least one element of decisions about sector roles and public values has an obvious appeal. Thus careful study of general views and values for the government role, studies performed apart from any specific decision, may be useful to our hypothetical governor making choices among potential managers of the state prison. This suggestion is not unlike the widespread practice, used especially in local governance, of citizen polling (Rogers and Friedman 1978; Van Houten and Hatry 1987) and, recently, in conjunction with new Internet and telecommunications technology (e.g., Budd and Connaway 1997). It is simply polling citizens about their most fundamental values.

Despite the apparent convenience of mechanism, the general approach of "simply asking" raises questions. Does it matter if choices of sector roles are ill informed or poorly rationalized? How does one deal with the likely variance in views according to region, class, education level, or interest identification? If the responses are relatively general (avoiding framing distortion), how does one apply general responses to specific cases?

Looking for Public Values in Scholarly Literature

Having provided a definition of public value in chapter 1 and having discussed in chapter 7 differences among types of values, one begins to appreciate the difficulties of setting out to identify particular public values. Where do we find public values, and how do we know them when we see them?

Much of recent public administration literature (e.g., Van Wart 1998; Jørgensen 1996; Van Deth and Scarbrough 1995; Kirlin 1996) has begun to move from philosophical discussion of the public interest to a concern with identifying aspects of publicness or public values. Not only is the public values topic compatible with public interest theory, but also, in fact, work on public values is one of the best routes to clarifying and advancing public interest theory, especially if one embraces a pragmatic approach to it. Work on public values is the "middle range" theory that has been absent in discussions of public interest and without which not even pragmatic approaches can expect to progress.

Public administration scholars examining public values take a variety of approaches. The work of Jørgensen and colleagues illustrates several different approaches. One approach is to posit public values, making no pretense of deriving them. For example, a recent article by Antonsen and Jørgensen (1997) concludes that Danish public values include, among others, due process, accountability, and welfare provision. Case studies (e.g.,

Table 8.1 Elicited Public Values, by Category

Value Category	Value Set
Public sector's contribution to society	Common good Public interest Social cohesion Altruism Human dignity Sustainability Voice of the future Regime dignity Regime stability
Transformation of interests to decisions	Majority rule Democracy Will of the people Collective choice User democracy Local governance Citizen involvement Protection of minorities Protection of individual rights
Relationship between public administration and politicians	Political loyalty Accountability Responsiveness

Relationship between public administration and its environment	Openness-Secrecy
	  Responsiveness
	    Listening to public
	    opinion
	Advocacy-Neutrality
	Compromise
	Balancing of interests
	Competitiveness-Cooperativeness
	Stakeholder or shareholder value

Intraorganizational aspects of public administration	Robustness Adaptability Stability Reliability Timeliness Innovation Enthusiasm Risk-readiness Productivity Effectiveness Parsimony Businesslike approach Timeliness Self-development of employees Good working environment
Behavior of public-sector employees	Accountability Professionalism Honesty Moral standards

Value Category	Value Set
Relationship between public administration and the citizens	Ethical consciousness
	Integrity
	Legality
	Protection of rights of the individual
	Equal treatment
	Rule of law
	Justice
	Equity
	Reasonableness
	Fairness
	Professionalism
	Dialogue
	Responsiveness
	User democracy
	Citizen involvement
	Citizen's self-development
	User orientation
	Timeliness
	Friendliness

Source: Adapted from Jørgensen and Bozeman (2007). Details about the literature examined and the means of identifying public values are discussed in the article.

Jørgensen and Bozeman 2002) focus on how public values are infused (or not) in public decisions.

In some instances public value is considered in connection with management, particularly how to infuse public value in management (e.g., Moore 1995). While much of the public administration literature advocates managing for public value through public service and moral and civic responsibility (see especially the work of Frederickson 1982, 1991, 1997), scholars have not much attended to the problem of discerning particular public values.

Another approach (Jørgensen and Bozeman 2007) is developing an inventory of public values from public administration and political science literature. This distillation of literature yielded a great many candidates for public values, many of which receive only oblique descriptions in their original sources. Despite this complexity, it is perhaps useful simply to identify the public values found in the literature. Table 8.1 provides the results for the literature analysis, grouping the public values by category.

A SURFEIT OF PUBLIC VALUES?

The answer to the question "Where does one find public values?" is that one finds public values in a great many places, nearly everywhere—formal scholarly literature, cultural artifacts and traditions, government documents, even some opinion polls (ones receiving valid and representative responses to questions about core values). Civil societies are necessarily permeated by public values as it is these that provide much of the structure of civil societies. The problem is not finding public values but understanding them in some analytically useful form.

In some cases a search for "analytically useful" public values may lead one to use close proxies. Public values statements are included in government agencies' strategic planning documents and mission statements and sometimes in budget justification documents. While the goals and objectives of government agencies are sometimes self-serving and not perfect embodiments of public value, they often prove a useful surrogate.

In some instances it may prove useful simply to posit public values. If one's interest is in gauging the extent to which some value has or has not been obtained, then positing it as a public value may be unobjectionable. Thus, "improvements in public health and longevity" would seem to entail only minimal controversy as would "decreased infant deaths" or "cleaner air." Even the latter example is unlikely to stir much controversy *as a public value.* One can expect disagreements on the need for and desirability of additional increments in air quality, about particular means to achieving air quality, and the value of air quality in relation to other values possibly diminished by the pursuit of air quality (e.g., economic development). But despite possible disagreement about quantity, means, and relational value, few would find the public value objectionable.

Positing other public values proves much trickier. Air quality can be precisely measured, and its meaning is relatively straightforward. But if one posits "freedom" as a public value, there is likely little agreement on either concept or measurement. Still other possible public values seem to be in an intermediate range of difficulty. For example, "humane treatment of animals" seems to provide more concrete meaning than freedom, and one can envision useful indicators, but the precise meaning of "humane" gives problems.

One recent study (Vrangbaek 2006) sought to identify the express public values of Danish public managers. Based on questionnaire responses to a survey sent to 4,962 middle- and upper-level public managers (sampled randomly from 2,873 public organizations and with responses received from 2,475), Vrangbaek found a great deal of consensus. Table 8.2 (adapted from Vrangbaek 2006) provides a summary of the values deemed important by Danish public servants. Perhaps surprisingly, we see that "innovation and renewal" are extremely important values, perhaps because these are so consistently emphasized in the public management rhetoric throughout the world. We also see that the study is not entirely a *public* values study as the items also included values that one would certainly consider individual values, especially career opportunities and networking.

Vrangbaek (2006, 12) summarizes his chief findings as follows:

> The overall picture is that the Danish public sector seems to be characterized by a remarkable agreement on the practical and normative importance of a number of values that are traditionally considered core elements of a hierarchical-democratic and professional-autonomous state. In addition we

see a strong tendency for organizations at all levels to point to innovation and flexibility as a dominating value. . . . The Danish public sector is dominated by a public ethos that includes traditional public sector values of judicial concern/due process, consideration for the public in general, equity, democratic hierarchy and openness. In addition comes a strong commitment to and acceptance of the need for constant innovation at all levels in the public sector.

We do not know as a result of this study the correspondence between the public values of Danish citizens and Danish public managers, and, of course, we cannot expect that Denmark, a small nation with a relatively homogeneous population and a distinctive political culture, resembles the public values in other nations.

Regardless of the approach one develops for distilling public values— positing public values, reviewing historical documents and traditions, opinion polling, surveying public managers, employing germane literature, or some combination of these—it seems unlikely that any approach will lead to unanimity. Public values are ubiquitous but, as is the case with so many fundamental social concepts, not subject to a single, obvious approach to either conceptualization, construct development, measurement, or analysis. *Fortunately, complete consensus about public values is not required to make headway toward public interest considerations.* A pragmatic approach to an ideal-based public interest requires (at least as envisioned here) attention to public values, but not monolithic public value constructs. The striving to identify, measure, and debate public values is inherently valuable to a procedurally oriented notion of public interest.

Table 8.2 Values Profile for Danish Civil Servants

Value	Reporting specified values are either "fundamental" or "usually very important" to their duties as public servants (%)
Innovation and renewal	89
Independent professional standards	87
Accountability to the society in general	85
Public insight/transparency	80
Judicial values (e.g., due process)	80
Efficiency	74
Satisfying user needs	72
Political loyalty (governability)	71
Equal opportunities	71
Continuity	66
User democracy	62
Balancing interests	57
Networking	54
Career opportunities	54
Listening to the public opinion	47

THE PUBLIC VALUE MAPPING MODEL

Disagreement about public values and their measurement proves less troubling in those instances when one has at her disposal public value *criteria*. Even when debates rage about choices of public value, concepts of public value, and the relevance of public values to particular states of affairs, one has hope of making headway if there are recognized public value criteria structuring arguments. Much of the remainder of this chapter is devoted to articulating a "public value mapping" (PVM) model that includes a set of criteria that may be useful for the analysis of public value.

The criteria presented in the PVM model are not, then, public values themselves, but rather a set of diagnostics. The PVM model provides quite general criteria applicable to virtually any set of putative public values issues or controversies. There is no implication that the criteria suggested here are exhaustive; instead, these criteria are presented in the spirit of deliberation, placed on the table, challenging others to criticize them and to suggest different public value criteria.

Similar to the market failure model and related concepts discussed throughout this book, the PVM approach seeks to identify public values failure. *Public values failure occurs when neither the market nor public sector provides goods and services required to achieve public values.* PVM criteria change the discussion of public policy and management by assuming that government (and market organizations as well) need to be more than a means of ensuring market successes and technical efficiency in pricing structures. A fundamental assumption of the PVM model is that market failure actually tells us little about whether government should "intervene." With PVM the key policy question becomes "Whether or not the market is efficient, is there nonetheless a failure to provide an essential public value?"

PVM is not a decision-making tool (à la cost–benefit analysis) but a framework to promote deliberation about public value (and its relation to economic value). The market failure approach to analyzing the allocation of goods and services, as discussed earlier, is widely used despite its limitations in providing meaning to economic value. As a diagnostic tool PVM requires no greater specificity than does the market failure model. To be sure, the PVM model is not premised on anything similar to the abstraction of a perfectly competitive market, nor does it have the convenient symbol of value, monetary indices. But neither is the utility of the market failure model entirely mitigated by its unrealistic assumptions of pure rationality and perfect information or the unrealized ideal of a perfectly competitive market. The facts that market failures are ubiquitous and that perfect competition is virtually unknown has not undercut the popular use of the market failure model's criteria (Faulhaber 1987). Similarly, the lack of consensus on particular public values and public values criteria should not greatly diminish the use of the public values model in identifying issues for policy deliberation and promoting public dialog.

THE PVM MODEL AND PUBLIC VALUE CRITERIA

Public values failure occurs when core public values are not reflected in social relations, either in the market or in public policy. Where do the public value criteria suggested here come from? To some extent they mirror the thinking of market failure. Thus there is a focus on problems of failure to ensure a legitimate government monopoly (as opposed to a failure to break up a private market monopoly), or benefit hoarding (as opposed to a failure of a firm to fully capture the return from its investments due to externalities). However, this is not somehow a canonical set of public value criteria. The only claim is that these criteria may prove useful complements to the standard market failure criteria now dominating so many social decisions. These criteria aim to enhance decisions about the allocation of responsibilities between public and private sectors. Table 8.3 summarizes the PVM model's public value criteria and provides brief illustrations.

VALUES ARTICULATION AND AGGREGATION

According to this criterion, public values failure may occur due to flaws in policymaking processes. If there are insufficient means of ensuring articulation and effective communication of core values, or if processes for aggregating values lead to distortions, then there is likely public values failure.

A crude but instructive way of conceptualizing the breakdown in values articulation and aggregation is to examine policy outcomes in the context of expressed public opinion. Consistently, public opinion has strongly favored a variety of forms of gun control, but state legislatures and the U.S. Congress have, time and again, followed at a snail's pace. This disjunction between

Table 8.3 Public Value Mapping Model

Public Value	Definition	Illustration of Public Value Failure
Mechanisms for values articulation and aggregation	Political processes and social cohesion should be sufficient to ensure effective communication and processing of public values.	Combination of U.S. Congress' seniority system and noncompetitive districts leading, in 1950s, to legislative bottlenecks imposed by just a few committee chairs who held extreme values on civil rights, national security, and other issues.
Legitimate monopolies	When goods and services are deemed suitable for government monopoly, private provision of goods and service is a violation of legitimate monopoly.	Private corporations negotiating under-the-table agreements with foreign sovereigns

(continued)

Table 8.3 *(continued)*

Public Value	Definition	Illustration of Public Value Failure
Imperfect public information	Similar to the market failure criteria, public values may be thwarted when transparency is insufficient to permit citizens to make informed judgments.	Public officials developing national energy policies in secret with corporate leaders of energy companies
Distribution of benefits	Public commodities and services should, ceteris paribus, be freely and equitably distributed. When "equity goods" have been captured by individuals or groups, "benefit hoarding" occurs in violation of public value.	Restricting public access to designated public use land
Provider availability	When there is a legitimated recognition about the necessity of providing scarce goods and services, providers need to be available. When a vital good or service is not provided because of the unavailability of providers or because providers prefer to ignore public value goods, there is a public values failure to due unavailable providers.	Welfare checks are not provided due to the lack of public personnel or failures of technology for electronic checking transactions.
Time horizon	Public values are long-run values and require an appropriate time horizon. When actions are calculated on the basis of an inappropriate short-term time horizon, there may be a failure of public values.	Policy for waterways that considers important issues related to recreation and economic development but fails to consider long-run implications for changing habitat for wildlife
Substitutability vs. conservation of resources	Actions pertaining to a distinctive, highly valued common resource should recognize the distinctive nature of the resource rather than treat the resource as substitutable or submit it to risk based on unsuitable indemnification.	In privatization of public services, contractors have to post bond-ensuring indemnification, but provide inadequate warrants for public safety.
Ensure subsistence and human dignity	In accord with the widely legitimated Belmont Code, human beings, especially the vulnerable, should be treated with dignity and, in particular, their subsistence should not be threatened.	Manmade famine, slave labor, political imprisonment

public opinion and policy outcome is not *necessarily* a public values failure. Legislators and public actors sometimes play Burkean roles rather than acting as instructed delegates. However, when a disjunction between public value and public policy is a result of the representative's dependence on the campaign contributions of political action committees representing values strongly at odds with the mainstream, then public values failure can be said to have occurred (Ackerman and Ayres 2002).

Another source of value aggregation public values failure occurs when political officials do not represent the core public values of a society. This can occur for a variety of reasons. For example, during several different periods in the history of the U.S. Congress, seniority rules have permitted small, unrepresentative factions to dominate entire policy domains for decades (Hinckley 1971). From the end of the Reconstruction era until the late 1970s, the states of the former Confederacy were known as the "solid South," because the Republican Party was all but invisible. As one-party Congressional districts returned the incumbent Democrat again and again, a small number of like-minded persons from the same region had an unbreakable hold on powerful committee House and Senate chairs. This minority of powerful committee chairs was often able to quash policies favored by the vast majority of their colleagues and by the majority of U.S. citizens, most notably civil rights policies (Fenno 1973).

Another reason public values sometimes have difficulty surfacing is that party recruitment generally results in candidates holding views more extreme than those held by the general public (Ryden 1996), with Democratic candidates tending to be more liberal than the rank-and-file Democratic voter, and Republican candidates tending to be more conservative than the Republican rank and file (McClosky 1964; McClosky, Hoffman, and O'Hara 1960). This is not to say that the best policymaking body is the one that is most representative. Legislators also tend to be unlike the general electorate because they are better educated professionals who are, in general, better informed about public issues. But when political recruitment results systematically in policies being developed by people who hold values outside the mainstream, there is clear potential for public values failure.

LEGITIMATE MONOPOLIES

In certain instances the breakdown of a government's legitimate monopoly in the delivery of goods and services can lead to public values failure. A relatively innocuous example is the inability of the U.S. Postal Service to control its first-class mail monopoly. An attempt to control it could result in higher postal prices and, at the same time, send mixed signals to carrier firms. But let us consider a more significant legitimate government monopoly. The U.S. government, according to the Constitution, retains a monopoly of foreign policy. James Q. Wilson (1989) uses the term *sovereign transactions* to characterize nations' dealings with other nations. Recently, the U.S. government has had some difficulty controlling its monopoly on foreign policy. When Reverend Jesse Jackson mediates in Yugoslavia, Bono in Africa, or Jimmy Carter in Iraq, one interpretation (assuming they are not authorized envoys) is a breaking down of a government monopoly. Even if there is a desirable short-term outcome from the role of individuals in U.S. foreign policy, we may nonetheless wish to consider possible implications for public values failure. The legitimate monopolies criterion at least serves as a red flag.

Another especially troubling example of possible public values failure due to imperfect monopoly is failure to retain an exclusive government monopoly on use of deadly force. Is there any greater public values failure than a high murder rate or instances of vigilante action? When schoolchildren in Littleton, Colorado, execute their classmates or Amish children are executed in Pennsylvania, or a Dutch film director is murdered on a city street by religious fanatics, or when thugs drag a Texas man to his death because of his race, one might argue that these are "private failures," perpetrated by persons who, at least temporarily, have no moral compass. But to the extent that acts of violence relate less to private maladjustment and more to failures of social relations or weapons policy, that is at least an aspect of public values failure.

IMPERFECT PUBLIC INFORMATION

A cornerstone of the market failure model pertains to information availability. The problem of imperfect information refers not to the amount of information available to the parties to a transaction but rather to the symmetry of the information. If one party has much more information than the other (information asymmetry), then a consequence is market failure. As explained by Grand, the classic example is medical care: "Doctors usually know more than their patients about the latter's state of health and are therefore in a position to exploit that knowledge by, for example, telling patients that they need more health care than they actually do. In this case, if, as in most markets in medical care, doctors' incomes depend on the amount of services they provide, medical care will be oversupplied relative to the efficient level" (1991, 426). One can think of many such examples, including the purchase of a used car. But the advantage is not always on the side of the seller. In some cases the buyer has more information. When one purchases insurance one may have more knowledge of his or her health status than does the insurance company selling the insurance.

Imperfect information is just as important with respect to public values, but information asymmetry tends to take a different form. Most important, the information asymmetry tends to be quite one-sided. With respect to public actions, policymakers and public officials almost always have much more information than citizens do. When policymaking is fully transparent, the citizen can exercise oversight and make judgments about policy alternatives. When policymaking is secretive then there is "imperfect public information" and a strong possibility of public values failure.

A well-known recent example of nontransparent policy development is the Bush administration's first-term deliberations about energy policy. Initially, there was no indication of the participants in Vice President Cheney's 2001 energy task force; all that was known, and controversial, was that their meetings were held behind closed doors, and lists of participants were not released. It was not until 2005 that suspicions were confirmed that the task force was dominated by oil industry officials. Documents obtained by the *Washington Post* (Milbank and Blum 2005) showed that participants included high-level officials from the Exxon Mobil Corporation, Conoco Corporation, Shell Oil, and BP America.

The task force became further controversial when many environmental groups complained that they had not been invited to participate, and the early conjecture (unproven until 2005) was that oil companies were closely involved in the proceedings. According to New Jersey senator Frank Lautenberg (D-N.J.), "The White House went to great lengths to keep these meetings secret, and now oil executives may be lying to Congress about their role in the Cheney task force" (Milbank and Blum 2005, A01).

While the case of the energy policy forum presents no clear illegality (with the possible exception of participants' lying while under oath before Congress about their participation), it seems clear that the public value criterion of imperfect public information was violated. This does not necessarily imply a breach of public value. Just as it is possible that one will have no information about an automobile and still obtain a good deal from the used car salesperson, so is it possible that an energy forum dominated by oil company officials will nonetheless result in an excellent, public-value-oriented energy policy. (Indeed, the two quite different cases seem about equally likely to result in a favorable outcome for the consumer or citizen.) The imperfect public information criterion, as other criteria in the PVM model, is used to signal possible public values failures, not verify them. The possibility of public values failure depends to a large measure on outcomes of the deliberations still unknown as of this writing.

DISTRIBUTION OF BENEFITS

A classic market failure problem is externalities, or spillovers. The costs and benefits of externalities thwart attempts at efficient pricing and result in market failure. Similarly, a public values failure occurs when there are public domain benefits—benefits that should be distributed freely throughout the population—which are for some reason not distributed. This can occur because of benefit hoarding—a group or segment of the population has managed to siphon benefits that are, by their nature, public domain. For example, in the annual distribution of flu vaccines in the United States (which sometimes are sold and other times given out for free), when vaccine shortages occur, benefit hoarding follows (Feeney and Bozeman 2007). In such cases the fact that a market structure has developed, whether an efficient one or not, is irrelevant and perhaps even insidious.

One of the more controversial instances of *possible* benefit hoarding arises in public education. In some societies public education is a core public value and every child is entitled to a quality public education. Perhaps the most extreme case is Japan, where there is at least one rural school district built entirely around the school district's single school-age child, this despite a cost of about $200,000 required for renovating an old schoolhouse and hiring a first grade teacher and principal (Kristof 1998).

The history of segregated education in U.S. public schools before *Brown v. Board of Education of Topeka* seems clearly to have represented a public values failure. Education-based maldistribution of benefits remains a contemporary problem, due less to overt racial discrimination than to the structure of school financing. In the United States there is a long tradition of locally financed and locally controlled schools, and there are enormous disparities in the amount spent per pupil according to (among other factors) the wealth of local homeowners and the willingness to pay for increased taxes to one's school district. If, due to maldistribution of educational financing, the public education available to many children is woefully substandard, benefit hoarding has occurred, and there is, arguably, a public values failure. State courts throughout the United States agreed, for example, following litigation in 1981, when the New Jersey Supreme Court ordered thirty-one school districts in economically disadvantaged municipalities be taken over by the state in order to ensure more equal distribution of educational financing (see *Abbott v. Burke I* [1985] and *Abbott v. Burke X* [2003]).

Benefit hoarding need not imply any particular pattern of exploitation (e.g., rich exploiting poor). In the case of flu vaccine distribution, benefit hoarding was related to the random luck of certain communities placing orders with the company Aventis, instead of Chiron, which pulled its contaminated vaccines from the market (Feeney and Bozeman 2007). A variety of circumstances can lead to benefit hoarding, and while it is generally the case that the hoarding segment exerts power, the power can be of a variety of types.

PROVIDER AVAILABILITY

Public values failure can occur because there is a deficit of providers for a core public value. A general instance of "provider scarcity" is the phenomenon of the hollowing out of government (Milward, Provan, and Else 1993; Rhodes 1994). Due to the rise of contracting out and the sale of public enterprise, there is in some cases insufficient government capacity to provide for public values (Kettl 1988, 1993). If the conferral of public value has been delegated to private contractors, there is no *necessary* failure in public value, but there is at least a potential hazard. If government does not have the capacity to ensure core public values and must rely on the lowest public bidder, then the possibilities for public values failure increase. Consider the case of Sandy Springs presented in chapter 2. What would happen if Sandy Springs citizens began to demand public services that were legitimated through public policy but that CH2M Hill, due to capacity limitations or profit motives, could not provide? A public values failure can occur if government becomes hostage to contractors, which can occur in the absence of a nonmarket means of providing public value and, from a practical standpoint, the inability of government to monitor contractors.

In some respects this problem is the "flip side" of the proprietary property rights problem. According to property rights theorists, government is less efficient because it lacks owner-operators conducing technical efficiency. But if government has no "owner-operators" conducing public value (Demsetz 1967; De Alessi 1969), there is an equivalent but more severe hazard. Riker and Sened (1991) provide an interesting view of government as the creator of property rights (not just the guarantor). In their study of airport space allocation, they found that "most property rights-holders waited passively for officials to thrust rights on them" (966). Dobbin and Dowd's (1997) case studies of railroad founding between 1825 and 1922 show a similar role for government in "pushing" property rights on relatively passive business founders.

A recent example of provider scarcity is nuclear waste cleanup. The current Department of Energy cleanup program is budgeted at more than $105 billion, but the total cost of nuclear waste cleanup may be five times that amount. This expenditure presents a considerable market opportunity for enterprising firms. However, the market has worked well in previous decades by regulating the supply of nuclear engineers. As a result of the greatly diminished use of nuclear power plants, and the subsequent lesser demand for nuclear engineers, the number of persons pursuing nuclear engineering degrees plummeted for more than a decade. Currently, there is no critical shortage of nuclear engineers. But the problem of nuclear waste cleanup and disposal will be with us for thousands of years while current markets are inadequate to the task of ensuring continued technical expertise and capacity. When the market is again sufficient to warrant increased numbers of nuclear engineers, there will likely be a significant and perhaps dangerous lag in capacity as the market seeks to catch up to the severity of the public problem. The problem of capacity and markets also relates to time horizons, as discussed in the next section.

TIME HORIZON

Market failure theory, as so much of positive economics, deals poorly with extended time horizons. Thus, if one is assessing market failure by, say, the criterion of monopolistic tendencies, what time band does one employ? Similarly, if there is currently no efficient pricing structure because of externalities, how long does one wait for one to emerge? Moreover, the most we can expect of a purely rational owner or operator of a firm is that she will consider implications for her own lifetime and those of her offspring. Human beings pay regard to unborn generations, but they do not do so out of economic rationality.

The time horizon public value criterion relates to many familiar problems of theory and policy practice (Frederickson 1994). For example, information economics remains stymied by the fact that returns to knowledge investments, especially basic research, sometimes occur in unpredictable ways and over distant (at least to contemporary decision makers and investors) time horizons. But the practical social implications of time horizons are dire. Intergenerational equity issues have begun to dominate a good deal of discussion about social security and other public welfare investments (for a review, see Wisensale 1999). Consider the case for privatizing Social Security discussed in chapter 2. Economists and policymakers face the challenge of predicting the future resources that will be available through the Social Security Trust Fund, the size of the future workforce, and the needs of retirees and their dependents and disabled persons.

Another area in which the time horizon criterion is often especially important is in environmental policy. In the case of ecologies and habitat, policymakers often grapple with unborn generations' environmental heritage (e.g., Howarth and Norgaard 1990). With such approaches as adaptive management (Norton, 2005), which focuses on cooperation and incremental learning, it is possible to pay heed to multigenerational environmental issues, but most standard approaches to environmental policy do not include the means to cope with long-term change and seemingly distant risks.

Food policy is a policy domain where environmental issues and agricultural issues often overlap and where time horizon issues are often important to public values. Let us consider another case from the agricultural realm— genetically altered food (an example developed extensively in the next chapter). Companies such as Monsanto have invested millions of dollars developing pest-resistant corn and soybeans and, generally, extending the shelf life of agricultural products (see Specter 2000). Demonstrably, the results can be applied in developing nations that have fewer soil nutrients, limited availability of effective pest control, and traditional means of food preservation. The applicability of genetically altered crops and foods to solving near-term problems of world hunger seems undeniable. Absent government intervention, this is a potential market success: worldwide need, expanding markets, and available suppliers with patented products (allowing them to reap rewards from their investment).

What is a short-term market (and perhaps public) success may prove a long-term disastrous public values failure. In the long term, the possibilities for ecological destruction may be enormous. It is not possible to predict the many calamities that might occur as genetically engineered plants begin to mingle with naturally occurring ones. However, one recent episode underscores implications on using a potentially sound near-term market solution (Specter 2000,

66–67). In the mid-1990s, a "Roundup Ready" canola was created that was resistant to Roundup pesticides. It had the enormous advantage of permitting applications of Roundup to the weeds surrounding the canola while the canola remained unaffected. In 1997, some of the genetically altered canola "escaped" from its controlled environment, cross-pollinated with related species of weeds and produced a Roundup-proof "superweed." While similar calamities have occurred before the era of genetic engineering, the episode underscores that near-term economic (and public) benefits must be weighed against much longer term benefits. There is clearly a public role in guaranteeing the "much longer term" perspective (witness the role of government in nuclear waste disposal), even in instances where there is no near-term market failure.

SUBSTITUTABILITY VERSUS CONSERVATION OF RESOURCES

Promoting conservation of natural resources has a relatively brief history of public concern. Only in about the last 150 years has much of the world begun to awaken to the exhaustibility of the planet's resources. Despite the fact that economics, at its very base, provides ways of thinking about resources and the exchange of resources, market failure models have proved problematical as frameworks for public values related to resources (Norton and Toman 1997).

The market failure model's central concern with efficient markets is generally neutral with respect to the commodity or asset valued or exchanged. This results in market-based solutions to resource scarcities that sometimes promote efficiency but have dubious effect on public value. Thus the economic solution to air pollution, the scarcity of clean air, is to make the market for clean air more "efficient," and the creation of a market for pollution credits seems a perfectly acceptable means to that end. There is much controversy (Moore 2004; Ribaudo, Heimlich, and Peters 2005) as to whether the approach is also a good means to the public value end of a cleaner environment. While market-based approaches have strong advocates (e.g., Stavins 1989), Kelman (1981) notes that the use of market incentives may actually encourage pollution. While taking no position on the pollution amelioration effects of this market approach, let us simply observe that it provides a useful representation of the impact of market-based thinking on public value.

The limitations of the market failure model are perhaps most compelling with respect to the sustainability of ecosystems (Toman, Pezzey, and Krautkraemer 1995). Standard economic accounting tends to focus on marginal well-being, paying heed to the substitutability of resources and paying limited heed to the irreversibility of diminished but substitutable resources. Risk is perceived in terms of efficiency and, indeed, is defined in cost–benefit terms to be as applicable to forests as to consumer goods. Much of cost–benefit analysis emerged in response to the need to value natural resources and public works (Krutilla and Eckstein 1958). However, ecologists and some economists (e.g., Victor 1991; Krutilla and Fisher 1985) have begun to note considerable faults in marginal cost–benefit accounting for natural systems. In the first place, standard economics tends to deal well with efficiency criteria but poorly with conservation issues. Economics is prone to search for substitutes for depletable assets and, if the assets are depleted and harm occurs, to indemnify with monetary assets. As environmental philosopher Brian Norton (1987) notes, the complex and multilevel interactions of ecological systems thwart human attempts to calculate what is and is not an acceptable substitute. Similarly, with unique habits it is sometimes virtually impossible to make satisfactory economic calculations of the impact of damage or the potential for reversibility. The economic approach to hazard relies strongly on indemnification and substitutability, a strategy requiring potential substitutes (when in some cases there are none) and exchange value (when in some cases there is no acceptable exchange).

While the point is especially clear in analysis of ecological issues, the characteristic approach of market failure models has much the same impact in other realms. It is commonplace for corporate strategists and insurance actuaries to calculate acceptable losses. Thus the manufacturer of an automobile must plan for the possibility of successful wrongful injury suits and is usually insured against such suits. We know from corporate histories that automobile manufacturers make strategic decisions that weigh loss of human life against a variety of other factors, including energy efficiency, steel content, and so forth. The market approach is to consider risk, including risk of human lives, against cost and profit. The approach focuses on insurance and indemnification policies. In especially pernicious cases, reason is distorted such that the loss of human life from trucks' exploding gas tanks is considered in terms of overall profit and levels of indemnification against expected lawsuits. While individual morality is really the issue in such decisions about the acceptability of exploding gas tanks, tobacco-related deaths, or the numbers of infants killed by the toxicity of baby formula, the analytical framework one uses has the potential to affect judgments as to whether human lives are substitutable assets.

THREATS TO DIGNITY AND SUBSISTENCE

Political philosophers have long recognized the role of government in ameliorating (in Thomas Hobbes's terms) the "War of All Men against All Men" (Oakeshott 1946). The sacrifice of individual autonomy is redeemed by the expectation that the sovereign will prevent the most brutal and rapacious activities of human kind (Laski 1930). Arguably, no greater public values failure exists than failure to provide human dignity and subsistence (think of the water case presented in chapter 2). The nation's relative resources play a role in gauging the extent of failure. In the poorest nations, threats to subsistence and human dignity have no less dire consequences, but they are less public values failures if the nation has few resources to distribute or if the nation is barely a "nation." In nations with a rich resource base, subsistence and human dignity threats are greater public values failures not only because resources afford choices but also because the failures give rise to or exacerbate social cleavages, thereby threatening not only the individual but also the nation.

Subsistence as a public value criterion can be traced to Aristotle and explanations as to why families come together to create communities and the polis. But there are several contemporary intellectual strains concerned with social issues relating to subsistence. In addition to the long-standing traditions in economics, including both the "basic needs" literature (Pigou 1920; Morris 1979; Kemp 1998) and social choice analyses of poverty and subsistence (e.g., Atkinson and Bourguignon 1982; Sen 1979), important analyses occur at the cusp of politics and economics. Rawls (1971) identified "primary goods," assets that any sane individual may be assumed to want (e.g., food, water, shelter).

One source to examine in connection with the public value criteria human dignity and subsistence is policy pertaining to vulnerable human medical subjects, a topic that came to the world's attention in the wake of World War II. In 1946, the Nuremberg trials provided information about experimentation on unwilling prisoners. During the prosecution of twenty-three German scientists, physicians, and administrators it came to light that unneeded surgery had been performed, purely for experimental purposes, on thousands of persons incarcerated in concentration camps (Bower 1987). Almost all of them died or were permanently maimed as a result of these curiosity-driven experiments. These human experimentation trials gave rise in 1948 to the Nuremberg Code, which was one of the first codified statements mandating what has come to be called "informed consent." This was articulated in more detail in the 1964 Helsinki Declaration, adopted by the World Medical Association (see Bozeman and Hirsch 2006 for an overview).

In the most instances of advances of medical ethics, progress has come only after one or more terrible violations of human rights. This is true in the United States. The most significant human subjects protection policies emerged in the wake of the abuses of the so-called Tuskegee Syphilis Study. In 1932, 399 African American sharecroppers living in Macon County, Alabama, were told by medical researchers that they suffered from "bad blood," a term that African Americans of the time and in that region used to describe a host of ailments including syphilis, anemia, and fatigue. The men had in fact been diagnosed with syphilis, but they were not informed of the diagnosis. Instead, they were invited to take part in a research study, funded in large part by the Public Health Service, of the effects of untreated syphilis on the African American male. As incentive, they were offered free meals, free medical exams, and burial insurance. Although the men had agreed to be examined and "treated," they were not informed of the real purpose of the study.

When the study began, there was no reliable treatment for syphilis. But even after penicillin came to be considered an effective treatment for syphilis in the 1940s, treatment continued to be purposely withheld from the research subjects so as not to interfere with the disease's natural progression. If the men in the study left Macon County or joined the military, penicillin was withheld from them via coordination between the Public Health Service and local health departments. Amazingly, the study continued without any significant changes in the methodology until 1972, after a series of news articles condemning the studies were published (Jones 1993).

The Tuskegee Study, which has come to be a symbol of exploitation of poor minority subjects, seems clearly a failure with respect to the human dignity and subsistence public value criterion. But the moral quandary presented in the Tuskegee Study gave rise in the United States to the National Research Act, which today provides extensive protections for human subjects. The act was passed in 1974 and created the National Commission for the Protection of Human Subjects of Biomedical and Behavioral Research. The commission was charged with developing guidelines for protection of human subjects, and its Belmont Report is one of the landmark documents of institutionalized science ethics.

The Belmont Report set forth three basic ethical principles for research involving humans: (a) respect for persons, (b) beneficence, and (c) justice. *Respect for persons* involves recognition of the personal dignity and autonomy of individuals and advocates special protection of people with diminished autonomy. The principle of respect for persons is achieved via the informed consent process in which potential participants are presented with comprehensible information in a manner that allows them to make an informed decision about whether or not to participate in a research study. *Beneficence* involves the obligation to protect participants from harm by maximizing anticipated benefits and minimizing possible risks of harm. The principle of beneficence is achieved through a careful analysis of the risks and benefits ensuring that the expected benefits outweigh the risks and that the risks are minimized. The principle of *justice* requires that the benefits and risks of research are distributed equally over the population and that participants are not chosen simply because they are conveniently accessible.

THE PVM GRID: A TOOL FOR ANALYZING NORMATIVE PUBLICNESS

Let us consider the relation of public values failure and market failure. The two are *not* single poles on a dimension or even two orthogonal dimensions. Instead, it is best to view the two as axes of a grid, as in Figure 8.1.

The notion of setting market values against other values not easily encompassed by market framework is not new. For example, Page (1977) suggested contrasting dimensions of market efficiency and conservation of resources. Norton and Toman (1997) speak of "two tiers," one an efficiency criterion, the other a conservation criterion. Figure 8.1 provides a highly simplified

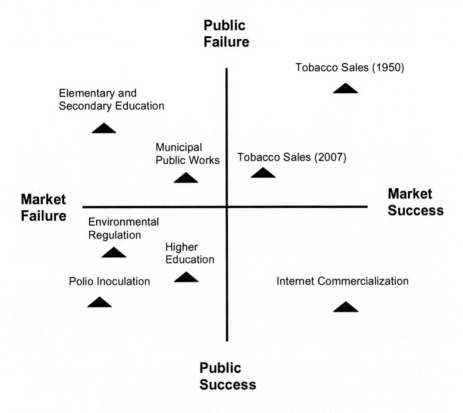

Figure 8.1   Public Value Mapping Grid

depiction of public values failure and market failure, illustrating the possibility of a virtually infinite range of outcomes among the extremes of complete public values failure, complete public success, complete market failure, and complete market success. One obvious point is that market failure and the concept of public values failure provided here need not be correlated at all. One can have one's cake and eat it too. One can be denied the cake and the eating.

Figure 8.1 gives some illustrative outcomes that I have assigned on the PVM grid. The actual location on the grid is not (and need not be) precise. Not only would an enormous amount of empirical information be needed for "accurate" location, but also the notion of success-failure (especially in the instance of public values) is bounded by individual preference.

In the PVM grid we see that tobacco policies in the United States are listed for two different times, indicating that success-failure "floats" and that the grid may look much different from one point to the next. In 1950, tobacco sales and profits were booming, tobacco-related health regulations were quite modest, and an obvious public value, public health, was greatly threatened. By 1999, the market for tobacco (at least in the United States and presumably in Ireland, where smoking is banned in public buildings) was diminishing somewhat, and government regulation in the interest of public health values was increasing from every quarter. Thus we moved from a "Market Success/Public Failure" to a moderate public and market outcome.

Perhaps the least common, but certainly the happiest outcome, is the "Market Success/Public Success," which seems to be the case with the late 1980s' commercialization of the Internet. After government agencies, first the Defense Department's Defense Advanced Research Projects Administration and then the National Science Foundation, had provided computing infrastructure for an Internet based on national security and scientific research needs, the decision was made to extend the Internet to commercial use (see Rogers and Kingsley 2004). While the Internet, much as any ubiquitous social phenomenon, has not been a success in every possible respect (witness controversies about privacy, pornography, and intellectual property), most observers would, on balance, assess the commercialization of the Internet as both a market and a public values success.

It is also useful to consider briefly the placement of municipal public works. Depending on the locality and historical experience, municipal public works could be at nearly any point on the PVM grid. A wide variety of service provision arrangements has been employed (Savas 1987, 2000) and, apparently, with an equally diverse set of results. The placement of municipal public services at the midpoint might need correction in the face of empirical survey, or in the case of developing versus developed nations, but at least represents the multiplicity of outcomes.

The simple logic and possible application of the PVM grid is straightforward. It matters not at all whether one concurs that, for example, elementary and secondary education in the United States is both a market failure (private schools and vouchers notwithstanding) and, generally, a public values failure. The point is that thinking in terms of public values failure (and public success) encourages a public interest perspective. Thinking in terms of market failure and government *intervention* conduces a view to efficiency. Efficiency is a vital consideration, sometimes an important public value, but there is no obvious reason for it to dominate policy deliberations simply by force of available analytical tools. In Bator's words (1958, 379), "Sometimes efficient markets may not do."

NOTE

1. This case and the following section on public values criteria are adapted from Bozeman (2002).

CHAPTER NINE

PUBLIC VALUE MAPPING: THE CASE OF GENETICALLY MODIFIED FOODS AND THE "TERMINATOR GENE"

We're progressing, to be sure, ever more deeply into the forest.

—FRANZ GRILLPARZER, "Natural Sciences"

The science and technology of genetically modified organisms (GMOs) is an especially compelling context for applying the Public Value Mapping model, in part because the stakes are high, in part because opinions are polarized, and in part because the issues touch on almost all the criteria of the PVM model. Some view GMOs as a means of saving the world from famine; others view GMOs as a likely route to exacerbated famine and to species and habitat destruction.

Never one to be accused of being an environmental Cassandra, President George W. Bush, speaking in 2003 at the Washington, D.C., annual meeting of the Biotechnology Industries Organization (BIO), lauded the conference attendees:

Your industry is helping this country and the world to meet a great challenge: sparing millions of people from starvation. . . . Through the work of scientists in your field, many farmers in developed nations are able to grow crops with high resistance to drought and pests and disease; enabling farmers to produce far greater yields per acre. In our own country, we see the benefits of biotech every day with food prices and good land conservation practices. Yet, the great advantages of biotechnology have yet to reach developing nations in Africa and other lands where these innovations are now most needed. Acting on unfounded, unscientific fears, many European governments have blocked the import of all new biotech crops. Because of these artificial obstacles many African nations avoid investing in biotechnology, worried that their products will be shut out of important European markets. (www.whitehouse.gov/news/releases/2003/06/20030623-2.html, downloaded July 11, 2004)

Almost a year after the Bush speech, the "artificial obstacles" relented somewhat. In May 2004, the European Commission, tasked by disagreeing members of the European Union (EU), voted to lift the six-year ban on genetically modified foods and backed a bid by Swiss-based Syngenta to sell Bt-11 sweet corn for human consumption (BBC News 2004). The change refers *only* to the variety of genetically modified sweet corn, both fresh and canned, to be imported into EU states for human consumption. Farmers are already allowed to use the sweet corn in animal feed; however, the sweet corn must be labeled as genetically modified before it can be sold for human consumption.

Even after the vote, many nations, including France and Germany, remained unenthusiastic about importing genetically modified foods. Many European nations maintain their highly restrictive laws about GMOs, reflecting their citizens' fear of "frankenfoods" and crop destruction.

Who is right? It is difficult to say. Most agree that it will take more time to determine the level of threat and the promise of GMOs. It is certainly the case that scientists working on GMOs have made great progress in developing crop strains that thrive in harsh conditions and that can protect themselves from predators and all manner of pestilence. Work is underway to enrich the vitamin content of crops and to infuse potatoes with extra protein. It is important to point out that millions of Americans, among others, have eaten GMOs with no obvious impact on public health.

THE SCIENCE BEHIND GMOs

An article in the *British Medical Journal* (Jones 1999) provides a succinct description of genetic medication. The fact that all organisms are composed of deoxyribonucleic acid (DNA) permits genetic modification. Modification involves the splicing of genes from two different organisms, forming a new combination, generally one not found in nature. DNA material contains restriction enzymes that cut DNA at specific points in the DNA sequences and create "sticky ends" that will adhere to sequences, including those from different genetic material, that are generated by the same enzyme. The DNA enzyme ligase rejoins the DNA backbone once the pairing of the sticky ends is accomplished.

In the case of bacteria, plasmids, short loops of DNA found naturally in bacteria, are used in genetic modification. First, the plasmid is cut open with a restriction enzyme and then mixed with another gene that was cut in the same way. The DNA ligase is then used to stitch the added gene into the plasmid. Finally, the resulting "recombinant" plasmid is mixed with bacteria. Once genetically modified, the new bacterial cells can be manipulated in a number of ways: they can be cultured, isolated, subcultured, and even grown to industrial scale (meeting, for example, requirements of fermenting industries).

In genetic medication of multiple cell plants and animals, bacterial plasmid and the cloned gene are sliced using a restriction enzyme. The resultant gene can then be introduced into individual plant and animal cells. This is accomplished in animals by injecting many millions or billions of copies of the gene into the nucleus of a fertilized egg. In most cases the fertilization will not "take." In only about 1 percent of cases does the cloned gene integrate into the zygote's chromosomes, passing along the new gene to each cell in the embryo. But that 1 percent of cells is then propagated, serving as a sufficient basis to begin the life of a new strain of organisms.

GMO: PANACEA OR PANDORA'S BOX?

With a projected world population of 9 billion in only fifty years, it seems reasonable to grasp at technologies that hold promise of feeding people. Indeed, green revolution technologies of the 1960s and 1970s have helped forestall hunger, and it seems likely that technological innovation will be a key to feeding people in the future. But the most prominent innovations entail genetic modification.

Some African scientists who are among those at the forefront of GMO research believe that GMOs are the only way to avoid sustained famine on the African continent. Kenyan researchers recently created a genetically modified sweet potato that they feel will increase yields by up to 80 percent. South African scientists have developed, through genetic modification, a cholera vaccine that can be grown in bananas (BBC News 2004).

Scientists working with GMOs have already made substantial gains in developing pest-resistant crops, thereby reducing the level of pesticides used for those crops. Furthermore, many common foods now have greater nutritional content because of genetic medication. Many other innovations appear to be just a few years away (BBC News 2004), including plant-based protein factories that can produce and harvest custom proteins with diverse applications including everything from biolubricants to replace current hydraulic fluids to nonpolluting automobile fuels based on flower extracts.

Opponents of GMOs are less impressed with the prospects for biotechnology innovation than with their potential hazards and uncertainties. Neither GMO opponents nor economic development experts see GMOs as the solution to world hunger, at least not in the short run. The major reason for this is that food shortage is not at the root of the world hunger problem. Experts note that the stumbling blocks to feeding the hungry in developing countries include an inability to provide access to water or to adequate systems for the storage, transport, and distribution of food (DeRose, Messer, and Millman 1998; Gittinger, Leslie, Hoisington 1987). In many cases these problems are caused or exacerbated by conflict, war, civil war, or civil unrest (Macrae and

Zwi 1994; Webb and von Braun 1994). In many instances food shortages are related to the increase in industrial farming and reduction of subsistence farming (McGregor 1990). Oftentimes food shortages relate to local political economy issues, including incentives for growing food crops versus cash crops and the structure of agricultural production taxation and government deficits responsible for reduced government expenditures on rural roads, fertilizer subsidies, irrigation, agricultural extension services, and other rural infrastructure (Mukherjee 1994).

According to GMO critic Andrew Rowell, author of *Don't Worry, It's Safe to Eat*,

> There's not too little food to feed the world now. Most famines are caused or exacerbated by political interference or civil war. The idea that it's going to feed the world is one of the most persistent myths about GM, but it's just one more techno-fix that won't work. The worrying thing is that hunger is being used as a marketing tool. Suddenly huge corporations are passionate about world hunger. The truth is they've sunk masses of money into GM and if Europe's closed to them they've got to find other markets. (Driscoll 2003, 8)

The argument that GMOs are not the entirety of the world hunger solution is not, of course, a strong argument against their development. A stronger argument is that relatively little of the GMO industry's attention is now devoted to problems of world hunger, and there is no reason to believe that this will suddenly change. Only about 1 percent of GMO research is aimed at crops that are staples in developing nations (Driscoll 2003). For example, approximately 40 percent of U.S. crops are now genetically modified—with soybeans and cotton leading the way—but few other nations have followed this lead. Two of the largest food-consuming nations, India and China, have not rushed to embrace GMOs despite having the technological ability to do so. Only about 2 percent of China's crops are GMOs and only about one-tenth of 1 percent of India's (Driscoll 2003).

The GMO food debate has led to some ironic political outcomes. For example, some famine-imperiled African nations, including Zambia and Zimbabwe, have refused food and agricultural aid because the aid included GMOs (Coghlan 2003). These developing nations, not wishing to have their own food exports banned from European markets (which only recently scaled back its strict rules against GMO imports) faced a Hobson's choice of current food shortages or suppression of future exports.

Despite the swarm of controversy, the evidence about the long-run safety of genetically modified foods and crops remains sketchy. In calling for additional research on the health impacts of genetically modified foods, Sir David Carter, chairman of the British Medical Association's Board of Science, said: "We have to move away from the hysteria that has often been associated with

GM foods and judge each genetically modified crop on a case-by-case basis. Decisions on whether to grow a particular GM crop in the UK should be made on the basis of whether the benefits outweigh the potential risk of harm to human health and the environment" (European Public Health Alliance 2004).

Following this advice, the controversy on genetically modified food is best viewed as ongoing, subject to research, testing, and revision, much like current approaches to review of new drugs. But many GMO critics, including some established scientists, do not endorse such an incremental approach. The reason why GMO critics urge conservative approaches to introduction of GMOs is that disaster scenarios seem plausible, even if there is no direct evidence for them. The feeling is that once the "genie is out of the bottle" there will be great difficulty putting it back. To see the trade-offs more concretely, let's consider the example of possible cross-pollinations of "pharm" crops with food crops, as reported recently in *New Scientist* (Pearce 2004). According to a study conducted by the Union of Concerned Scientists (USC), there is a strong possibility (supported by experimental trials) that crops genetically engineered to produce new drugs ("pharm" crops) could begin to cross-pollinate with natural crops grown for food (Rissler and Mellon 1996). This could result in, for example, "drug-laced cornflakes" (Pearce 2004). In trials conducted by microbiologists Margaret Mellon and Jane Rissler, crops have been genetically engineered to manufacture proteins for healing wounds and treating conditions such as cystic fibrosis, cirrhosis of the liver, and anemia. The strong regulations that control laboratory production of drugs do not pertain to genetically engineered crops that produce or harness drugs. The UCS study reports that two commercial laboratories have been contracted to test traditional varieties of maize, soybeans, and canola to determine the presence of DNA sequences in genetically modified crops. About 1 percent of all individual seeds, and more than half the seed batches tested, contained at least one genetically modified DNA sequence.

This is a typical case of GMO concern in the absence of a smoking gun. There was no evidence that any of the crops tested were unsafe. But, according to the study's lead author, Margaret Mellon, "seed contamination is the back door to the food supply," and there is the possibility of serious health risks. The study's coauthor, plant pathologist Jane Rissler, warns: "Until we know otherwise, it is prudent to assume that engineered sequences originating in any crop—including genes from crops engineered to produce drugs, plastics and vaccines—could potentially contaminate the seed supply" (Pearce 2004).

The problem is that no one knows the extent of the risk (*Nature* 2000; National Research Council 1989). Should this unknown risk, albeit a potentially dire one, forestall the advance of plants and drugs that could save lives, either through providing much needed nutrition or by attacking disease? Such questions are not unprecedented. For example, there was considerable debate during the development of the polio vaccine. Should an active culture vaccine be used, one that had a high probability of curing the disease, or should safer, but less effective, inactive cultures be used? Ultimately, the Salk vaccine, the active vaccine, was employed to the good result that polio was virtually eradicated with very few adverse reactions to the vaccine. But, in that case, the controversies battleground was somewhat narrower, and the decisions more easily reversed.

PUBLIC VALUE MAPPING AND THE CASE OF THE TERMINATOR GENE

A particularly interesting case for analyzing public values is the agricultural innovation known as "genetic use restriction technology" (GURT) or, by its more familiar name, the "terminator gene" introduced into plant seeds (Lambrecht 1998; Vidal 2005). Similar to the opposing arguments in the GMO debate, GURT is billed by some as a scientific savior in the face of ecological catastrophe, a means of staving off world famine, and by others as the progenitor of a new and deadly ecological catastrophe and a contributor to world famine (Leahy 2006). Because there are good arguments on all sides and because the case illustrates a number of possible failures in the public values model, it is an excellent case in point for public values analysis.

A BRIEF HISTORY OF AN AGRICULTURAL INNOVATION: GENETIC USE RESTRICTION TECHNOLOGY

In the early 1980s, following a decade of disappointing economic performance, U.S. policymakers were anxious to find ways to stimulate economic growth. One area of action focused on creating incentives to transfer the results of government-funded research to the private sector as a stimulus to technological innovation and resulted in such laws as the Stephenson-Wydler Act of 1980, the Bayh–Dole Act of 1980, and the Federal Technology Transfer Act of 1986. The Technology Transfer Act made legal public-private research partnerships, called "CRADAs" (Cooperative Research and Development Agreements) meant to stimulate collaboration between government and corporate laboratories. The "findings" that articulate the rationale for the act include brief mention of "social well-being," "increased public services," and "public purposes," but in fact focus almost entirely on economic arguments, for example: "Increased industrial and technological innovation would reduce trade deficits, stabilize the dollar, increase productivity gains, increase employment, and stabilize prices." While these are all laudatory goals, they make no mention of possible social impacts that could run counter to the public interest.

On March 3, 1998, The U.S. Patent and Trademark Office granted a patent jointly to the U.S. Department of Agriculture's (USDA) Agricultural Research Service and the Delta and Pine Land Co., a breeder of cotton and soybeans, titled "Control of Plant Gene Expression." This patent arose from joint work funded through a CRADA embodying the type of technology transfer envisioned by legislators more than a decade earlier.

As shown in the patent, the gene use restriction technology works in four major steps: (a) borrowing a seed-killing toxin from another plant, genetic engineers insert it into the genome of a crop plant; (b) in order to breed enough generations of the crop to produce a supply of seeds, scientists also insert blocker DNA that suppresses the production of the toxin; (c) before the seeds are sold they are immersed in a solution that induces the production of an enzyme that removes the blocker; and (d) after the seeds are planted and the crop matures, the toxin is produced, killing the new seeds the plants carry. Farmers who want the same crop line the next year must thus buy new seed.

The patent covered for the GURT process—at the time the process was referred to by the innocuous if ambiguous name Technology Protection System (TPS)—would allow seeds to be genetically engineered so that they did not give rise to fertile offspring. The intent was to protect the technological innovation embodied in new varieties of seeds (e.g., resistance to drought or herbicides), by ensuring that farmers could not plant second-generation seeds produced by the first-generation crop. Rather, they would have to buy new seeds for each planting. In the words of the USDA (ARS 2001, 12), the new technology "would protect investments made in breeding or genetically engineering these crops. It would do this by reducing potential sales losses from unauthorized reproduction and sale of seed."

The arguments advocating the GURT innovation were initially advanced in standard market logic:

> The knowledge that the seed companies could potentially recoup their investment through sales will provide a stronger incentive for the companies to develop new, more useful varieties that the market demands. Today's emerging scientific approaches to crop breeding—especially genetic engineering—could be crucial to meeting future world food needs, conserving soil and water, conserving genetic resources, reducing negative environmental effects of farming, and spurring farm and other economic growth. TPS technology will contribute to these outcomes by encouraging development of new crop varieties with increased nutrition to benefit consumers and with stronger resistance to drought, disease and insects to benefit farmers for example. (ARS 2001, 37)

The GURT technology held considerable interest for plant-breeding companies, and patents continue to be granted in the United States and abroad (ETC Group 2002). In essence, GURT makes protection of intellectual property a biological process rather than a legal one. At present, seed companies must count on farmers to honor intellectual property by not "brown-bagging" second-generation seeds, or the companies must resort to policing farms to enforce their intellectual property. Indeed, in pursuing the latter course, Monsanto suffered a public relations disaster when they sued a Saskatchewan rapeseed farmer for patent infringement (e.g., Margoshes 1999).

GURT is a testimony to amazing progress in genetic engineering. The process described in the original TPS patent involves enormously complex, integrated manipulation of transgenic components that are inserted into the DNA of the plant that is to be protected. In essence, a plant gene that would normally activate late in seed development must be fused with a "promoter to the coding sequence for a protein that will kill an embryo going through the last stages of development" and then coupled to a mechanism to repress the promoter until it is treated with a specific chemical (Crouch 1999, 27).

Fewer than two years after the TPS patent was granted, M. S. Swaminathan, one of the founders of the Green Revolution and an advocate of biotechnology in the service of global agriculture, declared that if TPS was widely adopted, "small farmers will then experience genetic enslavement since their agricultural destiny will be in the hands of a few companies" (Swaminathan 1999). The Consultative Group on International Agricultural Research (CGIAR)—the organization that provided much of the science for the Green Revolution—banned TPS from their research agenda (Service 1998) and Monsanto Company, which was attempting to acquire Delta and Pine Land Company (coholder of the original patent), pledged, under pressure from public interest groups and philanthropic foundations, "not to commercialize sterile seed technologies" (Shapiro 1999, 2).

The Rural Advancement Foundation International (RAFI), which mobilized opposition to TPS, coined the phrase "terminator technology" and asserted that the "seed-sterilizing technology threatens to eliminate the age-old right of farmers to save seed from their harvest and it jeopardizes the food security of 1.4 billion people—resource poor farmers in the South—who depend on farm-saved seed" (ETC Group 1998, 12). RAFI also argued that TPS would further contribute to diminution of global agricultural genetic diversity, especially for plant varieties of importance to developing countries. In response to protests and a UN report that was critical of the development of terminator seeds, in 2000 the United Nations Convention on Biological Diversity (CBD) issued a moratorium on the terminator seed, forcing Monsanto and other companies to halt terminator seed research.

In 2006, the Canadian government, with support from Australia and New Zealand, lobbied to end the moratorium on the terminator seed development and allow testing and commercialization of the technology. Individuals and groups around the world protested the Canadian proposal. For example, in India, farmers collected more than five hundred thousand signatures in protest; the European Parliament passed a resolution calling to uphold the CBD moratorium; indigenous leaders in Peru pushed the multinational company Syngenta to halt development of a terminator-like patent for potatoes;

and protesters gathered in front of the Monsanto offices in Madrid, at New Zealand embassies in London and New Delhi, and at the Canadian embassy in Berlin (Ban Terminator Campaign 2006).

The argument against TPS specifically and the GURT process generally is multifaceted (Visser et al. 2001; Eaton et al. 2002; Service 1998; ETC Group 1998, 1999). At the heart of the issue is the practice by many farmers, especially (but not only) in the developing world, to continually seek to find and create better plant varieties for local growing conditions through careful selection of kept seed, as well as through purchase of new varieties from seed distributors (private or public). GURT is alleged to threaten this process in many interconnected ways. First, it would allow commercial breeders to capture markets for crops that are not amenable to hybridization, including wheat, rice, and cotton. (Commercial breeders do not focus on such crops precisely because they cannot control farmers' use of kept seed. Hybrid seed, on the other hand, tends not to express its engineered attributes homogeneously in the second generation and thus offers some inherent protection of intellectual property.) This commercialization of seed varieties in turn would inevitably reduce the available sources of such seed due to advantages conferred to larger breeders and seed purchasers by economies of scale. Local plant breeders' access to new genetic materials would thus become increasingly restricted, and their ability to select for improved seed varieties would be impaired.

Because commercial plant breeders would be aiming their products at the most profitable markets—that is, those of rich countries—they would be unlikely to engineer plant varieties to meet the needs of poorer farmers—as is generally the case with hybrid products. At the same time, publicly funded plant breeding organizations, such as CGIAR, might be blocked from using engineered traits developed by private breeders unless they also accepted GURT. Such trends would exacerbate agricultural technology gaps between rich and poor. In addition, because poor farmers would find it increasingly difficult to acquire seed without terminator technology, their exposure to year-to-year food-supply disruption due to economic, political, climatic, or other factors would increase. Finally, genetic diversity of agricultural varieties would decline, because the largest source of such diversity is the seed-production activities of farmers themselves. Large breeding companies tend to reduce, not increase, genetic diversity.

As Eaton and colleagues (2002, 21) point out, these scenarios are speculative at present, but they note that "as with many [agricultural] technological innovations, richer farmers and richer farming countries are likely to reap most of the benefits." Existing international agreements governing biosafety or intellectual property do not offer mechanisms that could allow developing countries to legally block the importation of seeds with TPS, which means that if the breeding industry does decide to adopt the technology widely, its proliferation will be very difficult to prevent.

The USDA has not backed off its advocacy of GURT (ARS 2001, 4): "Loss of cost savings from brown-bagging also must be weighed against the productivity gains to the farmer from having superior new varieties that could increase crop values such as yield and quality, input cost reductions such as for fertilizers and pesticides, and reduced losses such as those due to pests or adverse soils and weather." Such arguments assume a level playing field, where the attributes of new, engineered seed varieties will be those needed by small farmers and poor farmers, where small farmers will be able to afford the new varieties, and where they will, therefore, no longer be dependent on their own seed selection skills to optimize crops for particular local growing conditions. But even should such an optimistic scenario transpire, it ignores the effects of reduced genetic diversity on the resilience of agricultural systems worldwide.

GURT technologies create a possibility for corporations to gain control of a process, seed selection, and a product, plant varieties, that have been in the hands of farmers for millennia. The effect is a private hoarding of previously public goods. A particularly troublesome element of this story is that the original GURT research was partly funded by public money and conducted at a public research laboratory. As such, it is an exemplar of the way that market values displace public values in justifying public funding of science and technology.

THE APPLICATION OF THE PVM MODEL

In keeping with the public interest model advanced in chapter 6, a pragmatic, deliberative, Dewey-style public interest, the aim of the PVM model is to encourage reflection concerning a set of public value criteria. The analysis should *not* prescribe *the* public interest nor, at least initially, prescribe particular public values or particular policy options.

Criterion: Mechanisms for Values Articulation and Aggregation

When there is a public failure related to values articulation and aggregation, political and social institutions and processes have failed to provide effective communication and processing of public values. To what extent, if any, does this seem to have been a symptom of the terminator gene case?

This public failure criterion does, indeed, seem to be a feature of the controversies pertaining to GURT, but it does not play out in a similar fashion to the examples in chapter 5. Let us consider two hypotheses about public failure. In the first place, perhaps the U.S. Department of Agriculture's early embrace of GURT did not reflect the range of values among U.S. citizens. Bureaucracies are notorious for the ease with which they are co-opted by well-organized business-supported interest groups. Even if this was a public failure, it was not necessarily a malevolent one. It is often much easier to respond to the persons front and center—the agribusiness and biotechnology lobbies—than to diffuse interests that have less information and are not so easily activated. In 2001, when the Agricultural Research Service was advocating GURT (in the form of the TPS patent), it seems likely that most Americans had no view at all about the terminator gene because they had no knowledge of its existence. This, itself, may be a form of public failure, one not easily remedied. It is a general failure of public policymaking, in the United States and elsewhere, that policy issues often crystallize before citizens are able to even develop an awareness of issues. If one has faith in pluralism, this is not so much a failure as a necessity.

Another possible public failure with respect to values articulation and aggregation pertains to the inability of developing nations to participate meaningfully in collective decisions that involve them. Often, developing nations find themselves pawns in the interplay between world markets and more powerful nations' political and economic self-interests.

Criterion: Legitimate Monopolies

The legitimate monopolies criterion fails when there is no adequate government monopoly despite the fact that the public interest is served by government monopoly. In the case of the terminator gene, this criterion is relevant, especially if one feels that government should play the key role in decisions about genetic products' intellectual property and the approval of GMOs in the marketplace. But if there is potential for failure on this criterion, it is not clear that it occurred in the GURT case. True, the U.S. government approved the technology, and it was taken off the market only because of public protests, not because of any government protection. Nonetheless, it is difficult to say whether government abrogated its responsibility to protect the public, and, moreover, if it did make a bad decision it was not because of a lack of decision-making authority or because private interests subverted government monopoly power of review. As noted, public values do not necessarily entail government action. In this case, the technology was removed from the market but not because of government action.

Criterion: Imperfect Public Information

From one perspective it seems clear that the imperfect public information criterion was not an issue in the GURT case. Interest groups around the world ultimately developed sufficient information about the terminator gene to organize generally successful political protests. Perhaps one advantage of early Agricultural Research Service partnership in developing the process and the patent was that information necessarily became publicly available. In developing a CRADA it is not possible to avoid disclosing information about research and technical processes. From another perspective, however, the information criterion was undermined. As is typically the case in corporate research and development (R&D), early planning and research are closely held secrets as companies strive to develop competitive advantage. As a general rule it seems clear that for many privately developed technologies early disclosure is not in anyone's interest. However, in the case of research that has the potential to affect literally billions of people, perhaps the rules should be different.

Criterion: Distribution of Benefits

Perhaps the key potential public failure in the case of the terminator gene is the benefit hording criterion. According to the distribution of benefits criterion, public values failure may occur if public goods and services have been captured by individuals or groups, limiting just distribution of vital resources, especially those resources required to sustain life.

Currently about 1.5 billion farmers, ranging from subsistence farmers to giant corporations, winnow one year's seed to produce the next year's crop. This practice has been employed, uninterrupted, for more than twelve thousand years. One could infer that agricultural subsistence relies on this practice. Even were the terminator seed to prove a great market success (now unlikely due to public outcry against it), it could remain a prodigious public failure if resulting in the hoarding benefits of seed replication for persons of means. Arguably, terminator seeds sacrifice potential for human sustenance to the ability to levy efficient pricing on a good (derived, second-generation seeds) that should not be priced at all.

Criterion: Provider Availability

As a public value criterion, failure may arise from a scarcity of providers. In the case of the terminator gene, there seems no obvious public values failure due to a scarcity of providers; indeed, providers were quite anxious were markets presumed viable. A better example of a genetically modified food issue pertaining to scarcity of providers is the inability to induce producers to focus on food staples when the greater profits lie with nonfood crops or with nonstaple foods.

Criterion: Time Horizon

Public value failure may occur when there is little heed given to long-term consequences. According to GMO critics, this is the most common problem with the introduction of GMOs in general and GURT in particular. There is limited evidence of GMO problems affecting existing crops, and there is little evidence of spillover effects from GURT (aside from the direct problem of genetic control of seeds). But there is great concern about long-term risks and about the irreversibility of potential damages. Similarly, critics argue that in the name of short-term profits and short-term perspective, GURT promoters ignore centuries of agricultural practice and the extent to which marginal farmers cannot subsist if they must depend on corporations for their crops.

GMO advocates can present their own time horizon argument for public failure. It is easy to construct an argument that overly cautious critics, thinking chiefly about disaster scenarios for which there is no proof, are standing in the way of development of GURT and other GMO technologies, ones that could potentially improve foods and ameliorate hunger, as well as provide for innovations that cannot yet even be imagined.

There is a historical parallel—nuclear energy. During the 1950s and since, the peacetime uses of nuclear energy have had strong advocates who promised cheap, clean energy. Opponents argued disaster scenarios. Both were right. Currently, at least in the United States, many of the dangers of nuclear energy have been diminished, chiefly through fewer operating plants, but the public benefits have also been reduced, including limiting the air pollution that now occurs as nearly 50 percent of public utility energy production relies on coal.

Criterion: Substitutability versus Conservation of Resources

According to this criterion, public failure can occur when policies focus on substitutability or indemnification even if there is no satisfactory substitute. The extent to which this criterion applies to the terminator gene case is difficult to determine. It is not yet clear that GURT will result in a substitution of genetically engineered crops and foods for natural ones. However, there is some evidence that cross-fertilization can occur such that naturally occurring plants will ultimately possess the DNA of GMOs. Whether or not this will result in a wholesale and uncontrolled substitution of GMOs for natural foods is not certain, nor is it easy to assess the damage that might occur. There seems no clear historical parallel. While it is certainly the case that one would be hard-pressed to find a potato that would have strong similarity to the much smaller, less robust potato of centuries ago, the changes have been desired, controlled, and (if there were ever need to do so) are reversible.

Criterion: Ensure Subsistence and Human Dignity

This criterion is a bit of a catchall but probably worth preserving inasmuch as some choices are repellent even if they do fail by either market standards or by the other criteria listed earlier. The example given in chapter 8, the free market sale of organs, is a good one. It does not obviously conflict with any of the other criteria presented previously, but, at the same time, some view the practice as repellent and laws are set against it, even when those laws abridge individual liberty and personal choice in a most fundamental way.

Certainly, if critics are correct, GURT seems to pose some threat to the ability of nonindustrial farmers to subsist. Does the terminator gene pose a threat to dignity? Perhaps. If we consider the extent to which the poor in developing nations and individual farmers in industrial nations are made even more powerless by multinational corporations' control of seed propagation, there does seem to be a prospect of a failure to human dignity.

THE TERMINATOR GENE AND THE PVM GRID

Chapter 8 presented a simple schematic, the PVM grid, useful in depicting the orthogonal relationship between public value success and market success. We apply that same tool to the case of the terminator gene, but the grid is developed further in order to illustrate more extensive applications. It should be reiterated that this is not presented or intended as a precise tool but as a means of stimulating thought and promoting discussion about public values and social outcomes. Obviously, there is no science to the positioning of policies on the grid, but it could prove a useful exercise to have different parties compare their positioning and discuss their rationales for doing so.

As a rough assessment, we can compare in Figure 9.1 the apparent market/public outcomes for GURT compared to other areas pertaining to science policy. For example, in this simple assessment, "high school science education," according to its placement on the grid, is both a public failure and a market failure. Academic research policy is a public value success but, to a large extent, an acceptable market failure (though that may be changing with the increasingly direct commercial relevance of academic research and with increasing ties between universities and business). The Internet is given, as before, as an example of an outcome that is to some extent both a market and a public value success.

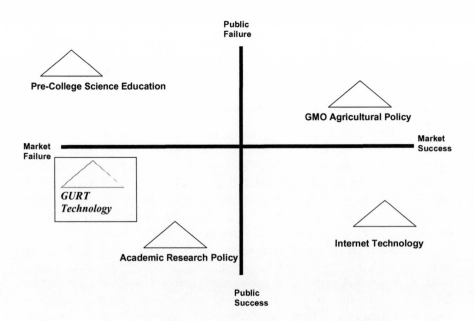

Figure 9.1 Public Value Mapping Grid for GURT and Illustrative Science Policies

Of greatest interest for present purposes is the contrasting position between GURT technology and GMO agricultural technology generally. The social outcome domains are in very different positions on the grid. GURT is listed as a substantial market failure and a modest public success; by contrast, GMO agricultural technology is listed as a substantial market success and a modest public failure. Why are these mirror images? In the first place, GMO agriculture has been a market boon, not only in terms of sales, productivity, and profit but in terms of the technical efficiency of transactions. By contrast, GURT has had minimal market impact thus far, chiefly because of the wariness of consumers and anti-GURT interest groups, but also because of government restrictions and the reluctant retreat of agribusiness corporations. GMO agriculture is assessed as a modest public failure because of the potential risks it presents; the benefits of GMO agriculture must also be recognized, including nutritional improvements. GURT is judged a modest public value success inasmuch as it has contributed to the advancement of knowledge and, as it has not been marketed successfully, there has been little ability thus far to generate "negative *public* externalities."

Figure 9.2 shows two very different public failure grid trajectories for GURT, each one defensible. Both scenarios are relatively optimistic with respect to the possible market outcomes for GURT, assuming that if the technology is disseminated in the market, it will generally meet with success. Because the intellectual property is, essentially, self-enforcing, this seems a

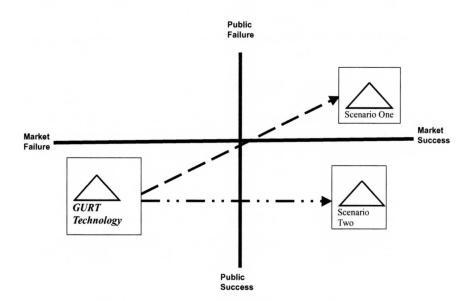

Figure 9.2 Public Value Mapping Grid Projecting GURT Outcomes

reasonable assumption, all else being equal. In scenario one, we have a more pessimistic public values assessment, one that could occur if critics' forecasts of disruption to subsistence farming occurs or if harm comes to the natural environment through cross-pollination. In scenario two, we have a more optimistic public values assessment, one that could occur if plant strains are improved, there is little interference with the natural environment or subsistence farming, and there are important advances in the qualities of seeds and in biotechnology innovation from the profits accrued from GURT.

CONCLUSION

The purpose of applying the PVM model to the genetically modified food and GURT case history is simply to show the very different routes one might take in analyzing public value failure than one might take analyzing market failure. From a simplified perspective, the GURT case is an ostensible market success (except for the "pigheadedness" of reluctant consumers!). The terminator gene certainly provides for technical efficiency, at least potentially, helping producers wring extra value from their intellectual property. But market failure analysis stops short of asking who *should* be the owner of property, and that, of course, is at the hub of the GURT controversy.

In the marketplace, externalities may distort prices and thus skew costs or benefits toward particular consumers. For example, the costs of cleaning up pollution are rarely included in the price of the polluting good. Thus those who produce and consume that good may benefit preferentially. But what if the "free rider" is not a polluter but a subsistence farmer whose very life, family, and community depend upon the ability to reuse seeds? By giving additional and systematic attention to public values, with application of the public values mapping model, questions of equity, individual worth, culture, and heritage are more likely to be privileged than they are in a decision framework dominated by the values of economic individualism.

The role of the public value grid and the public values mapping model generally is not in providing an answer to evaluations or forecasts but simply in suggesting a set of analytical tools that will keep public values deliberation on a par with discussions of market failure or success. It is a simple discipline, easily applied, and quite likely provocative. In many cases it is best used in connection with market failure models. Each model has the advantage of providing a potentially useful perspective, and when taken together, the two can stimulate the type of debate so useful in pursuit of public interest ideals.

CHAPTER TEN
MANAGING PUBLICNESS

Reform, v. A thing that mostly satisfies reformers opposed to
reformation.

—AMBROSE BIERCE, *The Devil's Dictionary*

Whether one embraces the public values model, a pragmatic public interest approach, or some entirely different public values framework, the question remains as to the most useful way to infuse public policy and public management with public values. This chapter presents the concept of "Managing Publicness" as an alternative to public management approaches, particularly New Public Management (NPM), rooted ultimately in assumptions of economic individualism.

We begin by asking what "Managing Publicness" means and discuss the managerial ethos associated with Managing Publicness. Then we differentiate Managing Publicness from NPM, ultimately moving from assumptions and philosophical grounding to some relatively concrete principles one might consider in implementing the Managing Publicness approach to governance.

Perhaps it seems strange even to consider how or why public managers might manage publicly. Does not the very name *public management* imply a commitment to Managing Publicness? But Managing Publicness, as the term is used here, is identical to managing for public value, and, of course, there is no necessity that public management, in its actual practice, seeks or achieves public values. Public management may seek economic efficiency, it may serve power, it may follow the dictates of narrow interests, or it may focus on "side-payments" and the self-interest of public managers, among other possibilities.

Before considering in any more than the most obvious meaning of Managing Publicness, the idea of infusing public management with public values, let us examine two very different meanings of public management to which Managing Publicness seems equally relevant.

TWO USAGES OF PUBLIC MANAGEMENT: ACTION VERSUS REGIME GOVERNANCE

"Public management" has two distinct usages that are quite far apart. One conceptualization of "public management" refers to specific actions taken by specific persons. The study of this sort of public management is the study of how managers manage and how they should manage. However, another usage of "public management" refers more to large-scale governance than to specific managerial activities. This grander conceptualization is much broader even than "strategic management" (see Moore 1995 for a public value conceptualization rooted in strategic management). Much of the discussion of NPM refers to public management regimes and governance approaches rather than to specific management strategies.

This chapter focuses on both concepts of public management, public-management-as-action, and public-management-regime governance. The idea of Managing Publicness refers to both usages. However, Managing Publicness is most relevant at the public management regime level, as an alternative to NPM. This is not to say that Managing Publicness requires NPM as a referent. Well before the NPM construct was developed there was ample justification for a focus on many of the ideas of Managing Publicness, though these ideas were not bundled into one concept. But the advent of NPM, along with similar privatization and quasimarket developments in the United States (but not under the then NPM banner, e.g., reinvention movement), have given an urgency to the ideas embraced by Managing Publicness.

THE MANAGING PUBLICNESS CONCEPT

As mentioned before, the most fundamental point about Managing Publicness, whether from the standpoint of a public management regime or a single public manager, is a focus on infusing public value into policy and management and, concomitantly, avoiding public value failure. But it is possible to provide some more specific principles.

Public Value as Starting Point

While most approaches to public management recognize the importance of public values, Managing Publicness differs in that public value is preeminent, not just one criterion to be balanced against others. Public value is the starting point. Oftentimes contemporary public managers seek public value within the limits of political constraints, budgets, discretion, neutral competence, and accountability mechanisms and controls. More likely than not, in the act of being realistic and practical the whole idea of public value is not simply compromised but, essentially, abandoned. Managing Publicness requires a statement of public value as a starting point, not as something to be negotiated on the fly, and an expectation that public value be sacrificed only by the most extreme and entirely uncontrollable events, events so extreme as to change the contemporary meaning of public value.

Managing Publicness is *not* the same as "managing in the public interest." As suggested elsewhere in this book, the most useful conception of public interest is a pragmatic one, based on deliberative processes shedding light on an ideal, but not seeking to attain an ideal that is either intersubjective or consensual. Public values, by contrast, are content based and can be consensual. Public values may be expressed in public policy, constitutions, public law, or social consensus, but whereas "the public interest" may only be approached, public values may be achieved. To put it another way, managing in the public interest presents no standard at all, but rather a declaration of intent. Managing Publicness, by contrast, involves specifiable values and, potentially, a standard against which public performance may be measured.

Managing for Citizens, Not Customers

Managing Publicness entails management for citizens within the confines of public law, and not customers. All of the trappings of "customer-oriented public management" have no place in Managing Publicness. There is not and cannot be a presumption that citizen equals customer, chiefly because this commonplace assumption disempowers citizens and devalues citizenship (Alford 2002; Frederickson 1997). Citizens have inalienable rights that customers do not have, and even if we grant that much of the "customerspeak" we see today is more rhetoric than substance, it is an unfortunate rhetoric. Customers are not the basis of legitimacy for the industries with which they have commerce. Customers are not sovereign. Customers have no bill of rights other than those granted temporarily through others' largesse.

To manage for citizens does not and cannot mean that each citizen's perceived self-interest is a paramount consideration in public management but, instead, that the guarantees to citizens embedded in public law provide a guidepost rather than just a consideration or a check and balance.

Managing Publicness Is Sector Neutral

One of the primary tenets of public value is easily misunderstood. Managing Publicness does *not* require one to eschew market or quasimarket approaches such as contracting and privatization. The concern with Managing Publicness is that public values are paramount. If it is more effective to achieve public purposes through the market, then there is nothing about Managing Publicness that enjoins market solutions. Approaches based on assumptions of economic individualism can be effective in achieving public value, especially in those cases where benefits can easily be disaggregated. However, Managing Publicness maintains skepticism about market solutions as solutions to public value problems. Moreover, market approaches often are "solutions" to politicians' needs to appear to be efficient or market friendly or to public servants' needs to find ways of compromising public value goals in the face of rampant cutbacks in resources or personnel freezes.

In the United States, sector neutrality is a radical idea. The most profound difference between Managing Publicness and many approaches to management, whether public or private, is that it does not privilege the market. There is no implication that government action is "interference" in the market or that market solutions are inherently better. Whereas market failure approaches assume that government should act only in instances of market failure (and not necessarily then), Managing Publicness makes no such assumption. Indeed, government action can be useful in cases where the market is working effectively. A considerable body of research and theory (see, for example, La Porta et al. 1999; Madrick 2002; Miguel 2004) suggests that one of the most important preconditions for strong economic development and economic prosperity is an effective, well-developed government.

In some cases, even as markets proceed effectively, the undergirding of government policies and structures enhances effectiveness, including achievement of public values (Boyne and Walker 2004). But Managing Publicness can also endorse those instances in which government is not just a support structure for market activities but, instead, "in competition" with the market. In some cases "being in competition" with the market is simply rhetoric. Sometimes in cases where government is pursuing the same ends as the private sector, but by alternative means, there is really no active competition but rather quite different routes to the same destination. In other instances, such as mail delivery or hospital management, government does literally compete with the market through "managed competition," an approach very much consonant with NPM. The essential points for managing publicness are (a) rhetoric and dogma get in the way; (b) rhetoric notwithstanding, there is nothing inherently superior about private-sector provision of goods and services (if the private sector were *always* effective, then why do about 80 percent of all businesses fail?); and (c) committed, talented people working in effective institutions produce good outcomes, regardless of sector, labels, or dogma.

We might consider, in passing at least, why Managing Publicness departs from what is generally the maintained truth of market superiority (see Bozeman 1987 for extensive treatment of this issue). The most important point is that ideas of market failure, property rights theory, and principal–agent theory, three of the strongest arguments for the inherent superiority of market approaches, are all based on assumptions that, remarkably, have rarely been submitted to strong empirical test and, when they have, yielded ambiguous results. It does not take much more than casual observation for one to reflect on life experiences to recall instances of extremely effective action by government agencies, extremely effective action by private firms, extremely inept action by government agencies, and extremely inept action by private firms. The supposed hallmark of market superiority is based on generally un-proven assumptions about the ultimate effects of rare instances of unfettered competition.

Let us consider the narrowest of possible claims. With respect to public values, would it be useful to privilege market approaches in those cases where we are comparing business and government providers that have equally tal-ented and committed individuals, equal institutional capabilities, and equal fi-nancial resources? The answer is still "no."

Managing Publicness Entails Advocating and Managing Capacity

The dogma of market superiority has been responsible for a remarkable amount of mischief, but it has nowhere been more harmful than in its effect of undermining government capacity. If government is to in any circumstances be a useful purveyor of public value, then it must maintain sufficient capacity to do its job, however that job is defined, even if its job is defined as nothing other than contract management (Bennett and Mills 1998; Grindle and Hilder-brand 1995). The related phenomena of government bashing (see Goodsell 2003 for detailed description) and market privileging have had the effect of encouraging the regular diminution of many government agencies' ability to perform their public-value-related functions. The loss of governance capacity is not entirely attributable to government bashing and dogma—such factors as recession and shifts in policy priorities contribute to capacity reduction—but the contribution of government bashing and dogma are certainly formida-ble (Lorentzen 1993).

Often knee-jerk antigovernment arguments are simply political cover, but that does not diminish their effects. Sometimes the result is that an attack on government agencies or "bureaucracy" causes a cutback in resources available to government agencies, which diminishes their capacity, which in turn con-firms the initial assumption in the chain of argument—that government is in-effective. It is difficult, of course, to know how to get out of this cycle so long as politicians continue to make reputations based on being actual enemies or, more often, pseudo-enemies of government (Rainey 2002). When political ca-reers are made by tax cuts and rollbacks of government employees, capacity building in government is a low priority or even a negative outcome (McSwite 2005).

Managing publicness requires *managers'* attention to capacity. Managing publicness does not require or expect that U.S. elected officials will wish to paint themselves as friends of government or that tax cuts will become unpop-ular with their constituents. It requires public managers to think of themselves as purveyors of public value and to do what they can, operating in a highly con-strained political system, to husband the resources necessary to accomplish the missions that these same elected officials have set for them. In most instances issues of capacity are reserved for upper echelon leaders, simply because these are the individuals who will be interacting with the elected officials who ultimately control resources. But Managing Publicness requires all public management leaders be prepared to make a case for capacity, a difficult task in a political culture that in most instances stacks the deck against providing sustained resources to government.

Managing Publicness Requires that Public Managers Not Be a Living Transactions Cost

If one reads serious criticisms of public bureaucracy one finds compelling arguments that government is less efficient because, variously, "side-payments" are more common (Bolton and Farrell 1990), transactions costs often are higher (Zerbe and McCurdy 1999), principal–agent problems are rampant (Horn 1995), and there is no private property for the trading (i.e., a citizen cannot easily alter her portfolio of government investments; De Alessi 1969).

However, these various theoretical condemnations of the government management are often flawed (Bozeman 1987) and their assumptions not often put to the test (Rainey and Bozeman 2000). Thus, for example, the claim that government cannot be efficient because, unlike private firms, there are no wealth-seeking entrepreneurs to act as a constant force for technical efficiency seems fatuous given the small number of modern corporations (the most appropriate basis of comparison to government agencies) that are actually run by wealth-seeking entrepreneurs. Further, the fact that stock prices, growth, and investment in the company are so often poorly correlated complicates findings about private firms' technical efficiency.

Likewise, the idea that government agencies are especially prone to side-payments (siphoning off resources that have no relation to organization goals and missions to achieve personal or coalition goals), as compared with private organizations, seems a flawed argument. The premise of government's alleged focus on side-payments is that government goals are more ambiguous and, ergo, contributions to productivity more difficult to trace. Indeed, the idea that government agencies' goals are more ambiguous is certainly widespread in the literature—*except* for the empirical literature. Almost all empirical research focusing on goal clarity shows that there is little or no difference in the extent to which public and private managers are clear about their goals (Chun and Rainey 2005; Lan and Rainey 1992; Rainey 1983; Rainey, Pandey, and Bozeman 1995). In one study of the relationship of goal clarity to managers' risk aversion (Bozeman and Kingsley 1998), it was shown that the lack of goal clarity is, indeed, associated with a tendency to avoid risk, but the tendency was just as strong in both sectors, and the goals were equally clear in both sectors.

Despite the difficulties of some of the premises, not to mention the empirical results, of literature claiming to show the inherent inefficiency of public organizations, it is certainly the case that market failure does not in any sense imply government success. Wolf (1993), among others, has provided some useful discourse on the reasons for "nonmarket failure" without retreating to the position that government is inherently inefficient. Managing Publicness asks that we forego universal indictments of government and, at the same time, recognize that there are particular challenges public managers face that sometimes make it more difficult for them to be efficient and effective. In particular, the vast differences in the accountability standards imposed on government and business influence their relative ability to proceed with dispatch to perform their required tasks (Kaufman 1956; Johnston and Romzek 1999).

As has often been pointed out (Pandey and Scott 2002; DeHart-Davis and Pandey 2005), the accountability requirements placed on government are not always best conceived as a burden or "red tape." Many accountability requirements are sensible and, in the long run, productive. However, it is also the case that almost all empirical studies comparing public- and private-sector organizations' red tape (for an overview, see Rainey, Pandey, and Bozeman 1995) show that the public sector tends to have more of it and that much of the red tape is due to accountability rules that are not sensible and productive.

The bottom line lesson for Managing Publicness is to understand both that public management is generally constrained in ways that private-sector management is not and that public-sector efficiency is nonetheless possible, even if sometimes more difficult than private-sector efficiency. Related, Managing Publicness requires an understanding that the technical efficiency and cost of the production of goods and services is not the only issue involved in managerial effectiveness. Many of the public values that provide the charter for public agencies, values such as national security or a social safety net, do not permit the types of learning curve production efficiencies experienced by manufacturers. Similarly, if a company wishes to enhance its value in the stock market, it is often the case that the quickest way is to "rationalize" employment (i.e., fire people). If we define efficiency as the greatest output for a unit of input, then there are only two possibilities for enhancing efficiency: the numerator or the denominator. Often the denominator is easier, at least for the people at the top. But this brings us to the truism that economic theorists have observed. There is no publicly traded stock in government agencies. As citizens we are often interested in government agencies (or private-sector purveyors of core public values) doing their jobs well and meeting recognized standards rather than insisting on maximum efficiency even if the result is poorer service. Doing more with less is a nice phrase, but doing less with less is a more common outcome. Naturally, it is a blessing, whether in government or business, when efficiency and effectiveness coincide.

Public Service Motivation

Efforts to "make government run like a business" often squander a precious resource—the public service motivation that many public managers bring to their job. Public service motivation is not a myth. Since Rainey's pioneering work (1983), many empirical studies have confirmed the commitment of public managers to public service. Using data from the General Social Survey, Crewson (1997) compared the attitudes and work preferences of public and private employees in similar occupations, reporting that public managers were much more interested in being "useful to society" and in helping others and were less interested than private employees in promotion. Other studies (Wittmer 1991; Perry and Wise 1990) have come to quite similar conclusions.

Whether or not public managers are supposed to be "neutral competence" bureaucrats, the fact is that they are not. As Moore (1995, 298) notes, "A false assumption is that those who choose to work for the government are content with putting their own moral views about the public interest and public value in abeyance. In reality, many people work for the government precisely because they want to enact some particular view they have of the public interest. Indeed, that is one of the small compensations that government provides in what is otherwise an uncompetitive effort to recruit some of societies most talented individuals."

If Moore's interpretation is correct, would we not expect that efforts to run government like a business or to reduce the role of public managers to contract management would lead to low morale and defection of some of the most able public managers? Certainly the U.S. government reforms under the *National Performance Review* (Gore 1993) recognized this problem and suggested remedies that would entail providing more autonomy for public managers.

None of this suggests that the prescription for effective public management is uncontrolled bureaucrats self-actualizing, each in his or her idiosyncratic way. But there seems little danger of masses of out-of-control bureaucrats in the contemporary climate of hierarchy and markets. More likely is that the public spiritedness that so many public servants bring to their first government job will be beaten down as public managers are removed from the frontlines and replaced by contractors and consultants.

Consider the NPM vision of governance and its likely impact on any public service motivation that public employees bring to their job: "In modern governance, government and its CEOs act on the demand side of the public household, facing a number of suppliers . . . looking for government contracts" (Lane 2000, 5). We can speculate that Lane, one of several advocates for "contractualism" as an approach to governance, would not be put off by likely impacts on public service motivation. Lane observes: "The idea (public service motivation) has long ago been abandoned. . . . Replacing the assumption about vocation with the assumption about self-interest maximization opens up entirely new ways of looking at motivation in the public sector. If people active in the provision of public services in the public sector are driven by self-interests, then what stops them from pursuing strategies which reduce public interests?" (2000, 184). Lane's answer: contracts. Advocates of NPM, many of whom are enamored of principal–agent theory, view contracting as a panacea with little if any role for the public manager as provider of public service. Interestingly, this conceptualization is in many ways redolent of Frederic Taylor's scientific management and "Schmidt," the ideal, entirely substitutable worker. According to Taylorism, the job can be engineered scientifically and, when it is, the characteristics of the steel cutter are generally not relevant. According to NPM, if a suitable contracting process and effective contract can be developed, the characteristics of the individual public manager are not particularly relevant, at least assuming a sufficient competence in contract management. Yes, public managers can become transactions costs (see earlier discussion), but that does not imply that it is useful to assume that they will be.

Public Interest as Endgame

As noted in chapter 4, market theories begin with the ideal of the perfectly competitive market. But the concept of public interest advanced here is as an ideal, one shaped by the quest for public values. A pragmatic public interest is about deliberation, fairness, and the "discovery" of the public interest, a process begun with a public problem or public value pursuit. Market theory starts with an ideal against which to measure problems (i.e., market failure). Public interest theory starts with the problem (a public values failure) and then addresses the public values failure by posing public policies (and other putative "solutions," including market and quasimarket approaches as well as public–private partnerships).

A pragmatic concept of the public interest not only allows for but also requires multiple meanings of public interest. What, then, does this imply for Managing Publicness? It implies openness and a respect for deliberation and discourse. If one embraces the notion of a pragmatic, procedurally based public interest centering on fairness in its pursuit of public values, it is difficult to simultaneously Manage Publicly and manage dogmatically.

COMPARING NPM AND MANAGING PUBLICNESS

Table 10.1 compares Managing Publicness to NPM, adapting the summary table ("emergent" NPM) presented originally in chapter 2. Table 10.2 compares "developed characteristics." The differences are stark.

Given that NPM is firmly rooted in economic individualism and that Managing Publicness largely rejects it, differences between the two come as no surprise. NPM privileges the market and market-related approaches to governance; Managing Publicness, which emphasizes pragmatic approaches to public value, does not. NPM focuses on "streamlining" (i.e., reducing) public employee rosters and achieving public ends through contract; Managing Publicness focuses on maintaining government capacity and using contracts to supplement that capacity when contracts serve identifiable public

Table 10.1 Emergent Characteristics of NPM versus Managing Publicness

NPM	Managing Publicness
Preference for "hands-on" professional management; active, visible control from top managers	Emphasis on participation from lower echelon and from citizens in addition to "hands-on" professional management; active, visible control from top managers
Preference for quantitative indicators and explicit standards and measures of performance	Preference for outcomes-based performance management with outcomes focused on explicit public values
Emphasis on output controls; resources linked to performance and decentralized personnel management	Preference for resources linked to public value prerequisites, rather than performance
Disaggregation of bureaucratic units; unbundling of management systems into corporatized units centered on products and service and with decentralized budgets, dealing with one another "at arm's length"	Emphasis on the integration of public duties, coordination, but recognizing that the coordinated networks may be (often *should* be) temporary
Shift to greater competition, term contracts, and competitive bidding	Focus on maintaining capacity, contracting augmenting existing capacity; competitive bidding only when there is "real" competition (multiple vendors)
Emphasis on private-sector style management practices; greater flexibility in hiring and rewards	Neutral on management style; pragmatic choice of management approach; reinforce public service motivation
Stress on greater discipline and parsimony in resource use; cutting direct costs, resisting union demands, limiting businesses' compliance costs	Emphasis on effectiveness in achieving public values and administrative effectiveness

Source: Adapted from Hood (1991, 4–5); Pollitt (2003, 27–28).

values. NPM moves from theory to prescription to action; Managing Publicness moves from problem specification (public value failure) to action (pursuit of public value) to provisional theory (context-specific concept of the public interest).

A FINAL WORD ON PUBLIC VALUE

NPM developed fully as both a term of art and as a management trend in the 1990s and the first part of the twenty-first century, but it is already in decline in many of the nations from which it sprang. NPM was, early on, a creature of Thatcherism, but it took root most firmly in New Zealand and Australia, having never been fully embraced (though it was much discussed) in Europe.

Table 10.2   Comparing Developed Characteristics of NPM and Managing Publicness

NPM	Managing Publicness
A shift in management focus from input and processes to output	A shift from input and output to outcomes and distributional equity
A shift toward more measurement and quantification, especially in the form of systems of performance indicators	A shift toward capacity-based and outcomes-based performance indicators
A preference for more specialized, "lean," "flat," and autonomous organization forms; "arm's length" relations among agencies	A preference for neutral on organizational design, pragmatically choose those that are most effective
Use of contracts or contract-agency relationships in lieu of formal and hierarchical relationships	Use of contracts to supplement agency capacity
Much wider than hitherto deployment of markets or marketlike mechanisms for the delivery of public services	Skeptical about marketlike mechanisms; judge on basis of public value achievements
Broadening and blurring of the frontiers between the public sector, the market sector, and the voluntary sector	Neutral on ownership arrangements and sector blurring
Shift in value priorities away from universalism, equity, security, an resilience toward efficiency and individualism	Shift in value priorities toward equity, community, and pragmatically determined public interest

With the evolution from Thatcherism to Blair's "third way" and the late 1990s' electoral change in New Zealand, the contract state seems less influential than before.

Of course, U.S. policymakers rarely use the term NPM, but why would they? As perhaps the world's strongest and most enduring experiment in economic individualism, the United States is largely inured to the market governance trends of nouveau riche market reformers. For more than forty years privatization and contracting out have continued to advance in the United States at all levels of government, as demonstrated by the few cases presented in chapter 2. These market approaches are so pervasive that they need no collective term such as NPM. Is privatization on the decline in the United States? At this turning point in political history, it seems too early to judge. However, economic individualism seems to be on solid ground.

One might argue that there has been only one period in U.S. history, the era of Franklin D. Roosevelt's administration to Lyndon Johnson's, a period of about thirty years, where the nation, recovering from economic depression, was not largely in the throes of economic individualism with respect to its policymaking assumptions, its policies, and its public management regime. In the United

States the federal bureaucracy has oftentimes posed the only check against the domination of economic individualism and the most steadfast and consistent pursuer of public value. If recent U.S. public management trends continue, however, the ideal of the public-manager-as-contractor and government-as-residual will surely find its apotheosis in this nation. Interestingly, the United States is also known for having only one truly original philosophical contribution—pragmatism. Perhaps a pragmatic conceptualization of public interest theory, when taken with a public management approach bent on achieving public value, can serve as a balance wheel to the even more fundamental philosophy of economic individualism.

REFERENCES

Abbate, J. 1999. *Inventing the Internet.* Cambridge, MA: MIT Press.

Abbott v. Burke I, 100 N.J. 269, 495 A.2d 376 (1985).

Abbott v. Burke X *(Maintenance Budget Order),* 177 N.J. 596, 832 A.2nd 906 (July 2003 M-976 September Term 2002).

Acemoglou, D., and T. Verdier. 2000. The choice between market failures and corruption. *American Economic Review* 90 (2): 194–211.

Ackerman, B., and I. Ayres. 2002. *Voting with dollars: A new paradigm for campaign finance.* New Haven, CT: Yale University Press.

Ackerman, B., and J. Fishkin. 2004. *Deliberation day.* New Haven, CT: Yale University Press.

Agricultural Research Service. 2001. Why USDA's technology protection system (aka "Terminator") benefits agriculture. *ARS News & Information* website, www.ars.usda .gov/is/br/tps/ (Accessed November 2, 2006).

Alchian, A. A., and H. Demsetz. 1972. Production, information costs, and economic organization. *American Economic Review* 62 (3): 777–99.

———. 1973. The property rights paradigm. *Journal of Economic History* 33 (1): 16–27.

Alford, J. 2002. Why do public-sector clients co-produce? Toward a contingency theory. *Administration and Society* 34 (1): 32–47.

Almond, G. A., and S. Verba. 1963. *Civic culture.* Boston: Little, Brown, and Company.

Anderson, C. J., and C. A. Guillory. 1997. Political institutions and satisfaction with democracy: A cross-national analysis of consensus and majoritarian systems. *American Political Science Review* 91 (1): 66–81.

Anderson, E. 1993. *Value in ethics and economics.* Cambridge, MA: Harvard University Press.

Antonsen, M., and T. Jørgensen. 1997. The "publicness" of public organizations. *Public Administration* 75 (2): 337–57.

Appel, H. 2000. The ideological determinants of liberal economic reform. *World Politics* 52 (4): 520–49.

Appleby, Paul. 1952. *Morality and administration in democratic government.* Baton Rouge: Louisiana State University Press.

Arthur, W. B. 1988. Self-reinforcing mechanisms in economics. In *The economy as an evolving complex system,* ed. P. W. Anderson, David Pines, and Kenneth Arrow, 33–48. Boston: Addison-Wesley.

Associated Press. 2003. Bush sticks with Iraqi contract ban: Annan sides with France, Germany, Russia, others. December 11. Available at www.msnbc.msn.com/id/ 3676000/ (Accessed August 4, 2006).

Atkinson, A., and F. Bourguignon. 1982. The comparison of multidimensional distributions of economic status. *Review of Economic Studies* 49 (2): 183–201.

Aucoin, P. 1995. *The new public management: Canada in comparative perspective.* Montreal: IRPP.

Austin, J., and G. Coventry. 2001. *Emerging issues on privatized prisons* (NCJ #181249). Washington, DC: Bureau of Justice Assistance.

Babcock, C., and M. Renaee. 2005. U.S. accuses pair of rigging Iraq contracts. November 18, p. A01. Available at www.washingtonpost.com/wp-dyn/content/article/2005/ 11/17/AR2005111701879.html (Accessed August 10, 2006).

Bannock, G., R. Baxter, R. Reese, and E. Davis. 2004. *Penguin dictionary of economics.* 7th ed. New York: Penguin Press.

Ban Terminator Campaign. 2006. UN upholds moratorium on terminator seed technology, March 31. www.banterminator.org/news_updates/news_updates/un_upholds_moratorium_on_terminator_seed_technology (Accessed November 2, 2006).

Barber, B. 1984. *Strong democracy: Participatory politics for a new age.* Berkeley: University of California Press.

Barber, W. J. 1999. The money interest and the public interest. *Economic Journal* 109 (4): 477–79.

Barnett, P., and S. Newberry. 2002. Reshaping community mental health services in a restructured state: New Zealand, 1984–97. *Public Management Review* 4 (2): 187–208.

Barry, B. 1965. *Political argument.* New York: Humanities Press.

———. 1967. The public interest. In *Political philosophy,* ed. A. Quinton, 122–34. Oxford: Oxford University Press.

Barzelay, M. 2001. *The new public management: Improving research and policy dialogue.* Berkeley: University of California Press.

Bator, F. 1958. The anatomy of market failure. *Quarterly Journal of Economics* 72 (3): 351–79.

BBC News. 2004. European Union lifts GM food ban. May 19. Available at http://news .bbc.co.uk/2/hi/europe/3727827.stm (Accessed July 12, 2006).

BBC News. 2006. Call to allow body organ selling. February 16. http://news.bbc.co.uk/1/ hi/health/4719374.stm (Accessed October 25, 2006).

Beach, W., A. Goyburu, R. Rector, D. John, K. Johnson, and T. Bingel. 2004. Peace of mind in retirement: Making future generations better off by fixing social security. Heritage Foundation, *Center for Data Analysis Report* No. CDA04–06, August 11. www .heritage.org/Research/SocialSecurity/CDA04-06.cfm (Accessed November 10, 2006).

Bearak, B. 2002. Bangladeshis sipping arsenic as plan for safe water stalls. *New York Times,* July 14, 2002, section 1, p. 1.

Becker, G. 1974. A theory of marriage. In *Economics of the family,* ed. T. W. Schultz, 299–344. Chicago: University of Chicago Press.

Becker, L. 1973. *On justifying moral judgments.* London: Routledge and Kegan Paul.

Beckett, J. 2000. The "government should run like a business" mantra. *American Review of Public Administration* 30 (2): 185–204.

Benditt, T. M. 1973. The public interest. *Philosophy and Public Affairs* 2:291–311.

Benn, S. I., and R. S. Peters. 1959. *Social principles and the democratic state.* London: Allen and Unwin.

Bennett, S., and A. Mills. 1998. Government capacity to contract. *Public Administration and Development* 18 (4): 307–26.

Benson, B. 1998. *To serve and protect: Privatization and community in criminal justice.* New York: New York University Press.

Bentham, Jeremy. 1977. *A fragment of government.* New York: Cambridge University Press.

Bentley, A. F. 1908. *The process of government.* Chicago: University of Chicago Press.

Berle, A., and G. Means. 1932. *The modern corporation and private property.* New York: Harcourt, Brace and World.

Birdsall, N., and J. Nellis, eds. 2005. *The distributional impact of privatization in developing countries.* Washington, DC: Center for Global Development, Brookings Institution Press.

Blancard, L., C. Hinnant, and W. Wong. 1998. Market-based reforms in government: Toward a social subcontract? *Administration & Society* 30 (5): 483–512.

Bohman, J. 2000. *Public deliberation: Pluralism, complexity, and democracy.* Cambridge, MA: MIT Press.

Boleyn-Fitzgerald, P. 1999. Misfortune, welfare reform, and right-wing egalitarianis. *Critical Review* 13 (1–2): 141–63.

Bolton, P., and J. Farrell. 1990. Decentralization, duplication, and delay. *Journal of Political Economy* 98 (4): 803–26.

Bond, E. 1981. On desiring the desirable. *Philosophy.* 56 (4): 489–96.

Booth, W. J. 1994. A note on the idea of the moral economy. *American Political Science Review* 88 (4): 653–67.

Boschken, H. 1992. Analyzing performance skewness in public agencies: The case of urban mass transit. *Journal of Public Administration Research and Theory* 2 (3): 265–88.

Boston, J., P. Dalziel, and S. St. John. 1999. *Re-designing the welfare state in New Zealand.* Auckland: Oxford University Press.

Bostrom, A., C. Atman, B. Fischhoff, and G. Morgan. 1994. Evaluating risk communications: Completing and correcting mental models of hazardous processes. *Risk Analysis* 14 (5): 789–802.

Bower, T. 1987. *The paperclip conspiracy: The hunt for the Nazi scientists.* Boston: Little, Brown.

Bowler, S., T. Donovan, and R. Hanneman. 2003. Art for democracy's sake? Group membership and political engagement in Europe. *Journal of Politics* 65 (4): 1111–29.

Box, R. C. 1992. The administrator as trustee of the public-interest: Normative ideals and daily practice. *Administration and Society* 24 (3): 323–45.

Boyne, G. 2002. Public and private management: What's the difference? *Journal of Management Studies* 39 (1): 97–122.

———. 2006. Strategies for public service turnaround: Lessons from the private sector? *Administration and Society* 38 (3): 365–88.

Boyne, G., and R. Walker. 2004. Strategy and content in public service organizations. *Journal of Public Administration Research and Theory* 14 (2): 231–52.

Bozeman, B. 1984. Dimensions of publicness: An approach to public organization theory. In *New directions in public administration,* ed. B. Bozeman and J. Straussman, 46–62. Belmont, CA: Crooks/Cole.

———. 1987. *All organizations are public.* San Francisco: Jossey-Bass.

———. 2000. *Bureaucracy and red tape.* Englewood Cliffs, NJ: Prentice Hall.

———. 2002. Public value failure: When efficient markets may not do. *Public Administration Review* 62 (2): 134–51.

———. 2004. *All organizations are public.* [Reprinted]. Silver Spring, MD: Beard Books.

Bozeman, B., and S. Bretschneider. 1994. The "publicness puzzle" in organization theory: A test of alternative explanations of differences between public and private organizations. *Journal of Public Administration Research and Theory* 4 (2): 197–224.

Bozeman, B., and L. DeHart-Davis. 1999. Red tape and clean air: Title V pollution permitting implementation as a test bed for theory development. *Journal of Public Administration Research and Theory* 9 (1): 141–77.

Bozeman, B., and M. Gaughan. 2002. Public value mapping of science outcomes: Theory and method. Report to the Rockefeller Foundation. Consortium for Science, Policy and Outcomes, Arizona State University. www.cspo.org/products/rocky/Rock-Vol2-3.PDF (Accessed July 14, 2004).

Bozeman, B., and P. Hirsch. 2006. Science ethics as a bureaucratic problem: IRBs, rules, and failures of control. *Policy Sciences* 38 (4): 269–91.

Bozeman, B., and G. Kingsley. 1998. Risk culture in public and private organizations. *Public Administration Review* 58 (2): 109–19.

Bozeman, B., and S. Pandey. 2004. Public management decision making: Effects of decision content. *Public Administration Review* 64 (5): 553–65.

Bozeman, B., and J. Rogers. 2002. A churn model of scientific knowledge value. *Research Policy* 31 (5): 769–94.

Bozeman, B., and D. Sarewitz. 2005. Public failure in science policy. *Science and Public Policy* 32 (2): 119–36.

Bozeman, B., and L. Wilson. 2004. Market-based management of government laboratories. *Public Performance and Management Review* 28 (2): 168–87.

Brandt, R. 1983. The concept of a moral right and its function. *Journal of Philosophy* 80 (1): 29–45.

Braybrooke, D. 1972. The public interest: The present and future of the concept. *Journal of Philosophy* 69 (2): 197–99.

Breton, A. 1965. A theory of government grants. *The Canadian Journal of Economics and Political Science* 31 (2): 175–87.

Bretschneider, S. 1990. Management information systems in public and private organizations: An empirical test. *Public Administration Review* 50 (5): 536–45.

Brewer, G. A. 2003. Building social capital: Civic attitudes and behavior of public servants. *Journal of Public Administration Research and Theory* 13 (1): 5–25.

Brewer, L. 1996. In the public interest: Symposium introduction. *Policy Studies Journal* 24 (1): 97–99.

Brooks, A. C. 2004. The effects of public policy on private charity. *Administration and Society* 36 (2): 166–85.

Brown, P. 1992. The failure of market failures. *Journal of Socio-Economics* 21 (1): 1–24.

———. 1994. *Restoring the public trust.* Boston: Beacon Press.

Bruce, N. 1998. *Public finance and the American economy.* Reading, MA: Addison Wesley.

Buchanan, J. 1978. Markets, states, and the extent of morals. *American Economic Review* 68 (2): 364–71.

Buchanan, J., and G. Tullock. 1962. *The calculus of consent.* Ann Arbor: University of Michigan Press.

Bucy, J. F. 1985. Meeting the competitive challenge: The case for R&D tax credits. *Issues in Science and Technology* 6 (2): 69–78.

Budd, J., and L. Connaway. 1997. University faculty and networked information: Results of a survey. *Journal of the American Society for Information Science* 48 (9): 843–52.

Burnett, J. 2003. Examining Halliburton's "sweetheart" deal in Iraq: Experts say lucrative contracts yield razor-thin profit margins. Business. *All Things Considered,* National Public Radio. December 22. www.npr.org/templates/story/story.php?storyId=1559574 (Accessed July 10, 2006)

———. 2006. Pentagon to change bid process for Iraq contracts. Nation, *All Things Considered,* National Public Radio. July 12. www.npr.org/templates/story/story.php?storyId=5552578 (Accessed July 14, 2006)

Burstein, P. 2000. Voices and echoes for the environment: Public interest representation in the 1990s and beyond. *American Journal of Sociology* 106 (2): 523–25.

Cadwallader, E. 1980. The main features of value experience. *Journal of Value Inquiry* 14 (3): 229–44.

Caiden, G., and P. Sundaram. 2004. The specificity of public service reform. *Public Administration and Development* 24 (5): 373–83.

Camm, F. 1996. *Expanding private production of defense service.* Washington, DC: RAND Corporation Press.

Campbell, H., and R. Marshall. 2000. Moral obligations, planning, and the public interest: A commentary on current British practice. *Environment and Planning B—Planning & Design* 27 (2): 297–312.

Card, R. F. 2004. Consequentialism, teleology, and the new friendship critique. *Pacific Philosophical Quarterly* 85 (2): 149–72.

Caspary, W. R. 2000. *Dewey on democracy.* Ithaca, NY: Cornell University Press.

Cassinelli, C. W. 1958. Some reflections on the concept of the public interest. *Ethics* 69:48–61.

Caulfield, J. 2006. The politics of bureau reform in sub-Saharan Africa. *Public Administration and Development* 26 (1): 15–26.

Champlin, D., and J. Knoedler. 2002. Operating in the public interest or in pursuit of private profits? *Journal of Economic Issues* 36 (2): 459–68.

Chandler, D. 2001. *Semiotics: The basics.* London: Routledge.

Chandra, P. 1991. Kidneys for sale. *World Press Review,* February, 53.

Choi, James J., David Laibson, and Brigitte C. Madrian. 2006. Why does the law of one price fail? An experiment on index mutual funds. www.som.yale.edu/faculty/jjc83/fees.pdf (Accessed August 8, 2006).

Chun, Y., and H. Rainey. 2005. Goal ambiguity and organizational performance in U.S. federal agencies. *Journal of Public Administration Research and Theory* 15 (4): 529–57.

Clarkson, K. W. 1980. Managerial behavior in nonproprietary organizations. In *The economics of nonproprietary organizations*, ed. Kenneth W. Clarkson and Donald L. Martin, 214–34. Greenwich, CT: Jai Press.

Cochran, C. E. 1973. The politics of interest: Philosophy and the limitations of the science of politics. *American Journal of Political Science* 17 (4): 745–66.

———. 1974. Political science and "the public interest." *The Journal of Politics* 36 (2): 327–55.

Coghlan, A. 2003. Zambia's GM food fear traced to UK. *New Scientist*, January 29, p. 19.

Cohen, E. 1978. Epistemology of value. *Auslegung* 5 (1): 176–98.

Cohen, J. 1997. Procedure and substance in deliberative democracy. In *Deliberative democracy: Essays on reason in politics,* ed. J. Bohman and W. Rehg, 407–37. Cambridge, MA: MIT Press.

Cointreau-Levine, S. 1994. *Private sector participation in municipal solid waste services in developing countries.* Washington, DC. Published for the Urban Management Programme by the World Bank.

Cooper, N. 1981. *The diversity of moral thinking.* Oxford, UK: Clarendon Press.

Coursey, D., and B. Bozeman. 1990. Decision making in public and private organizations: A test of alternative concepts of "publicness." *Public Administration Review* 50 (5): 525–35.

Cowen, T. 2006. *Public goods and externalities: The concise encyclopedia of economics.* www.econlib.org/library/ENC/PublicGoodsandExternalities.html (Accessed October 30, 2006)

Cox, J. W. R. 1973. The appeal to the public interest. *British Journal of Political Science* 1 (4): 229–41.

Crewson, P. 1997. Public service motivation: Building empirical evidence of incidence and effect. *Journal of Public Administration Research and Theory* 7 (4): 449–518.

Crouch, M. 1999. How the terminator terminates: An explanation for the nonscientist of a remarkable patent for killing second generation seeds of crop plants. Rev. ed. Edmonds, WA: Edmonds Institute, Occasional Paper.

Crow, M., and B. Bozeman. 1998. *Limited by design: R&D laboratories in the U.S. national innovation system.* New York: Columbia University Press.

Dahl, R., and C. Lindblom. 1953. *Politics, economics, and welfare.* New York: Harper Torchbooks.

Daniels, C. 2006. An invisible population: Sandy Springs' homeless increasing. *Atlanta Journal-Constitution*, August 24. www.ajc.com/search/content/metro/northfulton/stories/nfxhomeless0824.html (Accessed August 25, 2006)

Davies, D. 1971. The efficiency of public vs. private firms: The case of Australia's two airlines. *Journal of Law and Economics* 14 (1): 149–65.

———. 1977. Property rights and economic efficiency: The Australian airlines revisited. *Journal of Law and Economics* 20 (2): 223–26.

Davis, J. R., and J. Hulett. 1977. *An analysis of market failure.* Gainesville: University of Florida.

De Alessi, L. 1969. Implications of property rights for government investment choices. *American Economic Review* 59 (1): 13–24.

De Bruijn, H., and W. Dicke. 2006. Strategies for safeguarding public values in liberalized utility sectors. *Public Administration* 84 (3): 717–35.

DeHart-Davis, L., and S. Pandey. 2005. Red tape and public employees: Does perceived rule dysfunction alienate managers? *Journal of Public Administration Research and Theory*, 15 (1): 133–48.

deLeon, P. 1995. Democratic values and the policy sciences. *Policy Sciences* 49 (4): 886–905.

Demortain, D. 2004. Public organizations, stakeholders and the construction of publicness. *Public Administration* 82 (4): 975–93.

Demsetz, H. 1967. Toward a theory of property rights. *American Economic Review* 57 (1): 347–59.

———. 1969. Information and efficiency: Another viewpoint. *Journal of Law and Economics* 12 (1): 1–22.

Denzau, A., and D. North. 1994. Shared mental models: Ideologies and institutions. *Kyklos* 47 (1): 3–31.

DePaul, M., & Ramsey, W., eds. 1998. *Rethinking intuition: The psychology of intuition and its role in philosophical inquiry.* Lanham, MD: Rowman & Littlefield.

DeRose, L., E. Messer, and S. Millman. 1998. *Who's hungry? And how do we know? Food shortage, poverty, and deprivation.* New York: United Nations University Press.

Dewey, J. 1927. *The public and its problems.* New York: Holt.

———. [1927] 1988. *The public and its problems.* In *The later works of John Dewey, 1925–1953,* vol. 2, ed. J. A. Boydston, 238–372. Carbondale: Southern Illinois University Press.

———. [1935] 2000. *Liberalism and social action.* Amherst: Prometheus Books.

Dhiratayakinant, K. 1995. The impacts of privatization on distributional equity in Thailand. In *Privatization and equity,* ed. V. V. Ramandadham, 99–117. London: Routledge.

Diamond, P. 1977. A framework for Social Security analysis. *Journal of Public Economics* 8 (3): 275–98.

———. 1996. Proposals to restructure social security. *Journal of Economic Perspectives* 10 (2): 67–88.

Diggs, B. J. 1973. The common good as reason for political action. *Ethics* 83:283–93.

DiIulio, J. 1994. Principled agents: The cultural bases of behavior in a federal government bureaucracy. *Journal of Public Administration Research and Theory* 4 (2): 277–318.

Dobbin, F., and T. Dowd. 1997. How policy shapes competition: Early railroad foundings in Massachusetts. *Administrative Science Quarterly* 42 (3): 501–29.

Domberger, S., and P. Jensen. 1997. Contracting out by the public sector: Theory, evidence, prospects. *Oxford Review of Economic Policy* 134 (4): 67–78.

Donahue, J. 1991. *The privatization decision.* New York: Basic Books.

Dorrell, O. 2006. Some new cities outsource city hall. *USA Today,* September 15, pp. 1, 4.

Douglass, B. 1980. The common good and the public interest. *Political Theory* 8:103–17.

Downs, A. 1962. The public interest: Its meaning in a democracy. *Social Research* 29 (1): 1–36.

Driscoll, M. 2003. George Bush says GM food will be Africa's salvation. *Sunday Times (London),* June 29, p. 8.

Dryzek, John. 2002. *Deliberative democracy and beyond: Liberals, critics, contestations.* Oxford: Oxford University Press.

Duch, R., and H. Palmer. 2004. It's not whether you win or lose, but how you play the game: Self-interest, social justice, and mass attitudes toward market transition. *American Political Science Review* 98 (3): 437–52.

Dutta, D., and M. Heininger. 1999. Complementarity of market and state intervention in the context of Australia's structural reforms since the early 1980s. *International Journal of Social Economics* 26 (7–9): 955–62.

Easton, D. 1957. An approach to the analysis of political systems. *World Politics* 9 (3): 383–400.

Eaton, D., F. Van Tongeren, N. Louwaars, B. Visser, and I. Van der Meer. 2002. Economic and policy aspects of "terminator" technology. *Biotechnology and Development Monitor* 49:19–22.

Eisenhower, D. 1954. Special message to the Congress on old age and survivors insurance and on federal grants-in-aid for public assistance programs—January 14, 1954. www.socialsecurity.gov/history/pres.html (Accessed July 30, 2006)

Elcock, Howard. 2006. The public interest and public administration. *Politics* 26 (2): 101–9.

Eldridge, M. 1998. *Transforming experience: John Dewey's cultural instrumentalism.* Nashville, TN: Vanderbilt University Press.

Emmert, M., and M. Crow. 1988. Public, private and hybrid organizations: An empirical examination of the role of publicness. *Administration and Society* 20 (2): 216–44.

Engerer, H. 2001. *Privatization and its limits in Central and Eastern Europe: Property rights in transition.* London: MacMillan.

ETC Group. 1998. Terminator technology targets farmers. *Communique,* March 30. www.etcgroup.org/article.asp?newsid=188 (Accessed March 10, 2005).

———. 1999. The terminator's wider implications. *Communique,* January 30. www.etcgroup.org/article.asp?newsid+184 (Accessed March 10, 2005)

———. 2002. Sterile harvest: New crop of terminator patents threatens food sovereignty. January 31. www.etcgroup.org/article.asp?newsid=290 (Accessed March 10, 2005)

European Public Health Alliance. 2004. BMA calls for further research to address public concerns over gm foods. www.epha.org/a/1116 (Accessed July 13, 2004).

Evans, K. 2000. Reclaiming John Dewey. *Administration & Society 32* (3): 308.

Farber, S., and R. Costanza. 1987. Economic value of wetlands systems. *Journal of Environmental Management* 24 (1): 41–51.

Farmer, A., and R. Bates. 1996. Community versus market: A comparative investigation. *Comparative Political Studies* 29 (4): 379–99.

Faulhaber, G. 1987. Comment: The role of government in a mixed economy. *Journal of Policy Analysis and Management* 6 (3): 557–61.

Faulkner, W. 1994. Conceptualizing knowledge used in innovation: A second look at the science-technology distinction and industrial innovation. *Science, Technology, & Human Values* 19 (4): 425–58.

Feeney, M. K., and B. Bozeman. 2007. Public values and public failure: Implications of the 2004–2005 flu vaccine case. *Public Integrity* 9 (2): 175–90.

Feigenbaum, H., J. Henig, and C. Hamnett. 1998. *Shrinking the state: The political underpinnings of privatization.* London: Cambridge University Press.

Fenno, R. 1973. *Congress in committees.* Boston: Little, Brown.

Fesler, J. 1990. The state and its study: The whole and the parts. In *Public administration: The state of the discipline,* ed. N. Lynn and A. Wildavsky, 84–97. Chatham, NJ: Chatham House.

Festenstein, M. 1997. *Pragmatism and political theory: From Dewey to Rorty.* Chicago: University of Chicago Press.

Fisher, R., W. Ury, and B. Patton. 1992. *Getting to yes: Negotiating agreement without giving in.* New York: Penguin Books.

Flathman, R. E. 1966. *The public interest: An essay concerning the normative discourse of politics.* New York: John Wiley and Sons.

Flynn, N. 1990. *Public sector management.* Brighton, UK: Harvester Press.

Frank, T. 2004. *What's the matter with Kansas: How conservatives won the heart of America.* New York: Metropolitan Books.

Frederickson, H. G. 1982. The recovery of civism in public-administration. *Public Administration Review* 42 (6): 501–8.

———. 1991. Toward a theory of the public for public administration. *Administration and Society* 22 (4): 395–417.

———. 1994. Can public officials correctly be said to have obligations to future generations? *Public Administration Review* 54 (5): 457–64.

———. 1996. Comparing the reinventing government movement with the new public administration. *Public Administration Review* 56 (3): 263–70.

———. 1997. *The spirit of public administration.* San Francisco: Jossey-Bass.

Friedman, S., S. Dunwoody, and C. Rogers, eds. 1999. *Communicating uncertainty: Media coverage of new and controversial science.* New York: Lawrence Erlbaum Associates.

Furubotn, E. G., and R. Richter. 2005. *Institutions and economic theory: An introduction to and assessment of the new institutional economics*. Ann Arbor: University of Michigan Press.

Galiani, S., P. Gertler, and E. Schargrodsky. 2005. Water for life: The impact of the privatization of water services on child mortality. *Journal of Political Economy* 113 (1): 83–90.

Garrison, J. 2000. Pragmatism and public administration. *Administration and Society* 32 (4): 458–78.

Garza, R. 1996. Will the real Americans please stand up: Anglo and Mexican-American support of core American political values. *American Journal of Political Science* 40 (2): 335–51.

Gaus, G. F. 1990. *Value and justification: The foundations of liberal theory*. New York: Cambridge University Press.

Gawthrop, L. 1998. *Public service and democracy*. New York: Chatham House.

Gert, B. 1973. *The moral rules*. New York: Harper and Row.

Gest, David. 2006. Georgia county battles breakaway city over parkland. *Atlanta Journal-Constitution,* June 22. www.planetizen.com/node/20256 (Accessed July 10, 2006)

Gevers, L. 1979. On interpersonal comparability and social welfare orderings. *Econometrica* 47 (1): 75–89.

Ghosh, Palash R. 2006. Private prisons have a lock on growth: With state-run prisons overflowing, outfits such as Corrections Corp. of America stand to benefit. *Business Week Online,* July 7.

Gittinger, J. P., J. Leslie, and C. Hoisington, eds. 1987. *Food policy: Integrating supply, distribution, and consumption*. Baltimore: Johns Hopkins University Press.

Glanz, J. 2006a. Army to pay Halliburton unit most costs disputed by audit. *New York Times,* February 27.

———. 2006b. Auditors find widespread waste and unfinished work in Iraqi rebuilding contracts. *New York Times,* January 31.

Goldstein, S., and M. Naor. 2005. Linking publicness to operations management practices: A study of quality management practices in hospitals. *Journal of Operations Management* 23 (2): 209–28.

Goodin, R. 1995. *Utilitarianism as public philosophy*. New York: Cambridge University Press.

———. 1996. Institutionalizing the public interest: The defense of deadlock and beyond. *American Political Science Review* 90 (2): 331–42.

Goodman, A. 2005. Dahr Jamail on Iraqi hospitals under occupation, war profiteering and the "brain drain" out of Iraq. July 14. Transcript of interview with Dahr Jamail. www.democracynow.org/article.pl?sid=05/07/14/1345204 (Accessed August 3, 2006)

Goodsell, C. T. 1989. Balancing competing values. In *Handbook of public administration,* ed. James Perry, 575–84. San Francisco: Jossey-Bass.

———. 1990. Public administration and the public interest. In *Refounding public administration,* ed. G. L. Wamsley, 96–113. Newbury Park, CA: Sage Publications.

———. 2003. *The case for bureaucracy: A public administration polemic*. 4th ed. Washington, DC: CQ Press.

Gore, A. 1993. *National performance review*. Washington, DC: Plume.

Grand, J. 1991. The theory of government failure. *British Journal of Political Science* 21 (4): 423–42.

Grant, W. 2000. In the public interest: Competition policy and the monopolies and mergers commission. *Public Administration* 78 (4): 991–92.

Gregory, R. 2002. Transforming governmental culture. In *New public management,* ed. T. Christensen and Per Laegreid, 231–58. Hampshire, England: Ashgate.

Grindle, M., and M. Hilderbrand. 1995. Building sustainable capacity in the public sector. *Public Administration and Development* 15 (5): 441–63.

Groopman, J. 1999. Life by design: The moral way to pay for human organs. *New York Times,* May 7, p. 27.

Guttman, D. 1976. *The shadow government: The government's multi-billion-dollar give-away of its decision-making powers to private management consultants, "experts" and think tanks.* New York: Random House.

Habermas, J. 1996. *Between facts and norm: Contributions to a discourse theory of law and democracy.* Cambridge, Mass.: MIT Press.

Halvorsen, K. E. 2003. Assessing the effects of public participation. *Public Administration Review* 63 (5): 535–43.

Haque, M. 2001. The diminishing publicness of public service under the current mode of governance source. *Public Administration Review* 61 (1): 65–84.

Hare, R. M. 1952. *The language of morals.* Oxford, UK: Clarendon Press.

Harmon, Amy. 1999. Illegal kidney auction pops up on eBay's site. *New York Times,* September 3, A14.

Harmon, G. 2000. *Explaining value: And other essays in moral philosophy.* New York: Oxford University Press.

Harris, M., and A. Raviv. 1978. Some results on incentive contacts with applications to education and employment, health insurance, and law enforcement. *American Economic Review* 68 (1): 20–30.

Hart, S. 1949. *Treatise on values.* New York: Philosophical Library.

Hausker, K. 1992. The politics and economics of auction design in the market for sulfur dioxide pollution. *Journal of Policy Analysis and Management* 11 (4): 553–72.

Hausman, W., and J. Neufeld. 1991. Property rights versus public spirit: Ownership and efficiency of U.S. electric utilities prior to rate-of-return regulation. *Review of Economics and Statistics* 73 (3): 414–23.

Hefetz, A., and M. Warner. 2004. Privatization and its reverse: Explaining the dynamics of the government contracting process. *Journal of Public Administration Research and Theory* 14 (2): 171–90.

Heinrich, C., and E. Fournier. 2004. Dimensions of publicness and performance in substance abuse treatment organizations. *Journal of Policy Analysis and Management* 23 (1): 49–70.

Held, V. 1970. *The public interest and individual interests.* New York: Basic Books.

Helmer, O., and N. Rescher. 1959. On the epistemology of the inexact sciences. *Management Science* 6 (1): 25–52.

Hempel, C. G. 1966. *Philosophy of natural science.* Englewood Cliffs, NJ: Prentice Hall.

Henisz, W., B. Zelner, A. Bennet, and M. Guillen. 2005. The worldwide diffusion of market-oriented infrastructure reform, 1977–1999. *American Sociological Review* 70 (6): 871–97.

Herman, B. 1985. The practice of moral judgment. *The Journal of Philosophy* 82 (8): 414–36.

Herring, E. P. 1936. *Public administration and the public interest.* New York: McGraw-Hill.

Hertzberg, H. 2005a. Unsocial insecurity. *The New Yorker,* January 24. The Talk of the Town: 31.

———. 2005b. Untrustworthy. *The New Yorker,* March 28. Comment.

Hickman, L. 1996. Nature as culture: John Dewey's pragmatic naturalism. In *Environmental pragmatism,* ed. A. Light and E. Katz, 50–72. London: Routledge.

Hinckley, B. 1971. *The seniority system in congress.* Bloomington: Indiana University Press.

Hirsch, W. 1995. Contracting out by urban governments: A review. *Urban Affairs Review* 30 (3): 458–72.

Hood, C. 1991. A public management for all seasons. *Public Administration* 69 (1): 3–19.

Hood, Chris, and Guy Peters. 2004. The middle aging of new public management: Into the age of paradox? *Journal of Public Administration Research and Theory* 14 (3): 267–82.

Horn, M. J. 1995. *The political economy of public administration: Institutional choice in the public sector.* Cambridge: Cambridge University Press.

Howarth, R., and R. Norgaard. 1990. Intergenerational resource rights, efficiency and social optimality. *Land Economics* 66 (1): 1–11.

Hulbert, Mark. 2006. Same portfolio, higher cost: So why choose it? April 9, Money and Business/Financial Desk; Strategies: 11. *The New York Times.*

Hunter, James. 1991. *Culture wars: The struggle to define America.* New York: Harper Collins.

Hutchings, V., N. Valentino, T. Philpot, and K. Ismail. 2004. The compassion strategy. *Public Opinion Quarterly* 68 (4): 512–42.

International Consortium of Investigative Journalists (ICIJ). 2003. *The water barons.* Center for Public Integrity, Project details and publications available at www .publicintegrity.org/water (Accessed August 10, 2006).

Isett, K., and K. Provan. 2005. The evolution of dyadic interorganizational relationships in a network of publicly funded nonprofit agencies. *Journal of Policy Analysis and Management* 15 (2): 149–65.

Jaffe, W. 1972. Pareto translated: A review article. *Journal of Economic Literature* 10, (4): 1190–1201.

Jamail, D. 2005a. Iraqi hospitals ailing under occupation. Submitted as Evidence to the Jury of Conscience during the Culminating Session of the World Tribunal on Iraq. *Istanbul 23–27,* June. http://dahrjamailiraq.com/reports/HealthcareUnderOccupation DahrJamail.htm (Accessed July 16, 2006)

———. 2005b. On Iraqi hospitals under occupation, war profiteering and the "brain drain" out of iraq. *Democracy Now,* July 14. www.democracynow.org/article.pl?sid=05/07/ 14/1345204 (Accessed July 17, 2006)

James, M. 1981. Public interest and majority rule in Bentham's democratic theory. *Political Theory* 9 (1): 49–64.

James, O. 2000. Regulation inside government: Public interest justifications and regulatory failures. *Public Administration* 78 (2): 327–42.

Jennings, P. H. 1996. The effect of publicness on the energy technology decision process. *Journal of Technology Transfer* 21 (1): 27–33.

Jensen, M., and W. Meckling. 1976. Theory of the firm: Managerial behavior, agency costs and ownership structure. *Journal of Financial Economics* 3 (2): 303–60.

Jewkes, J., D. Sawers, and R. Stillerman. 1958. *The sources of invention.* New York: Norton Library.

Joassart-Marcelli, P., and J. Musso. 2005. Municipal service provision choices within a metropolitan area. *Urban Affairs Review* 40 (4): 492–519.

Johnson-Laird, P. N. 1983. *Mental models: Towards a cognitive science of language, inference, and consciousness.* Cambridge, MA: Harvard University Press.

Johnston, J. M., and B. Romzek. 1999. Contracting and accountability issues in a state medicaid reform: Rhetoric, theories, and reality. *Public Administration Review* 59 (5): 383–99.

Joint Center for Political and Economic Studies. 1999. *National opinion poll: Politics, 1998.* Washington, DC: Joint Center for Political and Economic Studies.

Jones, J. 1993. *Bad blood: The Tuskegee syphilis experiment.* New York: Free Press.

———. 1999. Science, medicine, and the future: Genetically modified foods. *British Medical Journal* 318:581–84.

Jørgensen, T. 1993. Modes of governance and administrative change. In *Modern governance: New government-society interactions,* ed. J. Kooiman, 219–32. London: Sage.

———. 1996. Rescuing public services: On the tasks of public organizations. In *Quality, innovation and measurement in the public sector,* ed. H. Hill, H. Klages, and E. Löffler, 161–82. Frankfurt: Peter Lang.

———. 1999. The public sector in an in-between time: Searching for new public values. *Public Administration* 77 (3): 565–84.

Jørgensen, T., and B. Bozeman. 2002. Public values lost? Comparing cases on contracting out from Denmark and the United States. *Public Management Review* 4 (1): 64–81.

———. 2007. Public values: An inventory. *Administration & Society* 39(3): 354–81.

Jurik, N. 2004. Imagining justice: Challenging the privatization of public life. *Social Problems* 51 (1): 1–15.

Kalleberg, A. 1969. Concept formation in normative and empirical studies: Toward reconciliation in political theory. *American Political Science Review* 63 (1): 26–39.

Kaplow, L., and S. Shavell. 2002. *Fairness versus welfare*. Cambridge, MA: Harvard University Press.

Kaufman, H. 1956. Emerging conflicts in the doctrines of public administration. *American Political Science Review* 50 (4): 1057–73.

Kelly, J. M. 2005. The dilemma of the unsatisfied customer in a market model of public administration. *Public Administration Review* 65 (1): 76–88.

Kelman, S. 1981. *What price incentives? Economists and the Environment*. Boston: Auburn House.

Kemp, S. 1998. Perceiving luxury and necessity. *Journal of Economic Psychology* 19 (5): 591–606.

Kennedy, G. 1958. The process of evaluation in a democratic community. *Journal of Philosophy* 56 (6): 253–63.

Kettl, D. 1988. *Government by proxy*. Washington, DC: Congressional Quarterly Press.

———. 1993. *Sharing power: Public governance and private markets*. Washington, DC: Brookings.

———. 2005. *The global public management revolution*. 2nd ed. Washington, DC: Brookings Institution Press.

Keynes, J. M. 1964. *The general theory*. New York: Harcourt Brace and World.

Kickert, W. J. M. 1996. *Public management and administrative reform in Western Europe*. London: Edward Elgar.

———. 1997. Public governance in the Netherlands: An alternative to Anglo-American "managerialism." *Public Administration* 75 (4): 731–52.

Kinver, Mark. 2006. Market forces stir up water debate. *BBC News,* March 16. http://news.bbc.co.uk/go/pr/fr/-/2/hi/science/nature/4813222.stm (Accessed August 4, 2006).

Kirkendall, R. S. 1997. Defender of the public interest: The General Accounting Office, 1921–1966. *Journal of American History* 84 (3): 1120–31.

Kirlin, J. 1996. What government must do well: Creating value for society. *Journal of Public Administration Theory and Research* 6 (1): 161–85.

Klein, D. 1987. Tie-ins and the market provision of public goods. *Harvard Journal of Law and Public Policy* 10 (2): 480–504.

Kobrak, P. 1996. The social responsibilities of a public entrepreneur. *Administration & Society* 28 (2): 205–37.

Kooiman, J. 1999. Social-political governance: Overview, reflections and design. *Public Management* 1 (1): 67–92.

Krane, J. 2003. Private firms do U.S. military's work. Associated Press. October 29. www.globalpolicy.org/security/peacekpg/training/1029private.htm (Accessed August 5, 2005)

Kristof, N. 1998. Japanese are torn between efficiency and egalitarian values. *New York Times*, October, 26, A1.

Krutilla, J., and O. Eckstein. 1958. *Multiple purpose river development: Studies in applied economic analysis*. Baltimore, MD: Johns Hopkins University Press.

Krutilla, J., and A. Fisher 1985. *The economics of natural environments*. Washington, DC: Resources for the Future.

Kumar, S. 1994. Curbing the trade in human organs in India. *Lancet* 344:750.

Kuttner, R. 1997. *Everything for sale: The virtues and limits of markets*. New York: Alfred Knopf.

Laird, J. 1929. *The idea of value*. Cambridge: Cambridge University Press.

Lambrecht, Bill. 1998. India gives Monsanto an unstable lab for genetics in farming. *St. Louis Post-Dispatch,* November 22.

Lan, Z., and H. Rainey. 1992. Goals, rules, and effectiveness in public, private, and hybrid organizations: More evidence on frequent assertions about differences. *Journal of Public Administration Research and Theory* 2 (1): 5–28.

Landry, C., and T. Anderson. 1998. The rising tide of water markets: Political economy research center. ITT Industries, Waterbook: Guidebook to Global Water Issues, pp. 71–75. www.itt.com/waterbook/tide.asp (Accessed May 14, 2007)

Lane, J. E. 2000. *New public management: An introduction.* London: Rutledge Books.

Lane, R. 1991. *The market experience.* Cambridge: Cambridge University Press.

Laski, H. 1930. *The danger of obedience and other essays.* New York: Macmillan.

Leahy, S. 2006. Ban endures on terminator seeds. *BROOKLIN,* Canada, February 11. www.bcpolitics.ca/enviro_terminator.htm (Accessed July 13, 2004).

Lee, S., and E. Webley. 2005. In search of the economic self. *Journal of Socio-Economics* 34 (5): 585–604.

Lemos, N., and W. Tolhurst. 1999. *Intrinsic value: Concept and warrant. Philosophy and Phenomenological Research* 59 (3): 829–31.

Lerner, R. 1996. *American elites.* New Haven, CT: Yale University Press.

Lewis, C. 1971. *An analysis of knowledge and valuation.* Lasalle, IL: Open Court.

Leys, W., and C. M. Perry. 1959. *Philosopher and the public interest.* Chicago: Chicago University Press, Committee to Advance Original Work in Philosophy.

Lindblom, C. E., and D. K. Cohen. 1979. *Usable knowledge.* New Haven, CT: Yale University Press.

Lindsay, C. M. 1976. A theory of government enterprise. *Journal of Political Economy* 84 (5): 1061–78.

Link, A. N. 1986. *Economics: A study of markets.* Englewood Cliffs, NJ: Prentice Hall.

Lippman, W. 1955. *The public philosophy.* London: Hamish Hamilton.

Lipset, S., and A. Pool. 1996. Balancing the individual and the community: Canada versus the United States. *Responsive Community* 6:37–46.

Lipsey, R., and K. Lancaster. 1956–57. The general theory of the second best. *Review of Economic Studies* 24:11–32.

Lohr, S. 2004 An elder challenges outsourcing's orthodoxy. *New York Times,* September 9. www.nytimes.com (Accessed October 30, 2006).

Lorentzen, P. 1993. Public administration and policy-making: The political career executive environment. *International Journal of Public Administration.* 16 (8): 1105–31.

Lowi, T. 1964. American government, 1933–1963: Fission and confusion in theory and research. *American Political Science Review* 58 (3): 589–99.

———. 1969. *The end of liberalism.* New York: W. W. Norton.

Machlup, F. 1962. *The production and distribution of knowledge in the United States.* Princeton, NJ: Princeton University Press.

Mackie, J. 1977. The third theory of law. *Philosophy and Public Affairs* 7 (1): 3–16.

Macrae, J., and A. Zwi, eds. 1994. *War and hunger.* London: Zed Books.

Madrick, J. 2002. *Why economies grow.* New York: Basic Books.

Maio, G. R., and J. M. Olson. 1995. Relations between values, attitudes, and behavioral intentions: The moderating role of attitude function. *Journal of Experimental Social Psychology* 31 (3): 266–78.

Marlow, M. 1995. *Public finance.* New York: Dryden Press.

Marmolo, E. 1999. A constitutional theory of public goods. *Journal of Economic Behavior & Organization* 38 (1): 27–42.

Marquis, S. M., and S. H. Long. 1999. Trends in managed care and managed competition, 1993–1997. *Health Affairs* 16 (6): 75–88.

Marsden, B. 2003. Cholera and the age of the water barons. *Public Integrity,* February 3. www.publicintegrity.org/water/ (Accessed August 8, 2006).

Martin, R. 2003. Introduction in ITT Industries, Waterbook: Guidebook to global water issues, p. 5. www.itt.com/waterbook/tide.asp (Accessed May 13, 2007)

Matouschek, N. 2004. Ex post inefficiencies in a property rights theory of the firm. *Journal of Law, Economics, and Organization* 20 (1): 125–47.

McCallum, J. 2001. Lockdown shutdown? *Mother Jones,* May 11. www.motherjones.com/news/feature/2001/05/cca_update.html (Accessed July 27, 2006)

McClosky, H. 1964. Consensus and ideology in American politics. *American Political Science Review* 58 (2): 361–82.

McClosky, H., P. Hoffman, and R. O'Hara. 1960. Issue conflict and consensus among party leaders and followers. *American Political Science Review* 54(2): 406–27.

McGregor, P. 1990. A model of crisis in a peasant economy. *Oxford Economic Papers*, n.s., 42 (4): 793–811.

McSwite, O. C. 2005. Taking public administration seriously: Beyond humanism and bureaucrat bashing. *Administration & Society* 37 (1): 116–25.

Mead, L. M. 2004. The culture of welfare reform. *Public Interest* 154 (3): 99–110.

Medical Industry Today. 1998. Suspected murder for organ trade probed in Philippines Sept. 9, pp. 127–28.

Menger, C. 1892. On the origins of money. *Economic Journal* 2:239–55, trans. by C. A. Foley.

Merton, Robert K. 1957. *Social theory and social structure.* Rev. ed. New York: Free Press of Glencoe.

Miguel, E. 2004. Tribe or nation: Nation building and public goods in Kenya and Tanzania. *World Politics* 56 (3): 327–47.

Milbank, D., and J. Blum. 2005. Document says oil chiefs met with Cheney task force. *Washington Post*, November 16, p. A01.

Miller, A. N. 1997. Ideological motivations of privatization in Great Britain versus developing countries. *Journal of International Affairs* 50 (2): 391–408.

Miller, G. 2005. The political evolution of principal–agent models. *Annual Review of Political Science* 8:203–25.

Miller, G., and A. Whitford. 2002. Trust and incentives in principal–agent negotiations. *Journal of Theoretical Politics* 14 (2): 231–67.

Mills, W. 1966. *American military thought.* Indianapolis: Bobbs-Merrill.

Milward, B., K. Provan, and B. Else. 1993. What does the "hollow state" look like? In *Public management: The state of the art*, ed. B. Bozeman, 309–22. San Francisco, CA: Jossey-Bass.

Mintz, E. 2001. Voices and echoes: Public interest representation in the 1990s and beyond. *Canadian Journal of Political Science* 34 (2): 422–23.

Mitchell, W. 1917. Weiser's theory of social economics. *Political Science Quarterly* 32 (1): 95–118.

Mohr, L. 1995. *Impact analysis for program evaluation.* 2nd ed. Thousand Oaks, CA: Sage Publications.

Monypenny, P. 1953. A code of ethics as a means of controlling administrative conduct. *Public Administration Review* 13 (3): 184–87.

Moore, C. A. 2004. Marketing failure: The experience with air pollution trading in the United States. *Environmental Law Reporter* 34 (3): 10281–88.

Moore, M. 1995. *Creating public value: Strategic management in government.* Cambridge, MA: Harvard University Press.

Moreno, L. 2006. Water works. *The Wall Street Journal*, March 9, p. A19. http://online.wsj .com/article/SB114195804548794425.html (Accessed July 17, 2006)

Morgan, G., B. Fischhoff, A. Bostrom, and C. Atman. 2001. *Risk communication: A mental models approach.* Cambridge: Cambridge University Press.

Morris, M. 1979. *Measuring the conditions of the world's poor.* Oxford, UK: Pergamon Press.

Mukherjee, A. 1994. *Structural adjustment programme and food security: Hunger and poverty in India.* Aldershot, England: Avebury.

National Research Council. 1989. *Field testing genetically modified organisms: Framework for decisions.* Washington, DC: National Academy Press.

Nature. 2000. Critics of "gene foods" reports are avoiding real issues. *Nature* 404 (6779): 689.

Nelson, R. 1959. The simple economics of basic scientific research. *Journal of Political Economy* 67 (5): 297–306.

————. 1987. Roles of government in a mixed economy. *Journal of Policy Analysis and Management* 6:541–57.

Netto, A. 2005. World water day: Private sector still eyeing to own every drop. Inter-Press Service. March 22. www.commondreams.org/cgi-bin/print.cgi?file=/headlines05/0322-06.htm (Accessed August 10, 2006).

Norton, B. 1987. *Why preserve natural variety?* Princeton, NJ: Princeton University Press.

————. 2005. *Sustainability: A philosophy of adaptive ecosystem management.* Chicago: University of Chicago Press.

Norton, B., and M. Tomen. 1997. Sustainability: Ecological and economic perspectives. *Land Economics* 73 (4): 553–68.

Nozick, R. 1974. *Anarchy, state and utopia.* New York: Basic Books.

Nurse, D. 2006a. City Hall Inc. a growing business in North Fulton: Rent-a-government: The upcoming city of Milton is following Sandy Springs' lead by hiring a company to run things. *Atlanta Journal-Constitution,* September 6. www.ajc.com/search/content/metro/stories/2006/09/06/metnewcities0906a.html (Accessed September 19, 2006)

————. 2006b. Recycled leaders: You might know their names, but now they're in new roles. *Atlanta Journal-Constitution,* September 19. www.ajc.com/search/content/metro/stories/2006/09/19/metnewcities0919b.html (Accessed September 19, 2006)

————. 2006c. Sandy Springs puts public services in private hands. *Atlanta Journal-Constitution,* September 27. www.ajc.com/metro/content/metro/northfulton/stories/2006/09/26/0927metprivate.html (Accessed September 28, 2006)

Nutt, P. 2006. Comparing public and private sector decision-making practices. *Journal of Public Administration Research and Theory* 16 (3): 289–318.

Nutt, P., and R. Backoff. 1993. Strategy for public and third sector organizations. *Journal of Public Administration Research and Theory* 5 (2): 189–211.

Nye, J. 1997. In government we don't trust. *Foreign Policy* 108 (2): 99–111.

Oakeshott, M. 1946. "Introduction" in Thomas Hobbes, *Leviathan,* vii–xvi. Oxford, UK: Blackwell's Political Texts.

————. 1975. *On human conduct.* Cambridge, UK: Clarendon Press.

Oddie, G., and P. Menzies. 1992. An objectivist's guide to subjective value. *Ethics* 102 (3): 512–33.

Okonski, K., ed. 2006. *The water revolution: Practical solutions to water scarcity.* London: International Policy Press.

Olson, M. 1971. *The logic of collective action.* Rev. ed. Cambridge, MA: Harvard University Press.

O'Neill, J. 2002. Deliberative democracy and environmental policy. In *Democracy and the claims of nature: Critical perspectives for a new century,* ed. B. A. Minteer and B. Pepperman Taylor, 257–75. Lanham, MD: Rowman & Littlefield.

Osborne, D., and P. Plastrik. 1997. *Banishing bureaucracy: The five strategies for reinventing government.* Reading, MA: Addison-Wesley.

Page, T. 1977. *Conservation and economic efficiency.* Baltimore, MD: Johns Hopkins University Press and Resources for the Future.

Pandey, S., and P. Scott. 2002. Red tape: A review and assessment of concepts and measures. *Journal of Public Administration Research and Theory* 12 (4): 553–80.

Parfit, D. 1984. *Reasons and persons.* Oxford, UK: Clarendon Press.

Parker, D., and C. Kirkpatrick. 2005. Privatisation in developing countries: A review of the evidence and the policy lessons. *Journal of Development Studies* 41 (4): 513–41.

Pearce, F. 2004. Crops "widely contaminated" by genetically modified DNA. *New Scientist On-line,* February 23. www.newscientist.com/hottopics/gm/ (Accessed July 13, 2004).

Peirce, C. 1956. *Collected papers.* Vol. 6. Cambridge, MA: Harvard University Press.

People's Daily [Online English Version]. 2006. China's regulation banning human organ trade takes effect. July 2. at http://english.peopledaily.com.cn/200607/02/eng20060702_279224.html (Accessed October 22, 2006).

Perry, J. 1996. Measuring motivation: An assessment of construct reliability and validity. *Journal of Public Administration Research and Theory* 6 (1): 5–24.

Perry, J., and H. Rainey. 1988. The public-private distinction in organization theory: A critique and research strategy. *Academy of Management Review* 13 (2): 182–201.

Perry, J., and L. Wise. 1990. The motivational bases of public service. *Public Administration Review* 31 (3): 302–16.

Pierre, J. 1995. The marketization of the state. In *Governance in a changing environment*, ed. B. G. Peters and D. Savoie, 64–91. Montreal: McGill-Queens University Press.

Pigou, A. 1920. *The economics of welfare*. London: Macmillan.

Pike, G. 1998. International trade in human organs for transplant. www.bio-ethics.com/newsc/trade.htm, p. 2 (Accessed December 4, 1998).

Piven, F. F., and R. Cloward. 1971. *Regulating the poor: The functions of public welfare*. New York: Pantheon.

Pollitt, C. 1990. *Managerialism and the public services: The Anglo-American experience*. Oxford, UK: Blackwell.

———. 2003. *The essential public manager*. London: Open University Press, McGraw-Hill.

Pollitt, C., and G. Bouckaert. 2000. *Public management reform: A comparative analysis*. New York: Oxford University Press.

Portney, P. 1994. The contingent valuation debate: Why economists should care. *Journal of Economic Perspectives* 8 (4): 3–17.

Posner, R. 2003. *Law, pragmatism, and democracy*. Cambridge, MA: Harvard University Press.

Prall, D. 1921. A study in the theory of value. *University of California Publications in Philosophy* 3 (2): 179–290.

Pressman, J., and A. Wildavsky. 1973. *Implementation: How great expectations in Washington are dashed in Oakland*. Berkeley: University of California Press.

Publius [James Madison, Alexander Hamilton, and John Jay]. 1996. *The federalist papers*. In *Princeton readings in political thought,* ed. Mitchell Cohen and Nicole Fermon, 335–46. Princeton, NJ: Princeton University Press.

Putnam, R. 2000. *Bowling alone: The collapse and revival of American community*. New York: Simon and Schuster.

Radcliff, B., and E. Wingenbach. 2000. Preference aggregation, functional pathologies and democracy: A social choice defense of participatory democracy. *Journal of Politics* 62 (4): 977–98.

Rainey, H. 1979. Perceptions of incentives in business and government: Implications for civil service reform. *Public Administration Review* 39 (5): 440–48.

———. 1983. Public agencies and private firms: Incentive structures, goals, and individual roles. *Administration & Society* 15 (2): 207–42.

———. 1989. Public management: Recent research on the political context and managerial roles, structures and behaviors. *Journal of Management* 15(2): 229–250.

———. 2002. What motivates bureaucrats? Politics and administration during the Reagan years. *Journal of Public Administration Research and Theory* 12 (2): 303–6.

———. 2003. *Understanding and managing public organizations*. 3rd ed. San Francisco, CA: Jossey-Bass.

Rainey, H., R. Backoff, and C. Levine. 1976. Comparing public and private organizations. *Public Administration Review* 36 (2): 233–46.

Rainey, H., and B. Bozeman. 2000. Comparing public and private organizations: Empirical research and the power of the a priori. *Journal of Public Administration Research and Theory* 10 (2): 447–70.

Rainey, H., S. Pandey, and B. Bozeman. 1995. Research note: Public versus private managers' perceptions of red tape. *Public Administration Review* 55 (6): 567–74.

Rawls, J. 1971. *A theory of justice*. Cambridge, MA: Harvard University Press.

———. 1982. Social unity and primary goods. In *Utilitarianism and beyond,* ed. A. Sen and B. Williams, 159–85. Cambridge: Cambridge University Press.

Raz, J. 1986. *The morality of freedom*. Oxford, UK: Clarendon Press.

Redford, E. 1954. The protection of the public interest with special reference to administrative regulation. *American Political Science Review* 48 (4): 1103–13.

———. 1985. Economists and policy analysis. *Public Administration Review* 38 (2): 112–20.

Rescher, N. 1969. *Introduction to value theory*. Englewood Cliffs, NJ: Prentice Hall.

Rhoads, S. 1985. *The economist's view of the world: Government, markets and public policy*. New York: Cambridge University Press.

Rhodes, R. A. W. 1994. The hollowing out of the state: The changing nature of the public service in Britain. *Political Quarterly* 65 (2): 138–51.

Ribaudo, M., R. Heimlich, and M. Peters. 2005. Nitrogen sources and gulf hypoxia: Potential for environmental credit trading. *Ecological Economics* 52 (2): 159–68.

Riker, W., and I. Sened. 1991. A political theory of the origin of property rights: Airport slots. *American Journal of Political Science* 35 (4): 951–69.

Rissler, J., and M. Mellon. 1996. *The ecological risks of engineered crops*. Cambridge, MA: MIT Press.

Rogers, J., and G. Kingsley. 2004. Denying public value: The role of the public sector in accounts of the development of the Internet. *Journal of Public Administration Research and Theory* 14 (3): 371–94.

Rogers, T., and N. Friedman. 1978. Decentralizing city government. *Administration and Society* 10 (2): 177–202.

Rokeach, M. 1973. *The nature of human values*. New York: Free Press.

Rose, N. 2000. Scapegoating poor women: An analysis of welfare reform. *Journal of Economic Issues* 34 (1): 143–57.

Rosen, Harvey S. 1999. *Public finance*. 5th ed. Boston: Irwin McGraw-Hill.

Rosen, Jan M. 2006. Richer retirement accounts aid small employers. *New York Times*. September 12, Small Business, Strategies:2.

Rosenberg, A. 1976. *Microeconomic laws: A philosophical analysis*. Pittsburgh: University of Pittsburgh Press.

Ross, S. 1973. The economic theory of agency. *American Economic Review* 63 (2): 134–39.

Rutgers, M. 1997. Beyond Woodrow Wilson: The identity of the study of public administration in historical perspective. *Administration and Society* 29 (3): 276–300.

———. 2001. Traditional flavors? The different sentiments in European and American administrative thought. *Administration and Society* 33 (2): 220–44.

Ryden, D. 1996. *Representation in crisis: The constitution, interest groups and political parties*. Albany, NY: SUNY Press.

Saari, D. 2003. Capturing the "will of the people." *Ethics* 113 (2): 333–51.

Sagoff, M. 1997. Can we put a price on nature's services? *Report from the Institute of Philosophy and Public Policy* 17 (3): 10–17.

Sahlins, M. 1972. *Stone age economics*. Chicago: Aldine.

Samuelson, P. 1954. The pure theory of public expenditure. *Review of Economics and Statistics* 36 (3): 386–89.

Sandel, M. 1996. *Democracy's discontent: America in search of a public philosophy*. Cambridge, MA: Harvard University Press.

Savas, E. 1987. *Privatization: The key to better government*. Chatham, MA: Chatham House.

———. 2000. *Privatization and public-private partnerships*. Chatham, MA: Chatham House.

Savoie, D. 1995. *Thatcher, Reagan, Mulroney: In search of a new bureaucracy*. Pittsburgh: University of Pittsburgh Press.

Sawyer, J. 1966. The altruism scale: A measure of co-operative, individualistic, and competitive interpersonal orientation. *The American Journal of Sociology* 71 (4): 407–16.

Schneider, H. W. 1956. *Three dimensions of public morality*. Bloomington: Indiana University Press.

Schubert, Glendon. 1961. *The public interest*. Glencoe, IL: Free Press.

Schueler, G. 1988. Modus ponens and moral realism. *Ethics* 98 (3): 492–500.

Sclar, Elliot D. 2000. *You don't always get what you pay for.* Ithaca, NY: Cornell University Press.

Scott, J. C. 1976. *The moral economy of the peasant.* New Haven, CT: Yale University Press.

Segerfeldt, Fredrik. 2005. *Water for sale: How business and the market can resolve the world's water crisis.* Cato Institute Publication.

Selgin, G. 1999. The money interest and the public interest: American monetary thought, 1920–1970. *Journal of Economic History* 59 (1): 256–57.

Sellers, Martin P. 1993. *The history and politics of private prisons: A comparative analysis.* Rutherford, NJ: Fairleigh Dickinson University Press.

Sen, A. 1970. *Collective choice and social welfare.* San Francisco, CA: Holden-Day.

———. 1979. The welfare basis of real income comparisons: A survey. *Journal of Economic Literature* 17 (1): 1–45.

———. 1995. Rationality and social choice. *American Economic Review* 85 (1): 1–24.

———. 1999. The possibility of social choice. *American Economic Review* 89 (3): 349–78.

Sen, A., and B. Williams, 1982. *Utilitarianism and beyond.* Cambridge: Cambridge University Press.

Service, Robert. 1998. Seed-sterilizing "terminator technology" sows discord. *Science* 282 (October 30): 850–51.

Shapiro, I. 2003. *The state of democratic theory.* Princeton, NJ: Princeton University Press.

Shapiro, R. 1999. Open letter from Monsanto CEO Robert B. Shapiro to Rockefeller Foundation president Gordon Conway. October 4. www.biotech-info.net/monsanto_letter .pdf (Accessed July 12, 2004).

Shavell, S. 1999. Why not sell organs? *New York Times,* May 11, p. 22.

Sheldon, R. 2005. Making profits out of human misery: The business of prisons. *Prison Service Journal* 157 (1): 29–35.

Shields, P. 2005. Classical pragmatism does not need an upgrade: Lessons for public administration. *Administration & Society* 37 (4): 504–18.

Short, T. 1997. Infrastructure visionaries. *Civil Engineering* 67 (8): 63–71.

Simon, H. A., D. W. Smithburg, and V. A. Thompson. 1950. *Public administration.* New York: Alfred A. Knopf.

Skocpol, T., and M. Fiorina, eds. 1999. *Civic engagement in American democracy.* Washington, DC: CQ Press.

Slack, K., J. L. Holl, B. J. Lee, M. McDaniel, M. L. Altenbernd, and A. B. Stevens. 2003. Child protective intervention in the context of welfare reform. *Journal of Policy Analysis and Management* 22 (4): 517–36.

Smith, Adam. 1976. *The theory of moral sentiments.* Indianapolis: Liberty Classics.

———. 2006. *An inquiry into the nature and causes of the wealth of nations,* ed. Edwin Cannan. Methuen and Co., Ltd. 1904. Library of Economics and Liberty. www .econlib.org/library/Smith/smWN1.html (Accessed December 9, 2006).

Smith, M. G. 1960. Social and cultural pluralism. *Annals of the New York Academy of Science.* 83 (4): 763–79.

Smith, S. R., and M. Lipsky, 1993. *Nonprofits for hire: The welfare state in the age of contracting.* Cambridge, MA: Harvard University Press.

Snider, K. 2005. Rortyan pragmatism: "Where's the beef" for public administration? *Administration & Society* 37 (2): 243–47.

Social Security Administration. 2006a. *Annual statistical supplement to Social Security Bulletin.* Washington, DC: U.S. Government Printing Office.

———. 2006b. *National average wage index.* www.ssa.gov/OACT/COLA/AWI.html (Accessed December 10, 2006).

Solow, R. 1991. Discussion notes on "formalization." *Methodus* 3 (1): 30–31.

Sorauf, F. 1957. The public interest reconsidered. *Journal of Politics* 19 (4): 616–39.

Specter, M. 2000. The Pharmageddon riddle. *New Yorker,* April 10, 58–71.

Spence, M., and R. Zeckhauser. 1971. Insurance, information and individual action. *American Economic Review* 61 (2): 380–87.

Starr, P. 1988. The meaning of privatization. *Yale Law and Policy Review* 6:6–41.

Stavins, R. 1989. Harnessing market forces to protect the environment. *Environment* 1, (1): 28–35.

Stein, M. S. 2003. Utilitarianism and conflation. *Polity* 35 (4): 479–90.

Stephan, P. 1996. The economics of science. *Journal of Economic Literature* 34 (3): 1199–1235.

Stern, P., L. Kalof, T. Dietz, and G. Guagnano. 1995. Values, beliefs, and pro-environmental action: Attitude formation toward emergent attitude objects. *Journal of Applied Social Psychology* 25 (18): 1611–27.

Stoesz, D. 1999. Unraveling the welfare state. *Society* 36 (4): 53–61.

Stone, D. 1997. *Policy paradox: The art of political decision-making*. New York: W. W. Norton.

Sturgeon, N. 1996. Anderson on reason and value. *Ethics* 106 (3): 509–24.

Susskind, L., and J. Cruikshank. 1990. *Breaking the impasse: Consensual approaches to resolving public disputes*. Chicago: Basic Books.

Suzumura, K. 1997. *Competition, commitment, and welfare*. Oxford: Oxford University Press.

Swaminathan, M. S. 1999. Genetic engineering and food, ecological livelihood security in predominantly agricultural developing countries. Speech to CGIAR/NAS Biotechnology Conference, October 21. www.cgiar.org/biotechc/swami.htm (Accessed July 10, 2004).

Talvi, S. 2006. Follow the prison money trail. In these times. *Frontline*, September, p. 12.

Tanyi, G. 1997. *Designing privatization strategies in Africa*. New York: Praeger.

Taylor, C. 1989. *Sources of the self: The making of the modern identity*. Cambridge, MA: Harvard University Press.

Toman, M., J. Pezzey, and J. Krautkraemer. 1995. Neoclassical economic growth theory and "sustainability." In *Handbook of environmental economics*, ed. D. Bromley, 121–47. Oxford: Blackwell.

Toner, Robin, D. Schemo, and R. Pear. 2006. On education and health, costly plans face hurdles. *New York Times*, February 1, p. 16.

de Toqueville, A. (1965). *Democracy in America*. Repr. ed. New York: Oxford University Press.

Treise, D., K. Walsh-Childers, M. Weigold, and M. Friedman. 2003. Cultivating the science Internet audience: Impact of brand and domain on source credibility for science information. *Journal of Communication* 24 (3): 309–32.

Trubac, E. 1995. Managed competition and school choice. *Business and Professional Ethics Journal* 4 (1): 33–64.

United Nations Environment Programme. 2002. GEO-Global Environment Outlook 3, Past, Present and Future Perspectives. Nairobi, Kenya: United Nations Environment Programme.

United Nations World Water Development Report 1. 2003. Water for people, water for life. World Water Assessment Programme. Paris: Berghahn Books, UNESCO Publishing. www.unesco.org/water/wwap (Accessed July 17, 2006)

United Nations World Water Development Report 2. 2006. Water, a shared responsibility. World Water Assessment Programme. Paris: Berghahn Books, UNESCO Publishing. www.unesco.org/water/wwap (Accessed July 17, 2006)

U.S. Congress. 1984. Stevenson-Wydler Technology Innovation Act of 1980. United States Code, Title 15, Section 3701-3714, 96–517. Washington, DC: U.S. Government Printing Office.

———. 1986. Federal Technology Transfer Act of 1986. 99th Congress, 2nd sess. Washington, DC: U.S. Government Printing Office.

———. 1993. *Government Performance and Results Act of 1993*, PL 103-62.

U.S. General Accounting Office. 1991. Private prisons: Cost savings and BOP's statutory authority need to be resolved. February 7. GAO/GGD-91-21.

———. 1996. Private and public prisons: Studies comparing operational costs and/or quality of service. Report to the Subcommittee on Crime, Committee on the Judiciary, House of Representatives. August 16. GAO/GGD-96-158.

———. 1998. *Privatization in state and local government.* Report GAO-98-97. Washington, DC: U.S. Government Printing Office.

———. 2000. District of Columbia: Issues related to the Youngstown prison report and Lorton closure.

Useem, B., and J. A. Goldstone. 2002. Forging social order and its breakdown: Riot and reform in U.S. prisons. *American Sociological Review* 67 (4): 499–525.

Vallentyne, P. 1988. Teleology, consequentialism, and the past. *Journal of Value Inquiry* 22 (2): 89–101.

Van Deth, J. W., and E. Scarbrough. 1995. *The impact of values.* Oxford: Oxford University.

Van Dyke, Vernon. 1982. Collective entities and moral rights: Problems in liberal-democratic thought. *Journal of Politics* 44 (1): 21–40.

Van Houten, T., and H. Hatry. 1987. *How to conduct a citizen survey.* Washington, DC: American Planning Association.

Van Slyke, D. M. 2003. The mythology of privatization in contracting for social services. *Public Administration Review* 63 (3): 296–315.

Van Wart, M. 1998. *Changing public sector values.* Hamden, CT: Garland.

Vickers, J., and G. Yarrow. 1991. Economic perspectives on privatization. *Journal of Economic Perspectives* 5 (2): 111–32.

Victor, P. 1991. Indicators of sustainable development: Some lessons from capital theory. *Environmental Economics* 4 (2): 191–214.

Vidal J. 2005. Canada backs terminator seeds. *Guardian,* February 9. www.guardian.co.uk/ gmdebate/Story/0,2763,1408821,00.html (Accessed November 2, 2006).

Visser, B., I. van der Meer, N. Louwaars, J. Beekwilder, and D. Eato. 2001. The impact of "terminator" technology. *Biotechnology and Development Monitor* 48: 9–12.

Vrangbaek, K. 2006. Public sector values in Denmark: Results from a survey of public managers. Paper prepared for European Group on Public Administration, Workshop of Public Values, Milan, Italy, September.

Walford, G. 1990. *Privatization and privilege in education.* London: Routledge.

Walker, R. 1994. Privatisation: A reassessment. *Journal of Australian Political Economy* 34 (1): 27–52.

Wamsley, G. L., and J. F. Wolf. 1996. *Refounding democratic public administration: Modern paradoxes, postmodern challenges.* London: Sage.

Warren, M. E. 1992. Democratic theory and self-transformation. *American Political Science Review* 86 (1): 8–23.

———. 1995. The self in discursive democracy. In *The Cambridge companion to Habermas,* ed. S. K. White, 167–200. Cambridge: Cambridge University Press.

Weatherford, M. S. 1992. Measuring political legitimacy. *American Political Science Review* 86 (1): 149–66.

Webb, P., and von Braun, J. 1994. *Famine and food security in Ethiopia: Lessons for Africa.* Chichester, UK: John Wiley.

Weimer, D., and A. Vining. 1999. *Policy analysis: Concepts and practice.* 3rd ed. Englewood Cliffs, NJ: Prentice Hall.

Wheeler, G., and N. Brady. 1998. Do public-sector and private-sector personnel have different ethical dispositions? A study of two sites. *Journal of Public Administration Research and Theory* 8 (1): 93–116.

White, Louise. 1994. Policy analysis as discourse. *Journal of Policy Analysis and Management* 13 (3): 506–25.

White House, The. 2005, February. *Strengthening Social Security for the 21st century.* www.whitehouse.gov/infocus/social-security/200501/strengthening-socialsecurity .html (Accessed November 10, 2006).

Williams, B. 1972. *Morality: An Introduction to ethics.* Cambridge: Cambridge University Press.

Williamson, O. 1979. Transaction cost economics: The governance of contractual relations. *Journal of Law and Economics* 22 (3): 233–61.

———. 1981. The economics of organization: The transaction cost approach. *American Journal of Sociology* 87 (4): 548–77.

Wills, G. 1999. *A necessary evil: A history of American distrust of government.* New York: Simon and Schuster.

Wilson, J. 1989. *Bureaucracy.* New York: Basic Books.

Wilson, Woodrow. 1955. *The study of administration* [*reprinted* 1913]. Washington, DC: Public Affairs Press.

Wisensale, S. 1999. Grappling with the generational equity debate. *Public Integrity* 1 (1): 1–19.

Wittman, D. 1995. *The myth of democratic failure: Why political institutions are efficient.* Chicago: University of Chicago Press.

Wittmer, D. 1991. Serving the people or serving for pay: Reward preferences among government, hybrid sector, and business managers. *Public Productivity & Management Review* 14 (4): 369–83.

Wittmer, D., and D. Coursey. 1996. Ethical work climates: Comparing top managers in public and private organizations. *Journal of Public Administration Research and Theory* 6 (4): 559–72.

Wolf, C. 1993. *Markets or governments: Choosing between imperfect alternatives,* 2nd ed. Cambridge, MA: MIT Press.

Wright, D. 1971. *The psychology of moral behaviour.* Hammondsworth, UK: Penguin Books.

Yeoman, Barry. 2000. Steel town lockdown. *Mother Jones.* May/June. www.motherjones.com/news/feature/2001/05/cca_update.html (Accessed August 4, 2006)

Young, I. 1996. Communication and the other: Beyond deliberative democracy. In *Democracy and difference,* ed. S. Benhabib, 120–36. Princeton, NJ: Princeton University Press.

Zerbe, R., and H. McCurdy. 1999. The failure of market failure. *Journal of Policy Analysis and Management* 18 (4): 558–78.

Zifcak, S. 1994. *New managerialism: Administrative reform in Whitehall and Canberra.* Buckingham, UK: Open University Press.

Ziman, J. 1968. *Public knowledge: The social dimension of science.* Cambridge: Cambridge University Press.

INDEX

CPSIA information can be obtained at www.ICGtesting.com
Printed in the USA
BVOW071721080112

279945BV00001B/9/P